The Bundesbank Myth

The Bundesbank Myth

Towards a Critique of Central Bank Independence

Jeremy Leaman
Senior Lecturer
Department of European Studies
Loughborough University

© Jeremy Leaman 2001

First published 2001 by
PALGRAVE
Houndmills, Basingstoke, Hampshire RG21 6XS and
175 Fifth Avenue, New York, N.Y. 10010
Companies and representatives throughout the world

PALGRAVE is the new global academic imprint of
St. Martin's Press LLC Scholarly and Reference Division and
Palgrave Publishers Ltd (formerly Macmillan Press Ltd).

ISBN 0–333–73862–4

A catalogue record for this book is available
from the British Library.

Library of Congress Cataloging-in-Publication Data
have been applied for.

10   9   8   7   6   5   4   3   2   1
10   09   08   07   06   05   04   03   02   01

Printed and bound in Great Britain by
Antony Rowe Ltd, Chippenham, Wiltshire

Contents

List of Charts

List of Tables

Box

Preface

The issue of central bank independence gained sudden prominence in political and academic circles in the 1980s and the 1990s. Before this time it had been regarded as an idiosyncrasy of the economic cultures of the United States, Germany and Switzerland or as a chance feature of federal systems of government. The sudden popularisation of autonomous central banking coincided with the stagflationary period which hit the OECD and other countries in the wake of the collapse of Bretton Woods and the two oil crises. The apparent and relative success of the German Bundesbank in steering the Federal Republic through stagflation elevated the principle of independent monetary policy to an article of faith among both neo-liberal economists and their political allies. The dragon of inflation became the primary public economic enemy. Othe 1980s, one or two smaller states (Netherlands, New Zealand) transformed their dependent central banks into autonomous agencies, largely free from interference from elected governments, but it was in the wake of the collapse of communism, German unification and the resurrection of European Monetary Union that the trickle became a torrent and Germany's idiosyncratic model of monetary policy-making became the blueprint for most central banks in the OECD and in the emerging states of central and eastern Europe.

This remarkable transformation of the institutional shape of economic policy-making encountered very little resistance. It is this process and the case, upon which it was based, which have motivated this study. I make no secret of my extreme scepticism about the efficacy and appropriateness of independent monetary policy for the complex political economies of the modern world. The problems facing mankind in the twenty-first century demand not less but more participation by informed democratic forces at every level and in every field of policy-making. The unanswerable quango, like the Bundesbank or its European clone, the ECB, seems to point in the opposite direction: in the direction of the disenfranchisement and disempowerment of civil society. It does not simply remove democratic control of one area of policy from the purview of voters, but generates a fatalism about the very nature of democratic influence.

Examining the mythology of the Bundesbank's apparent success could help to generate a new debate about the nature of civil society and the need to restore and strengthen instruments of democratic control which have either been removed or weakened by the dominant economic and political forces of the outgoing century. It might be naïve to suggest that the dragon of inflation has been finally slain; the power of global corporations to exploit the potential for monopolistic pricing has, if anything, increased. However, it would seem legitimate to assert that the problems of humanity in this century will be those of distribution in the broadest sense: who enjoys what share of available resources, jobs, rewards, private and public goods, leisure, travel opportunities, health, nature. Answering such questions demands refined and painstaking participation by people at local, regional, national and supra–national level. In this author's view, monetarism and its flagship institution, the autonomous central bank, contributed to one of the most disastrous episodes of economic 'management' in the modern world, namely the Third World debt crisis of the 1980s, the effects of which will still be felt for many years to come. The adoption of the independent central bank as core institution of economic policy could risk repeating such disasters.

Jeremy Leaman
Loughborough, April 2000

Acknowledgements

This book would not have been completed without the support of family, colleagues and friends. This is a truism which nevertheless needs repeating in situations like this. Another truism, occasionally forgotten by scholars eminent or otherwise, is that analysis and discourse are collective activities. Writing a book like this one draws on the work and ideas of hundreds of other individuals, in their published work in their contributions at conferences, their questions at seminars or their queries over lunch. Even though I am critical of the ideological positions represented by the Bundesbank, it would be churlish to deny that it has been incredibly helpful in supplying information, in providing statistical sources and well researched papers. Friends/colleagues at work have likewise been extremely helpful in exploding some of my dafter lines of argument and guiding me into safer intellectual waters. My family has also been extraordinarily patient watching the often slow progress of the book. Above all, my wife Cheryl has been a source of great encouragement and support throughout. Finally, the book would not have been completed without the help of Karel Thomas in copy–editing, proof–reading and indexing the rough old word–processed manuscript with which she was confronted.

1   Why is Money a Problem?

The context of monetary policy is multi-faceted and complex. It is a context which has changed and will continue to change over time, differing from one territory, one state, one zone to another, differing from one system of social reproduction, from one socio-economic culture to another. Few observers would deny that differences in monetary policy are determined to a greater or lesser degree by differences in the operational context of that policy. Institutions of monetary policy have accordingly changed over time in terms of their modes of operation, the instruments employed, the length and intensity of their application and their position within political structures. Many of the arguments supporting the latest reforms in monetary institutions and monetary policy are indeed informed by the perception of such changes and the need to adapt to them: globalised financial markets, intensified world trade, international corporate strategies of production and distribution. Any decent account of monetary policy must thus define such a context, however broad or narrow. A central hypothesis of this chapter is that most mainstream accounts of monetary policy define their contexts too narrowly and, even if they admit to changes over time, still produce absolutised, a-historical prescriptions. These in turn are based on 'articles of faith' which have 'served to justify errors of perception and organization in the implementation of monetary policy whose consequences are occasionally calamitous and almost always unintended'. [1]

Many theories of money suffer from an extreme selectivity of diagnosis which predefines an extreme and crude quality of prescription. One can take a zoological metaphor to illustrate the point: tree shrews and elephants are both mammals belonging to the same evolutionary line, sharing countless common genetic characteristics. They nevertheless differ in significant respects: habitat, territorial range, familial structures, nourishment, size and power to name but a few. Circulatory disorders in elephants and tree shrews may manifest similar symptoms, but a zoo vet who prescribed identical treatments, be they drug-based or surgical, would arguably not be taken seriously by

---

[1] Thus Nigel Dodd, *The Sociology of Money,* New York 1994, xxviii

anyone above the age of three. The same applies to social formations of different size, different structural characteristics, different trading relations, different geographical position, climate, natural resources, different patterns of social culture, different levels of economic and technological development. And yet orthodox economists in the late 1970s and early 1980s urged the crude prescriptions of monetarism on to all countries via the dominant institutions wielding global political power – IMF, World Bank, Federal Reserve and Bundesbank – unleashing one of the most destructive periods of global economic development this century: the Third World debt crisis, ecological despoliation, famine, war and mass migrations can be ascribed in part to the pernicious rise in real interest rates, to the one-club cure for inflation. One feature of global economic problems – price rises in the advanced countries of the North – was elevated to the status of economic enemy No. 1, marginalising or even dismissing other features of crisis as secondary or irrelevant. Furthermore, the lines of transmission were so dominated by the key agencies of monetarism and neo-liberalism that few countries or communities could escape. No question of carefully calculated doses of medicine here: the global cost of credit was raised surprisingly uniformly, but the effects differed in every case. While the industrialised countries of the OECD were able by and large to recycle petro-dollars via trade and financial institutions, developing countries were forced to service their vast debts via cash-cropping and indirectly through the empoverishment of their populations.

The message of this introduction and one of the core points of departure for this book is simple: one man's meat is another man's poison, there is no policy cure-all, no institutional panacea. Policy has to be applied in relation to the particular circumstances of a given economic space, institutional agencies have to be tailored to achieve the best outcome for the inhabitants of that space. Above all, the architects of monetary policy must proceed from the assumption that 'money' is a problematic phenomenon, whose social value, function and significance varies from one social formation to another.

Orthodox monetary theory has, however, tended to regard money as an ontological given, whose forms may change over time (specie, notes, promissory notes, bills of exchange, credit cards, memory traces in bank computer systems) and where the share of each form in the 'money stock' varies, but where its functional essence remains unchanged. This functional essence encompasses the notion of money as both a store of value and as a means of economic transaction. The notions of the *logical* and *political 'neutrality'* of money dominate classical and neo-classical theories and are linked to the ontological view of money whose functional essence remains constant despite (often radical) changes to the operational context of economic systems based on production and exchange. The *logical neutrality* of money expresses its supposed pure instrumentality, 'it mediates the production and exchange of goods, making no intrinsic difference to real economic variables'.[2] Marxian economics, for all its differences to orthodox theories, retains this classical view of money as means, while rooted in a labour theory of value and an economy of commodity production and exchange:

'It is not money that renders commodities commensurable. Just the contrary. It is because all commodities, as values, are realised human labour, and therefore commensurable, that their values can be measured by one and the same special commodity, and the latter be converted into the common measure of their values, i.e., into money'.[3] Marx would not argue with the classical assertion that money is logically neutral, since its function as a 'special commodity' which is universally exchangeable within a given territory is identical whether performed by transactors in feudal, capitalist or collectivist states. The significance of money in Marxist analysis is not that its definition alters within different social formations but that, as a constant, it is 'nothing but a particular expression of the social character of labour and its products',[4] the understanding of which makes the process of capitalist accumulation more transparent.

Arguably Marx's analysis of capitalism, which marginalizes human agency as a social psychological feature of an economic system, and employs the structural abstractions of capital and labour as the pivotal elements of production and exchange (relations of production), is more amenable to the notion of money's logical neutrality. But it is precisely this assumption which would seem to be flawed, both in epistemological and in historical terms. Marx' view of the structural dynamics of capitalist accumulation, of exchange processes which operate according to an inexorable logic of social behaviour corresponds in a strange way to the classical and neo-classical assumption of rational self-interest as the driving force behind economic activity: they are both essentialist, the one in terms of the

---

[2] N.Dodd, *The Sociology of Money,* op. cit. p.3.

[3] K.Marx, *Capital* Vol. 1, London 1954, p.57.

[4] Ibid, vol III, p.607.

transactional structures, the others in terms of the transactional agents, and they are both syllogistic, i.e. they only admit a limited set of causal determinants and set others aside, arriving at conclusions which suit their assumptions.

In this context the attitude of the individual to the use or the holding (non-use) of money is a problem which neither Marx nor orthodox schools of economics wish to acknowledge. Others – be they philosophers, like Simmel, psychoanalysts like Freud or sociologists like Dodd – would assert at the very least that there are significant differences in individual attitudes to money which interfere with the comfortable notions of logical (and thus predictable/ manageable) processes. As Dodd suggests, these differences have much to do with the tension between the functions of money as a (mere) means of exchange and as a store of value. However crude the categories, there would seem to be some sense in accepting the differences between the gambler, the spendthrift and the hoarder, to name but three when seeking to produce a theory of money. Whereas Marx shared the limited and limiting view of money's logical neutrality, he was one of the first to formulate a theory of domination which questioned the political neutrality of money, i.e. the notion 'that money can express inequalities of wealth and power but can never generate them'.[5]   In contrast to Adam Smith, John Stuart Mill and later Menger and Polanyi, Marx' theory of capital and surplus value proceeds from the contextual idea of a 'capital relation', which both requires inequality in order to generate accumulation and in turn cultivates inequality. Adam Smith's account of money admittedly did not descend to the crude abstractions of neo-classical theory which, as abstractions (utility, equilibrium, maximisation, rationality) allow the easy assumption of the political neutrality of money as the medium of transaction between utility-maximising individuals. Firstly, Smith provides Marx with the beginnings of a labour theory of value, of work as the original money with which all commodities can be bought, which he then proceeds to qualify in terms of his own social pragmatism.[6]   Secondly, Smith places

---

[5] N.Dodd, *The Sociology of Money,* op.cit. p.3.
[6] 'But though labour be the real measure of the exchangeable value of all commodities, it is not that by which their value is commonly estimated', *Wealth of Nations,* Vol. 1 (London 1904), p. 34; Smith then describes the difficulties of valuation in complex processes of production and sale as the imperfect but unavoidable basis for the the production of wealth.

money into a moral context in which 'wealth ... is power': 'the power of purchasing a certain command over all the labour or over all the produce of labour which is then in the market'.[7] Smith derives from these perceptions both the need to control monopolies and the obligation of the state to tax progressively, i.e. redistributing social wealth and power according to a set of moral principles.[8]

Marx' labour theory of value develops the notion of money ('labour time as a general commodity')[9] as the source of a general commodification of labour and the vehicle for the exploitation of dependent workers, where the abstract price of labour is necessarily less than the value of the labour-product. Marx' political economy of money thus proceeds from the insight of the functional abstraction/anonymity of money for the capitalist, and its indispensable role in maintaining property inequalities. It should also be underscored that the commodification of labour and other social relations and the accompanying complexity of immaterial, abstract exchange transactions involves and depends on a process of descriptive abstraction on the part of agents or observers which is potentially mystifying. In other words, the language of commerce or of economics is abstract, non-immediate and frequently confusing. As such it can provide an ideological barrier of protection which the untrained or uninitiated outsider is frequently unwilling to penetrate. It can help to conceal a hierarchy of property relations in terms of a hierarchy of knowledge.

The money economy – as a real and ideological system – may facilitate social liberties and social mobility, but it is not politically neutral. It follows that the political management of money cannot be neutral either, as assumed by the advocates of autonomous central banking (see below).

THE EPISTEMOLOGY OF MONEY: THE LANGUAGE OF ECONOMICS

The problems associated with the orthodox assumptions of the logical and political neutrality of money are at root epistemological problems. In turn, the primary problem in all epistemologies is the elusiveness of language, whereby economics manifests such difficulties constantly.

---

[7] A.Smith, ibid. Vol. I, p.33.
[8] A.Smith, ibid. Vol.II, 388ff and 472ff.
[9] Marx, *Grundrisse*, London 1973, 133ff.

Words are not fixed measurable items as one encounters in pure and applied sciences but vehicles of social meaning, the value of which resides not in the fixed, quantifiable and testable equivalences of maths or engineering but in the continuous process of social usage. The relationship between words and physical or abstract phenomena is and will always be approximate; the metaphoricality of abstract concepts increases their approximate and elusive character.[10] The metaphoricality of economics (management/nomos of the house/oikos) is very rich but very rarely acknowledged by economists: inflation, deflation, liquidity, circulation, equilibrium, price mechanism, market, competition, overheating, boom, slump etc. are at best imaginative attempts to convey a plasticity of concrete experience about invisible and abstract processes; they are heuristic tools providing the comfort of association with known phenomena. At worst, however, they replace the invisible abstract and complex process with a caricature image, with all its simplifying associative force. The free and fair struggle of equivalent contestants on an even playing field with the purpose of winning the favour of generalised consumers is thus the (thoroughly misleading) ideal-typical account of competition in orthodox textbooks, from which deviation can occur but which remains the core image and belief. Similarly misleading would be the 'demand' for 'liquidity' as a unitary phenomenon in monetary economics. Likewise, the relational and causal linkages of language are highly simplified renderings fundamentally dependent on the subject-predicate structures of grammar and syntax; they can provide at best adequate but not exact accounts of events and states of affairs.

The Quantity Theory is a perfect example of the epistemological problems attached to any abstract social science: the equation supporting quantity theory (MV=PT) is precise and mechanistic and functions as a prescriptive axiom in monetary institutions, like the Bundesbank, which practises orthodox monetarism. A direct causal link is postulated between the quantity of money in circulation and the aggregate level of prices, such that increases in the money stock (M),

---

[10] In one of his early works (*Ontologie der Arbeit*, repr. Darmstadt, 1973), Georg Lukacs stresses firstly the determinate nature of syntax, where an artificial subject-predicate structure is imposed on reality as a heuristic means of understanding that reality (in line with Nietzsche), and goes on to indicate the difficulties attached to the further metaphorical leap from this fundamental teleology of syntax to the figurative use of language in philosophy, religion and myth (13ff).

multiplied by the velocity of circulation (V) is seen to generate increases in the price level (P) adjusted by the number of transactions (T). The causal chain operates one way, from left to right, in this theorem (MtoP). Calculating monetary outcomes should accordingly be relatively simple, likewise preventing potential negative outcomes. However, there are serious theoretical reasons for questioning both the selection of the determinants and the direction of causal determination in the equation.

While the extreme example of hyperinflation clearly confirms the negative influence on inflation rates of a continuously expanded money stock, open-house discounting and give-away interest rates, linked to production shortages (e.g in Germany 1914–23), there is no obvious or exact correlation between money stock growth and inflation rate that could deliver fine-tuned prescriptions for delivering low inflation or price stability. Even Milton Friedman was prepared to concede that monetary policy is unimportant in relation to longer-term economic equilibria.[11] Indeed the money stock in 1923 in Germany, i.e. in the final stages of hyperinflation, failed to keep up with the process of devaluation.[12] Other factors, including negative international demand for the Reichsmark and the desperate flight into Dollars, as well as the suspension of public trust in domestic monetary networks, must have played a strong role, enough at least to question the validity of monetarist doctrine.

Quantity theory also has problems with the actual definition of what constitutes the money supply. Neither in theory nor in practice is there a pre-defined money stock, upon which other calculations are based. Rather, central banks committed to the quantity theory (and their academic advisors) have taken a variety of narrow and broad definitions of money stock. While the monetary authorities in the United States and in Britain abandoned attempts to target M3 in the early 1980s, the Bundesbank has (ostensibly) maintained a strict adherence to monetary targets, eschewing the less orthodox inflation targetting preferred by other independent central banks like the Bank of New Zealand and,

---

[11] Milton Friedman, 'Inflation and Unemployment', *Journal of Political Economy*, Vol.85, 1987; see also Arne Heise, *'Geldpolitik im Disput'*, *Konjunkturpolitik*, Vol. 38, No.4, 1992, 178ff.
[12] Claus-Dieter Krohn, *Die große Inflation in Deutschland 1918–23*, Cologne 1977.

more recently the Bank of England.[13] The flimsiness of Bundesbank
theory is exposed by the fact that it has shifted its preference from M1
to its own narrow Central Bank Money Stock and more recently to a
much broader M3; the failure to hit M3 targets has led to the inclusion
recently of data on M3 Extended to account for failures. Quite rightly,
the Bank is attempting to take account of changing circumstances but,
in the eyes of Keynesian and other critics (viz Tobin), the enterprise
remains a-historical and self-defeating.

THE EPISTEMOLOGY OF MONEY: MONEY AND VALUATION

One example of the difficulty of precise definitions of the function of
money is the area of the money valuation of goods or services, where
that valuation can reflect scarcity preference, taste, vital or non-vital
interests etc. Scarcity as a function of natural limitations (finite
availability, difficulty of extraction) of geography and cost of transport,
of ownership and control (of part or whole markets) of the symbolic
representation of the purchaser's market power – describes or implies a
variety of quite different relations. Scarcity is not an abstract absolute,
pre-defining value and value scales, but a crude metaphor covering a
range of distinct or indistinct linkages: relations between humans and
nature, notions of geographical and technical access of human beings to
goods; relations between owners of goods and services and customers
of greater and less means, of greater and less need, with greater, less or
no choice; of social power relations where ownership, consumption and
life style are norms by which power, merit, authority, legitimacy are
represented. Conspicuous obesity in Renaissance Europe or less
developed countries today, the number of horses in one's carriage team,
the size of one's house, the number of servants, cars, Gucci suits – are
all demonstrative representations of the social psychological value and
function of money which are distinct from but co-defined by the value
of money in fulfilling the vital needs of shelter, warmth, clothing and
food. The symbolic representation of money power reinforces social

---

[13] There is a strong body of opinion which asserts that the
Bundesbank's espousal of money stock targetting has been largely pro
forma, and that in practice it has pursued a non-orthodox approach of
exchange rate targets: Herr, Hansjörg and Voy, Klaus,
Währungskonkurrenz und Deregulierung der Weltwirtschaft, Marburg
1989; Herr, Hansjörg, W., *Währungswettbewerb und Währungssysteme*, Frankfurt am Main 1992.

power relations and the rationalisation of powerlessness and disparity as fate, the natural order of things, the reflection of divine or material merit.

Scarcity thus also represents opportunity as well as relative misfortune. It is the opportunity to increase money-value earnings via price changes in commodities and services by those who control the production and distribution of those commodities and services. Scarcity is the source of higher profit, archetypally provided in the growth phases of the trade cycle in market economies, the opportunity rationally to be exploited according to text books, in order to cushion the recessive phases of those cycles. Within advanced capitalist economies it is more frequently the opportunity which can itself be acquired by increasing market power via the cartel, the monopoly and the monopsony. Given that in pure theory and pure practice 'markets are inherently anti-monopolistic', the money-price advantage of reducing the fluctuations of competitive trading, according to Wallerstein, means that 'all capitalists seek to monopolize'.[14] The monopoly gatekeeper of supply can stabilise the price advantage of cyclical expansion throughout and beyond the cycle by regulating the volume of supply, but can also exploit the market power of demand (monopsony power) by taking advantage of the competition of the suppliers of pre-products. This in turn affects the attitude of the monopoly/monopsony to the cost of money (credit interest – see later sections), in that marginal increases in that cost can be accommodated via its power to regulate supply and/or demand processes.

The function of money as a 'store of value' in a 'normal' situation of dynamic disequilibrium (Schumpeter) is thus distinct from the function of money in the situation of regulated asymmetrical disequilibrium of monopolized/monopsonized markets. This is before any consideration of the function of money in the 'abnormal' modern context of 'decoupled' financial markets [Altvater, Strange]; (see below).

The variable and ambivalent translation of scarcity into value illustrates the contingent nature of valuation as such; the scarcity of firewood in rural India is mediated psychologically into a money-value in a quite different way to the scarcity/rarity of a Fabergé egg at a Sotheby's auction. Conversely, the one commodity like water enjoys a higher premium for the inhabitants of dry zones than for those of

---

[14] Immanuel Wallerstein, *Historical Capitalism and Capitalist Civilization*, London 1983, p.142.

temperate zones.[15]   Equally, as economic cultures in general become
more developed, as subsistence becomes less pressing and lifestyle
becomes the dominant priority in individual self-development, so the
valuing process involved in acquiring money is altered; as the
opportunities for social mobility – upwards and downwards – increase,
so the function of money in the objectified form of goods and life-style
alters. Simmel, in his *Philosophy of Money*, was one of the first
contemporary social theorists to recognize that money takes on the
function of affirming a changed or unchanged social status in the new
'material culture'.[16] Simmel also links the changing social function of
of money to developments in philosophical approaches to social reality:
    'Money, as an institution of the historical world, symbolizes the
behaviour of objects and etablishes a special relationship between itself
and them. The more the life of society becomes dominated by monetary
relationships, the more the relativistic character of existence finds its
expression in conscious life, since money is nothing other than a special
form of the embodied relativity of economic goods that signifies their
value. Just as the absolutist view of the world represents a definite stage
of intellectual development in correlation with the corresponding
practical, economic and emotional conditions of human affairs, so the
relativistic view of the world seems to express the momentary
relationship of adjustment on the part of our intellect.'[17]
    The relativism of valuation can be seen in the fact that the poorer
east Germans in the immediate aftermath of unification in 1990 spent
more than their western counterparts per capita on cars. The
demonstrative preference of east Germans for everything western, to
the exclusion of home-made goods of equal or greater value, reveals the
complex and varying nature of cultural valuation; collectively, it
achieved (or was intended to achieve) a public sense of economic and
cultural convergence, of unity; one can speculate also that the
phenomenal and rapid disgorging of savings converted (generously)
into DM also signified the enjoyment of an unfamiliar social power,
long associated with the richer western neighbour and now suddenly

---

[15] It is interesting to note that Adam Smith takes water to be a
commodity with a use-value but not an exchange value, in contrast to
the less useful diamond (*Wealth of Nations*, I/31); historians of the
global political economy of water in the 20th and 21st centuries will
undoubtedly have a different tale to tell.
[16] Georg Simmel, *The Philosophy of Money*, London 1978, 448ff.
[17] Georg Simmel, *The Philosophy of Money*, London 1978, p.512.

conferred on a population starved of a consumerist lifestyle, but exposed to its attractions via western television and western advertising. The fact that it was self-destructive, diverting demand away from east German enterprises, contributing to the wave of reduncancies in 1990 and 1991, should give theorists of money and of rational choice pause for thought.

This underscores the problems associated with the money-valuation of goods and of money itself. In the Middle Ages, money valuation was rendered more straightforward because of the static nature of economic production and by the simple nature of labour, consumption and exchange; 'it was assumed that there was a direct relation between object and money-price, i.e. a relation based upon the independent value of each.'[18] 'Mediaeval theory regarded value as something objective. It required the seller to ask the 'just price' for his commodity and occasionally attempted to fix this price by regulation.'[19] Mediaeval economic culture was still dominated by the notion of use-value in Adam Smith's or Marx' sense which found direct expression in the common system of barter or indirect representation in the constancy of money-price, where money functions were frequently paralleled by common goods like salt. As production, exchange, consumption and general lifestyles become more complex, the valuation process becomes increasingly refined and untransparent, subject as it is to a wide variety of cultural determinants. As payment in kind or by work gives way to wage labour and money exchange, so the simple equivalents of the use-value system give way to the money-valuations of the system of exchange value.

The exchange value system, combined with the dynamics of capitalist growth and mass consumption creates the cyclical 'necessity' of price changes and, with the advent of monopoly price-'stickiness', the structural feature of price inflation; while inflation was not unknown in pre-capitalist societies, emerging in particular in times of war and poor harvests, all economic histories chart the entry of inflation as a structural feature of economic culture from the early 19th century.[20] Price rises in industrial capitalism have thus reflected both scarcity and the dynamism of growth. Constant technological improvements and the growth of labour skills allow increased labour

---

[18] Georg Simmel, *The Philosophy of Money*, London 1978, p.126.
[19] Georg Simmel, ibid.
[20] See in particular, Roger Bootle, *The Death of Inflation*, London, 1997.

productivity, higher wages and higher prices; increased nominal wages can be eroded in part by higher prices (the 'money illusion') but still leave an increase in real income. Central bankers in recent years, particularly during and after the abnormal period of stagflation in the 70s and early 80s, frequently urge the need to banish the culture of 'inflationary expectations'. However, it is also well known that, even in the havens of monetary stability like Germany or Switzerland, mild inflation of some 2 per cent per annum is the norm (or maybe even the target). There is consequently an inbuilt culture of inflationary expectations which accepts (mild) increases in prices because they are a) offset by increases in productivity and nominal incomes and b) the tokens not of misfortune but of success. This paradoxicality of inflation is arguably reflected in all state economic policy, including monetary policy; inflation must be and is deliberately allowed. (See below)

The measurement of inflation has always been a rather haphazard affair, varying over time and between individual countries, depending very heavily on the selection of goods and services which are included in the indices of price movements. Measurement is simpler when the basket contains the staples of subsistence (basic foodstuffs, fuels, clothing and shelter) and when the price rises are extreme, as in Germany's two hyperinflations following World War One and World War Two. The measurement of inflation, and therefore of money as a store of value, becomes much more problematic as the selection of goods and services in the basket is wider and more refined. This applies to the current period of rapid technological progress, increased labour productivity and quality improvements.

Recent studies by Boskin (1997) and Hoffmann (1998) draw attention to systematic errors in the calculation of aggregate annual rates of inflation deriving from changes in consumer behaviour and the emergence of new or qualitatively better products. Both studies suggest a consistent overestimation of inflation. Apart from having significant consequences for monetary and fiscal policy (see below) the findings raise questions about perceptions of money and value and the determinant role of the state as fiduciary guarantor of money and statistical adjustments to money values. If there is a systematic over-compensation for inflation over time because of changes in the nature and quality of the 'standard' basket of commodities (i.e. because of the inadequacies of state measurement techniques), a dichotomy between real objective money value (adjusted for changes) and apparent official money value (unadjusted) opens up. When unknown to the economic agent as subject, this dichotomy is socially irrelevant. If made known and particularly if adjustments are made in indexed benefits, tax allowances, salaries, pensions etc. the fiduciary element in individual expectations of fiscal and monetary authorities is potentially undermined, the logical neutrality of money exposed as a delusion.

Similarly subversive of the concept of money's logical neutrality is the contrast between the internal and external value of currencies, where the former is managed and ensured by territorial monetary authorities and where the latter (under the current conditions of flexible exchange rates and capital mobility) is determined by a variety of determinants via currency markets (current and future bond yields, current and future disparites of central bank rates, current account balances, 'professional' and amateur predictions of currency movements, associated derivatives etc.), not to mention the very nature of monetary regimes, targetting money stock, inflation or exchange rates. The sale or purchase of one currency as a variable store of value by means of another currency in a process of exchange itself intended to alter the nominal and real value of the currency acquired or disposed of, at the very least undermines the fiduciary relationship of nation state to the residential population, holding and using the national currency, but it also reinforces the contradiction between the commodity function and the exchange function of money. Money as a global means to modify the value of specific monies and to provoke defensive acts of exchange from national guarantors of stability is precisely the paradox of contemporary currency market activity. Furthermore, global currency markets reveal clear hierarchies of currencies, some which are held long-term as reserves, others which are targetted as objects of speculative attacks.[21] 'Currency competition' means that the exchange rate of weaker currencies needs to be more actively defended with higher than average real interest rates and regular market interventions.[22] The existence of international money markets (xeno markets) which are accessible in practice to a limited number of agents who in part operate quite separately from markets in goods and services but who nevertheless affect the operation of normal exchange markets and normal state activity, is a modern phenomenon which was predicted neither in classical nor Marxist economics in the 19th century. However, it is in part foreshadowed in Marx' concept of the fetishisation of money and the development of commodified systems of exchange in which value is located in the exchangeability of a

---

[21] Herr, *Währungswettbewerb und Währungssysteme*, op.cit.132ff.

[22] Ibid. 225ff

commodity rather than in its use. Money, as the purest abstract commodity, thus has the potential to free itself from the normal sphere of productive accumulation.

The fact of a decoupled global capital market is demonstrated:

a) by the disparity of the volume of monetary transactions and current account (traded) transactions. Guttmann calculated in 1996 that the volume of daily transactions on Forex markets averaged $1400 billion, of which a maximum of 15 per cent are concerned with trade and long-term capital flows.[23]

b) by the high rates of growth achieved by equity values compared to GDP; in Germany the DAX rose by 45 per cent in 1997 compared to real GDP growth of just 2.2 per cent; this translates into a clear income disparity if equity gains were to be calculated on an annual basis;

c) so-called derivative markets have developed, selling bonds and other 'products' which are not even tangentially related to productive assets but to speculative bets on the movement of other fictitious values.

****

If we accept Marx' and Simmel's view of money facilitating the commodification of economic and social existence and helping to define power relations in society in which (among other things) labour power is reduced to a commodity, one is half-way to understanding the need for a proper historical sociology of money. A fundamental insight of such an approach would be that the money economy evolves along with processes of technological refinement, specialization, industrialisation, internationalisation, communication etc. Rentier income, for example, in the eighteenth and nineteenth centuries predefined a distinct set of social relations: work (non-work), inheritance, marriage ('She has but £300 a year'), housing, servants, education and recreation. The rentier classes were virtually wiped out in Germany as a result of the First World War and post-war hyperinflation: bank deposits and fixed interest securities, as the predominant sources of rentier income, were rendered worthless by devaluations of 12000 and 30000 per cent, by the failure of the Reichsbank to prevent the process through credit controls and high interest rates and by the refusal of the state to allow the revaluation of

[23] Robert Guttmann, 'Die Transformation des Geldkapitals. *Prokla* 103, 1996, p.183.

old debts after stabilisation. This process clearly undermined the temporary allegiance of the middle classes to democracy and contributed to the rise of fascism as the ostensible defender of the petit bourgeoisie.

The modernisation of production since World War I and a further bout of hyperinflation after 1945 prevented the development of a socially or politically significant rentier class. However, since the emergence of in the late 1970s of deregulated, decoupled and technoligically refined global capital markets and the simultaneous accumulations of inherited wealth in the hands of an already comfortable post-war generation, rentier income has reappeared as a significant socio-economic phenomenon which needs to be serviced in terms of both policy and politics.[24] However, in contrast to the relatively low yielding financial assets from which earlier rentier income was earned, and which represented in the main the normal savings loop of bank deposits and other fixed interest securities, the new modern form of rentier income derives from a wide variety of sources, including bonds and time deposits but also incorporating investment trusts, commodity, currency, equity and bond futures as well as 'derivative' products; the latter, as observed above, no longer belong to the standard savings-investment loop but to the globalised casino which is self-referential and self-perpetuating.[25] The distinct quality of the new sources of rentier (unearned) income is that they function separately from and despite conditions on normal trading markets (see above). They represent the sluggishness or inadequacy of traditional forms of accumulation (investment, production, trade, profit), the resulting growth of vast reserves of corporate and private money wealth and the need to find an alternative means of capital reproduction. Financial markets have provided a new home for these large and increasing reserves and, as indicated above, they have generated a dynamism which is maintained not just by the rates of return but by the

---

[24] 'If inherited wealth and savings from the great post-war boom have so altered the political economy of the 1980s and 1990s, that is a trend which will continue. Furthermore, it is the old who as a group are most homogeneously in favour of high interest rates and stable money and most opposed to inflationary stimuli'; thus Alan S. Milward, 'The Social Bases of Monetary Union', in: Peter Gowan and Perry Anderson (eds), *The Question of Europe*, London 1987, p.157.
[25] Thus Michael Zapf, 'Good news is bad news. Kapitalmärkte als paradoxe Systeme', *Kursbuch*, Nr.130, December 1970, p. 129f.

knowledge that there is no alternative to a new monetary accumulation (see Chapter 6). The disparity between the increase in equity values and the income/profits growth of the corresponding enterprises underlines the dilemma and the general deformation of capital accumulation in which, as Milward observes, increasing numbers of the population have a vested interest. It is not just the stockbrokers and currency dealers that cannot afford to question the fictitious quality of financial accumulation, but the financial managers of corporate reserves, the pension fund managers, the insurance companies. They are only able to maintain their own rates of growth and benefit by not crying out that the emperor has no clothes, that the spiral of 'value growth' is not much less spurious than the pyramid-selling scams of Rumania and Albania.

The loyal self-perpetuation of the markets in fictitious values is, of course, damaging to the needs of those excluded from their benefits, who would benefit from the redirection of investment funds out of financial markets and into real, productive investments: the social, educational and economic infrastructures of developed and developing countries, for example. This is a broader feature of the deformation of economic life which will be examined in later chapters. The importance of the above remarks for this stage of the argument is that it underscores the very different stage which the money economy has reached and the different forms which money and monetary networks take.

These networks are determined by a variety of factors. Firstly, the technology of communication and transmission has revolutionised systems of payment and speculation in a way which would have unimaginable thirty years ago; information systems allowing immediate and constant knowledge of currency market movements in the major centres of currency trading have clearly contributed to the emergence of the very modern form of speculative accumulation. Secondly, however, the speculation networks have been aided by a set of political decisions, based on radical market beliefs: the collapse of the Bretton Woods system between 1971 and 1973, the gradual lifting of exchange controls and increasingly benign tax regimes have provided the networks with the preconditions for in part computer-driven currency trading, the volume of which dwarfs the commodity markets they used to serve. The subsequent attempts to reconstruct more stable currency systems, like the EMS, created yet further opportunities for predatory attacks by international currency speculators.[26] This was particularly noticeable in the period following the signing of the Maastricht Treaty (December 1991), when EMS members were keen to maintain the parities of participant currencies and were committed to intervene on their behalf. As a result, vast fortunes were earned from the Treasuries of Britain, Italy, Ireland, Spain, Portugal, France and Germany because of their intramarginal interventions. Unless currencies were withdrawn from the EMS or formally devalued within the system, the speculator could rely on being able to play one EMS currency off against another, buying cheap (at EMS floor margins) and selling dear, after central banks had been forced (by treaty) to sell strong currencies to buy weak ones. The EMS proved to be a speculators' paradise up until August 1993, the losses to national treasuries were prodigious.[27]

Contemporary currency markets are paradoxical phenomena; if commercial banks are involved in their transactions, only the profits and losses from such transactions appear on the balance sheets; they are self-referential, largely divorced from trading accounts, but – inasmuch as industrial corporations are also dependent on rentier income – they affect their operational surpluses and deficits; they depend essentially on imperfect information networks, on the knowledge/luck of some participants and the ignorance/bad luck of others. As Michael Zapf correctly observes: 'A judgement which all share has an index potential of zero';[28] In the case of concerted predatory attacks on national currencies, the losses are frequently socialised via state interventions and the profits privatised (viz. the example of George Soros). Above all the fictionality of the 'added value' (where no work has been done, no product produced, no service rendered) demands a 'dynamic of non-reflection': 'Since a contemplative and disorientated pause for thought is more dangerous for economic systems than marching in the wrong

---

[26] See, in particular, Eichengreen, B/ Rose, A.K. and Wyplosz, C, 'Exchange market mayhem: the antecedents and aftermath of speculative attacks', in: *Economic Policy*, No 21, pp.251–312.

[27] Aeschimann and Riché calculate that the Banque de France spent the equivalent of $27.5 billion supporting the FF up to the end of July 1993, the cost of two tunnels under the Channel! (Aeschimann, E and Riché, P. *La Guerre de Sept Ans. Histoire Secrète du franc fort 1989–1996*, Paris 1996, p.219.

[28] Michael Zapf, 'Good news is bad news', op.cit. p.136.

direction, the whole thing makes sense'[29], at least to the little boy in the crowd.

If one takes the idea of currency hierarchies one step further, one raises the question of the cultural value and the social psychological function of a strong currency, compared to a weaker one, particularly if that strength is recent, unaccustomed and growing – the position of the Mark today. The cultural history of the Mark as national currency is both short and marked by critical disjunctures which tend also to be the examples most often cited in general histories of money and central banking. The Mark became the general currency of united Germany in 1873, replacing the nine distinct denominations in circulation in Germany's regional states before that and, thanks to French reparations in gold Francs, struck in part in gold. Of the 48 years of the Second Empire's existence (1871–1918), no less than 19 were marked by zero or below zero inflation. On the other hand, the final years of the Reichsmark from 1914 to 1923 – after the suspension of the gold standard prior to the outbreak of war – saw the effective destruction of the RM as an internal and an external currency.[30] The misery of post-war inflation was repeated after World War Two but under the conditons of occupation and ostensible external control of fiscal and monetary affairs. Three years of a massive currency overhang and underproduction reduced the money economy nevertheless to a farce and created both a ruthless barter economy (where a canteen of silver cutlery could be exchanged for a dozen eggs) and the adoption of foreign cigarettes as a substitute currency (qua stable store of value). The introduction of the DM in the West in 1948 and its subsequent appreciation against all other currencies (with the exception of the Yen and the Swiss Franc) was arguably a matter of considerable social psychological importance for the western state, its monetary institutions and its population, particularly when set against 34 years of mayhem between 1914 and 1948. It took DM 4.20 in 1949 to buy one unit of the world's strongest reserve currency, the Dollar; in May 1998 one Dollar, still the world's primary reserve currency, costs just DM1.76. This has

---

[29] Michael Zapf, ibid. p.131.

[30] Domestic (wholesale) prices doubled between 1913 and 1918, while the Dollar exchange rate declined by about a third. In the next five years external devaluation progressed faster than domestic inflation (a disparity which yielded clear benefits – see below) but the final end position showed the Dollar rate 6 billion times the 1913 and the wholesale index 7 billion times higher than a decade earlier.

to be the source not just of international economic power (as fiscal contributor, trader or tourist) but also of cultural pride.

In the absence of other strong collective bonds of tradition or stability, neutralised in large measure by the German catastrophe of two world wars, the importance of 'our money' (Nölling)[31] must be considerably greater than that of the French Franc or the Pound Sterling. 'For hardly any other country does the currency have such value. The Mark became the symbol of German strength and independence'.[32] In the new context of international subordination, half-sovereignty and pooled sovereignty, 'the new currency was' according to a popular view, 'the precondition for the economic miracle, it was the entry fee which eased the Germans' path into the circle of western civilisation after their Nazi-madness'.[33] Adenauer even used the monetary metaphor of 'creditworthiness' which the Germans needed to develop in their international relations.[34] Franc and Pound have been subject to marked processes of devaluation internally and externally, in particular in relation to the Mark,[35] but France and Britain also have a righteous tradition of continuity and resistance to the 'enemies of democracy'. For Germany, accordingly, 'currency reform' is seen/presented as the key event in the establishment of economic order in 1948; a key driving force of unification was the urgent desire of east Germans to swap their 'Alu-Chips' (the insubstantial and unconvertible Ostmark) for Deutschmark; the slogan 'If the DM doesn't come to us, we will go to it', was the key accelerator of

---

[31] Unser Geld is the title of the book by the EMU opponent, Wilhelm Nölling, formerly President of the Hamburg Land Central Bank, (1993) which was translated into English under the rather anodyne title *Monetary Policy in Europe before and after Maastricht*, Nölling's opposition to EMU was/is based both on a reasoned scepticism towards the historical context, timing and modalities of the programme and on an unconcealed and convincing prejudice in favour of the national currency. See also his pamphlet *Goodbye to the Deutschmark, Hamburg 1993*.

[32] Thus Michael Schmidt-Klingenberg, 'Der schwere Abschied', *Der Spiegel*, 18/1998, p.114.

[33] Ibid.

[34] See Hallgarten/Radkau, *Deutsche Industrie und Politik*, Cologne 1974.

[35] For example the purchasing power of the Pound in 1998 is 5 per cent of its 1948 value, the Franc's 6 per cent, but the Mark's 27 per cent.

currency union in 1990. There has been much talk of a so-called DM-Nationalism, perceived in both the scepticism of the population towards the Euro-Project and the desire to ensure at the very least that the new European currency is as 'hard as the Mark', by insisting that the institutional arrangements for EMU are identical to those applying to the Mark: independent bank, stability culture, Frankfurt headquarters. Poll after poll confirms the reluctance of Germans to relinquish the Mark.[36] Embracing the EURO is thus seen not as an enthusiastic strategy for economic advancement, but rather as the collective price to be paid for German unification.[37] If one ascribes to Germany's money a particular function of national-cultural cement, as objectifier of success and reliability, its disappearance within EMU should reveal a corresponding vacuum and the need for substitute sources of cultural identity.

Deriving identity from money and money-power was itself to become a problem in the young culture of post-war Germany, in particular after the establishment of a new affluence and the emergence of a younger, questioning generation, the children of affluence who no longer needed the diversionary comfort of hard work. Again, it is not possible to quantify the effects of a social culture where – for better or worse – 'only money, only the D-Mark was and is the measure of all things' (Grass), or the intergenerational tensions this produced, but it does help to illustrate in this introductory chapter how money and its functions can only be understood in the specific historical and cultural context of its usage, that it cannot be regarded as a unitary, abstract, neutral phenomenon with a corresponding set of immutable regulatory principles. Neither the economic nor the social understanding of money is a simple affair. To assume this, as monetarism and its practitioners do, is to remain wedded to a dangerous ahistorical dogmatism. To apply

---

[36] Schmidt-Klingenberg notes that, up until 1998, opinion polls showed a consistent two thirds of the German population sceptical of or hostile to EMU, 'Der schwere Abschied', op.cit.

[37] This view was frequently uttered by academics (e.g. Alan Milward, 'The Social Bases of Monetary Union?', op.cit. p. 156; Stephan Schulmeister, 'EURO-Projekt', op.cit. p.299; the premature publication of documents dealing with unification *(Dokumente zur Deutschlandpolitik*, Munich 1998) would seem to confirm that Helmut Kohl bowed to pressure from François Mitterrand to accelerate European monetary union in exchange for French compliance in the unification project; summarized in *Der Spiegel*, 19/1998, 108ff.

German cultural norms relating to monetary policy to a set of other economic cultures takes this dangerous dogmatism one step further.

In the following chapters, we will examine firstly the ideological context within which the preference for central bank autonomy developed, the operation of independent central banking in Germany, the popularisation of independent central banks within the 'developed' world and the observable consequences of this trend.

2 Autonomy and German Traditions of Liberalism

LIBERALISM AS A CONTEXT

'Market democracy, in its silent precision surpasses the most perfect political democracy'. This key statement by one of the intellectual fathers of German ordo-liberalism, Wilhelm Röpke,[1] expresses in a very obvious way the fundamental ambivalence within liberal intellectual traditions towards 'freedom' and 'democracy' as social phenomena. The power to act as a free economic agent, to produce, buy and sell in a market driven by supply and demand, is presented by Röpke as more 'democratic' than the power to elect political representatives and hold them answerable. There is a greater 'equality' for Röpke in the aggregate of market decisions, because all economic agents are involved all of the time, whereas elections are sporadic, electoral majorities leave sizeable minorities unrepresented and political processes of influence and decision-making are haphazard. It follows that market 'freedom' must be the core measure of a culture's democratic credentials, supported to a greater or lesser degree by the 'less precise' institutions of political democracy. This ambivalence as to what constitutes true liberal democracy is by no means confined to the idiosyncratic German tradition of liberalism but is shared by early British exponents of liberalism from Hobbes through to the younger Mill, indeed by modern exponents of 'neo-liberalism'. The ambivalence derives from differing perceptions of the central theoretical concepts of liberalism, namely of liberty, equality and property and from associated problems of defining the role of the state as a social institution in the framework of an ideology directed towards the individual.

Döhn goes as far as to say that an adequate, self-contained definition is impossible: 'Liberalism is not a closed theory, nor is it a unitary political movement, but rather a *function* of bourgeois society which

---

[1] W. Röpke, *The Social Crisis of our Time*, Erlenbach-Zürich 1942, p. 103

has developed in the relationship of tension between freedom and equality as political principles of democracy and private ownership of the means of production (including the freedom associated with this ownership) as a social principle of capitalism.'[2]

The historical origins of core liberal principles reinforce the scope for ambivalence: Hobbes derivation of the modern state from a rational subordination of individual freedom to the necessity of constraint via a social contract involving all members of society, as a means of maximising residual individual freedoms, differs from Locke's view of the liberal state as guarantor of the freedom of property-owning classes as agents of a putative common good. Hobbes' views prioritised the political and social rights of all, albeit within an absolutist state, while Locke emphasised the economic rights of property-owning classes, implying the exclusion of both subordinate classes and Hobbes' absolutist guarantor, where the latter is supplanted by the rule of law. Theories of the liberal capitalist state based on class analysis identify the primacy of bourgeois economic interest and the need to establish a regulatory framework for commercial contracts and the disposition of property as the origin of the categories of equality (before the law) and liberty (to dispose freely of property).[3] The centralisation of political controls over currency, units of measurement, customs duties and taxation, and the establishment of an independent judiciary within a unitary territory were thus economic in motivation and fundamental in the emergence of entrepreneurial capitalism, trade and industrialisation. The economic essence of the categories of 'liberty' and 'equality' correspond therefore more closely to Locke's exposition of liberalism as hierarchical (and politically non-egalitarian), even if the particular transitions from absolutism to 'liberal' constitutional states took a variety of very distinct forms in the history of industrialising nations. The primacy of the economic categories of liberty and equality nevertheless is very convincing. The translation of these essentially economic categories to the level of non-economic civil rights, to

---

[2] Lothar Döhn, 'Liberalismus', in: Neumann, F (ed.) *Handbuch politischer Theorien und Ideologien*, Opladen 1995, p.173

[3] See, for example, Blanke, B., Jürgens, U. and Kastandiek, H. *Kritik der Politischen Wissenschaft*, (2 vols), Frankfurt 1975; Dieter Langewiesche, in contrast, asserts that 'social liberalism' preceded any 'economic liberalism', at least within the German tradition, but does not explain the historical parentage of 'social liberalism'; viz *Liberalismus in Deutschland*, Frankfurt am Main 1988, p.7

political constitutions and political processes thus creates the immanent tension between a specific and a general interest, between the propertied classes (aristocracy and bourgeoisie) and other social classes. It is a tension which accompanies the whole of the modern history of constitutional liberalism in all national contexts. Within these contexts liberalism as an ideology performs historically determinate functions: legitimating the rights and freedoms of anti-feudal, middle class economic agents in the seventeenth and eighteenth centuries, underpinning the economic and political rights of (the white) man in the eighteenth and nineteenth centuries and then legitimating a variety of political liberations from perceived bondage to perceived freedom in the twentieth. The twentieth century variants arguably seek to defend the civil rights and 'liberties' of all members of society, but there is still a wide scope for ambivalence: European social liberalism has more in common with democratic socialist traditions than with Chilean neo-liberalism under Pinochet, for example.

Within the very broad church of liberalism there has thus predictably been an extraordinary variety of selective interpretations of what constitutes liberty: whose liberty, from what, to what, how much of it, how is it chosen, how is it valued, how is its value imparted to others, how much coercion is necessary to guarantee one or more freedoms?

German liberalism, in the two centuries of its emergence and development, conforms to the broad church model, accommodating conservative monarchists, radical anti-monarchists, bureaucratic 'statist' liberals, economic liberals, national liberals, 'progressive' 'free-thinking' social liberals, ordo-liberals and more recently neo-liberals, to mention only those (political) movements that marched under the 'liberal' banner; some commentators argue convincingly that other groupings embody some significant features of liberalism, even if they were programmatically opposed to parties who describe themselves as 'liberal'; the liberal constitution of the Weimar Republic[4] was accordingly upheld by both the Social Democratic Party as the main party of state and by trade unions before any other social groupings; furthermore, post-1945 Christian Democracy is seen as a

---

[4] While the first Weimar Coalition was dominated by the Social Democrats, the chief author of the August 1919 Constitution was Hugo Preuß, a member of the German Democratic Party, the left liberal junior coalition party.

blend of social catholicism and liberal economics (be it ordo- or neo-liberal[5] in nature).

Thus, it is impossible to define a specific liberal archetype, let alone a specific German liberal archetype; the label 'liberal' and the key categories of 'freedom', 'autonomy' and 'equality' are deployed to justify a wide variety of, often contrasting, policies (free trade or mercantilism, civil liberties and repression, slavery and slave emancipation, for example). Such paradoxes are generated by the immanent tension between economic individualism and constitutional liberalism and the particular preferences accorded to the one or the other, but also by the opportunism involved in claiming a general 'interest' when pursuing sectional or individual interests. It is nevertheless possible to provide a rough assessment of where the pendulum of ideological interpretations swung within particular liberalisms in the course of German history. This will act as a backdrop to a closer analysis of the particular place of the autonomy principle within the history of German liberal ideas and within the political praxis of liberal and other states and state parties. It is my contention that, for a variety of historical reasons, Germany's ruling elites have demonstrated a stronger preference for the principle of autonomy in the structures and hierarchies of the country's political economy than is typical of other modern industrial societies. This is not intended to exculpate other national liberalisms in terms of their ambivalence towards democracy, but rather to inform the specific debate surrounding the issue of central bank autonomy; analysis of specific institutions of economic policy (Reichsbank, Bundesbank) in the framework of social, economic and intellectual history shows to what degree they are contextually determinate and hence how easy/difficult it would be to transplant the model onto other cultures.

Why should we suddenly be so concerned about the ideology of autonomy, when discussing contemporary central banking? Essentially because the principle of an autonomous monetary policy is being institutionalised at a European level and for a number of reasons:

---

[5] A.J.Nicholls makes no distinction between 'ordo-liberals' and 'neo-liberals' in his account of the origins of the 'social market economy' (*Freedom with Responsibility. The Social Market Economy in Germany 1918–1963*, Oxford (Clarendon) 1994; this represents a significant misreading of the peculiarities of the German school of economists around the journal *Ordo*, and their particular policy preferences, according to this author.

1) at the practical level, it would have been impossible to get the German state to commit itself to EMU without the adoption of similar/identical institutional arrangements as they have obtained in Germany since 1948, where currency union is seen from both a German and a European perspective as a means of anchoring Germany more strongly to the EU;

2) at the technical level, a number of studies have seemed to indicate that central bank autonomy ensures a lower level of price inflation than provided by dependent central banks;

3) at the theoretical level central bank autonomy accords with neo-liberal precepts of market-driven political processes, in this instance in relation to the national and international demand for money;

4) at the political level it corresponds to recent preferences for quasi autonomous agencies of policy implementation, on whom the state confers executive power for reasons of technical and economic efficiency.

'Only independence guarantees success',[6] is an increasingly popular dictum of monetary theorists; above all it implies that central bank 'dependence' upon the instructions of central government and finance ministry opens up monetary policy for potential abuse by elected administrations. European history undoubtedly reveals significant examples of such abuse, where a democratic state seeks to ameliorate the shocks of war or reconstruction and to avoid the legitimacy crises of severe deflation by resorting to unconsolidated central bank credits; likewise, there are examples of governing parties creating convenient pre-election pro-cyclical booms by relaxing monetary policy when it should be tightened or left as it was. Unfortunately, the nature of this 'abuse' does not provide convincing evidence to support the theoretical case for autonomisation. The hyperinflations of the early 1920s or after 1945 in Europe, of Latin America in the 1970s or of post-communist societies in the 1990s have by and large been the exceptions that prove the rule (within democratic societies at least) of relative stability. They can be ascribed primarily to large exogenous shocks which are not typical of organised, democratic capitalism; the same is in part true of the most recent outbreak of stagflation in 'western' democracies resulting from the two oil crises. Secondly, the most notorious hyperinflation of 1923 in Weimar Germany was presided over by a Reichsbank which had been 'autonomised' in May 1922; the

---

[6] Thus Dieter Balkhausen, *Gutes Geld und Schlechte Politik*, Düsseldorf, 1992, 72ff

failure/refusal of its then President, Havenstein, to end the disastrous policy of open-house discounting was not the result of instructions from elected authorities but of a dominant view within the Central Council of the Reichsbank that currency reform (stabilisation) would be counter-productive as long as the perceived cause of Germany's whirlwind devaluations, the reparations 'dictat' of the London Schedule of Payments, remained in place.[7] This position has been underpinned theoretically by the perfectly respectable (if flawed) balance of payments theory. Conversely, the debate about the advantages and disadvantages of German inflation reveals at the very least convincing arguments of the exceptional nature of the two exogenous shocks of war (domestic debt) and defeat (reparations obligations) making hyperinflation inevitable or even desirable.[8] Herbert Ehrenberg suggests convincingly that the effects of monetary deflation during the Great Depression were far more damaging economically and politically than Weimar hyperinflation.[9] Thirdly, the implication that autonomous central banks are 'de-politicised' or immune to the attractions of the

---

[7] Thus Havenstein, president of the Reichsbank, in two separate meetings of the Central Committee of the Bank (22 October1922 and 25 August 1923), cited in: Claus-Dieter Krohn, *Die große Inflation in Deutschland 1918–1923*, op.cit., p.23

[8] The virtual expunging of the German state's colossal domestic debt and the legislative bar on revaluing debts after stabilisation, freed the state budget from the levels of debt-servicing still endured by Britain and France; Germany's merchant fleet, railway system and telephone network were all rebuilt using inflationary (free) credit; in addition, even before the strong rationalisation wave of 1924–29, German industry had used cheap Reichsbank credit to reequip factories, mines and distribution networks. Furthermore, the inflation economy had helped to reintegrate demobilised workers, keep unemployment at far lower levels than in France and Britain and to conduct a very effective export-drive. Notwithstanding the misery (and subsequent political alienation of both the working class and the rentier elements of the middle class) the macro-economic benefits of inflation seemed clearly to outweigh the disbenefits. C.f. D. Graham, *Exchange, Prices and Production in Hyper-Inflation: Germany 1920–1923*, Princeton 1930; K. Laursen and J. Pedersen, *The German Inflation 1918–1923*, Amsterdam 1964

[9] H. Ehrenberg, *Abstieg vom Währungsolymp*, Frankfurt 1991, 85ff

political cycle defies the evidence.[10] Most recently, the Central Bank Council under the Christian Democrat Hans Tietmeyer managed to lower interest rates in the first half of 1994 in advance of the crucial federal elections despite a continued and rapid expansion of the money supply, ostensibly the key trigger of interest rate rises; Tietmeyer's party colleague Helmut Kohl was successfully re-elected. In a broader sense, the centrality of central bank reform and monetary policy to the political debates of the 1990s has politicised the institutions, their leading personnel and academic discourse like this current study.

If, as I contend, the evidence in support of the principle of central bank autonomy is intellectually flawed, the question then arises how it can gain such a strong foothold in contemporary economic and political thinking, what cultural and ideological filters are in operation to ease its passage and to neutralise the preference for alternatives. Clearly, the crisis in economic policy which accompanied the end of Bretton Woods and the onset of stagflation in the 1970s was the catalyst. Keynesianism was seemingly discredited; monetary policy instruments appeared to be more effective in coping with the vicissitudes of deregulated world capital markets in contrast to fiscal regimes. Nevertheless, the triumph of central bankism has taken place within an historical context in which the central banks of two leading and successful industrial economies were already independent (USA and Germany), where the principle had already taken firm root, facilitating the transition from simple monetarism in the seventies and eighties to autonomisation in the 1990s.

Autonomy in its predominant forms in liberal theory is a metaphor for self-determination, self-authorship; literally, it means self- (auto-) legislation (nomos = law). The metaphor is applied to the individual human being as the locus of rational will. Kant confers an ethical essence on the concept: 'The autonomy of the will is the sole principle

---

[10] Studies by both Roland Vaubel and Susanne Lohmeier present evidence of a changing party-political bias of the Bundesbank Central Council relative to its composition; S. Lohmeier, *Federalism and Central Bank Autonomy: The Politics of German Monetary Policy 1957–1992*, Mimeograph, University of California at Los Angeles; Roland Vaubel 'The Bureaucratic and Partisan Behaviour of Independent Central Banks: German and International Evidence', ms. December 1995

of all moral laws and associated duties'.[11] Conversely, according to John Gray, the market derives its moral foundation 'as an enabling device for the protection and enhancement of human autonomy'.[12] In both accounts, autonomy denotes a process of individual human activity, facilitated by the freedom from coercion (negative freedom), where freedom is simply a state of affairs. Autonomy becomes the end, towards which liberty, as means, leads: 'The value of negative liberty must therefore be theorized in terms of its contribution to something other than itself, which does possess intrinsic value. In truth, it seems clear that the chief value of negative liberty is in its contribution to the positive liberty of autonomy'.[13] The pivot of liberal theory is the autonomous individual, 'individualism' is 'the metaphysical and ontological core' of liberalism,[14] the core prescription of liberal politics is the optimisation of the individual's opportunities for self-determination:

According to Dahrendorf, '[l]iberalism is in principle a perfectly clear and simple orientation of political action: It depends upon doing everything to extend the individual's opportunities in life.'[15] The sum of individual opportunities is the yardstick for the liberality of society in Mill's sense of collective utility,[16] while the collectivity is judged by the degree to which it does or does not constrain the individual's

---

[11] Immanuel Kant, *Kritik der Praktischen Vernunft*, Werke VII, Frankfurt 1948, p.144. Vol. 1 §8

[12] John Gray, 'The Illusions of Libertarianism', in: Gray, *The Moral Foundations of Market Institutions*, London 1992, p.19

[13] Gray, ibid. p. 22. Gray's closer definition of autonomy is revealing in terms, firstly of the gendered nature of his language, secondly in terms of the relativisation of the liberty involved: 'By autonomy is meant the condition in which a person can be at least part author of his condition, in which a person can be at least part author of his life, in that he has before him a range of worthwhile options in respect of which his choices are not fettered by coercion and with regard to which he possesses the capacities and resources presupposed by a reasonable measure of success in his self-chosen path among these options.'

[14] Thus A. Arblaster, *The Rise and Decline of Western Liberalism'*, London 1984, p. 15

[15] Thus Ralf Dahrendorf, *Die Chancen der Krise*, Stuttgart 1983, p.37

[16] Dahrendorf provides a modern version of the doctrine of liberal utitlity: 'The greater the number of people that have more opportunities in life, the more liberal is a society', ibid.

autonomy. The sanctity of the autonomous individual accords with the image of man in Protestant theology, created in the image of the 'Creator', no longer caught in the ineluctable power pyramid of Catholicism and absolutism, but freed to operate above all as an economic agent, where usury and accumulation are not sins but virtues.[17]

Creative autonomy is arguably also the dominant cultural virtue of Renaissance Europe up to this day; the cult of the heroic autonomous male in the fine arts, in literature, drama, music, opera, popular legend has likewise been a common form of artistic creation: Prometheus, Laokoon, Herkules, Wallenstein, Faust, Robinson Crusoe, El Cid, Napoleon, Parsifal, Gulliver, Superman, Popeye, Mickey Mouse reflect the core of a cultural canon which continues to inform relationships and social structures in the late 20th century. The 'universal man' of Renaissance and post-Renaissance high culture corresponds to other models of dynamic male autonomy, like Schumpeter's heroic entrepreneur in economic theory,[18] or to mythologized adventurers like Francis Drake, Marco Polo and Columbus, best ironised in Brecht's 'Questions of a Reading Worker': 'Caesar invaded Gaul. Didn't he even have a cook with him?'

The context of individual action, the network of relations, the technical infrastructure are set aside in the typical liberal view of things, creating an artificial antinomy. The values of autonomous male agency are thus another illustration of the epistemological problems raised in the previous chapter in relation to the function of money. Language, as a human and social construct, imposes a simple and simplifying notion of agency and causality onto a highly complex and multi-causal reality; subject-predicate views of agency conceal the socio-structural origins of both action *and* language and produce rather a dichotomy between

---

[17] Viz. R.H. Tawney, *Religion and the Rise of Capitalism*

[18] See Joseph Schumpeter, *Theorie der wirtschaftlichen Entwicklung*, (2. Edition), Munich 1926; Schumpeter's entrepreneur also appears in the rhetorical guise of the 'Führer' whose innovative force breaks the equilibrium and ensures dynamic progress. This led one later commentator to caricature Schumpeter's symbolic figure as his 'superman', thus Gottfried Eisermann, *Bedeutende Soziologen*, Stuttgart 1968, p. 58; for a cogent and fair discussion of the significance of Schumpeter's entrpreneuer, see: Dieter Haselbach, *Autoritärer Liberalismus und soziale Marktwirtschaft*, Baden-Baden (Nomos) (1991), 25ff, 238ff.

the autonomous will (the linguistic subject) and the constraining influence of the Other, of social rules, of 'structure'.[19] In the simple mythical world of self-determination and leadership, the polar (and negative) concept is that of determinateness, external determination ('Fremdbestimmung') of heteronomy. There are unavoidable inherent problems within both the cultural mythology of liberalism and the social reality of liberalisms concerning the balance between self-determined individuals, i.e. in terms of the power relations between more and less self-determined individuals, between Robinson Crusoe and Man Friday, between gentry and peasantry, employer and employee, between husband and wife, but also between knowledge and ignorance, ignorant power and knowing powerlessness, between liberty and democracy, or in Röpke's analysis between political and market democracy. The sanctification of autonomy as objective of human existence inevitably produces hierarchies of control and influence at the top and self-subordination and deference at the bottom.

In the case of German economic and social culture, there have been and arguably still are very specific hierarchies of knowledge which underpin its (successful) functioning. These involve both technical and technocratic expertise, represented in a variety of fields:

1. the tradition of guild-based, self-regulated skills training which still requires a majority of blue collar workers to have artisanal qualifications;

2. the traditions of scholarship and academic research, associated closely with industrial innovation;

3. the tradition of industrial entrepreneurs being, first and foremost, engineers rather than accountants;

4. the tradition of bureaucratic efficiency and loyalty to the state, maintained by a generous, hierarchical set of privileges.

These traditions are not absent in other cultures, but they are certainly highly developed and persist to a stronger degree in Germany than in many other highly industrialised economies. They can be used

---

[19] Elizabeth Frazer and Nicola Lacey (*The Politics of Community*, Toronto 1993, 171ff) examine the syllogisms involved in the 'agency structure dichotomy' in relation to the 'liberal-communitarian debate'; they talk rightly of the grammatically determined binary oppositions of agency and structure and of the need to conceive of a notion of autonomy which is rooted in rather implicitly opposed to social structures; this in turn requires 'a reconstructed theory of the subject' (p.180) as an epistemological/ linguistic project.

to explain the particular direction of Germany's political economy in its rapid development in the last thirty years of the nineteenth century. They can also be used to explain the particular development of social and political class relations. The relative impotence of bourgeois political forces until 1918, at least at regional and national level, the failure of 1848, the shrewd bonapartism of the German but especially the Prussian aristocracy, prolonged the transition to a modern civil society based on 'liberal' norms and human rights. Artisanal skill, scholarship, industrial innovation and success, technocratic efficiency became the dominant sources of middle-class self-advancement and pride. The hierarchies of skill and influence within particular fields of middle class activity imposed a stronger imprint on the norms of social existence than in other already industrialised countries with their normal colonial cushions. A highly ordered and economically functional education system reflects this imprint very clearly, reflects the central value placed on education as the vehicle for individual (bourgeois) advancement, for self-determination: specific grammar schools providing different weightings for different discipline channels: classical languages, modern languages or natural sciences, 'Realschulen' providing a channel for white collar occupations in the state service and commerce and for lower-middle class trades, the Volks- and Hauptschulen offering channels towards blue-collar training.[20] The German education system contrasted markedly with its British counterpart, the former elitist but economically effective, the latter elitist but economically paralysing.

In Germany, the skills culture with its associated hierarchies of knowledge, power and influence, its carefully graded wage and salary differentials, its sectoral economic effectiveness, reinforced the faith in technical agency and technical demarcation, particularly in the context of seemingly unalterable political facts: an authoritarian Prussian-German state and the geo-political dominance of other European colonial powers. The organisation of the skill society was conducted in large measure on the basis of sectoral self-administration, sectoral autonomy by any other name. It was aided, nevertheless, by the enlightened self-interest of the mercantilist aristocratic state. This produces an interesting kind of interdependence: the state needed

---

[20] An excellent introduction into the functionalism of the German education system in its developmental stage is: Detlef K. Müller, *Sozialstruktur und Schulsystem. Aspekte zum Strukturwandel des Schulwesens im 19. Jahrhundert,* Göttingen (Vandenhoeck) 1977

skilled engineers and technocrats but within a structure which resisted democratic forces, while engineers and commercial leaders needed the orders, the trade diplomacy and the social control of the state, while retaining significant powers of self-determination. Within this corporatist interdependence, however, the engineer, as specialist, was keen to present an 'a-political' face.[21] The craft chambers, the chambers of commerce, the trade associations had and still have legislating powers of self-promotion and self-defence, functioning in part as para-public institutions, particularly in the fields of training, education and industrial relations. Right through to 1945, the trade association functioned typically as a vehicle for cartel arrangements,[22] the cartel being vigorously defended as a means of promoting efficiency and avoiding waste,[23] but they also promoted the positive virtues of contractual probity, reliability and prompt payment.

The sanctification of autonomy within German economic culture has a distinct dimension of 'order' about it, in which individual skill and merit is organised within acknowledged professional structures, where initiative is promoted according in part to sets of rules, drafted and administered by the professional group, the craft chamber or trade association. This is not the improvisatory, amateurish risk-taking seen to have characterised the Anglo-Saxon approach to commercial and industrial development, extending over two or more centuries. It is not the Schumpeterian heroic entrepreneur. It is a more restrained entrepreneurship which has not enjoyed the advantages of relatively slow organic development or captive colonial markets but, as a latecomer culture, is obliged to minimise risk, to overcome the limitations of less developed capital markets and to make the best of an autocratic constitutional monarchy not designed to preside over free

---

[21] Viz. Gerd Hortleder, *Das Gesellschaftsbild des Ingenieurs. Zum politischen Verhalten der Technischen Intelligenz in Deutschland*, Frankfurt (Suhrkamp), 1970, 18ff
[22] Viz. Robert J. Bennett, 'Trade Associations: new challenges, new logic', in: Bennett (ed.), *Trade Associations in Britain and Germany: responding to internationalisation and the EU*, London 1997, p.3
[23] 'Under the precondition of healthy and responsible cartel activity, the Reich Federation of German Industry considers cartels to be indispensable'; this statement is taken from the 1925 Economic Programme of the Federation, quoted by Kurt Pritzkoleit, *Das kommandierte Wunder*, Vienna/Munich/Basle 1959, p.613

markets.[24] Germany's managed transition to 'organised capitalism' thus produces a more complex view of economic autonomy and liberty, matching the lateness of that transition and reflecting a unique set of circumstances. Notwithstanding the problems of a *Sonderweg* account of modern German history (with its implied postulation of an archetype from which the 'special path' deviates), the material and ideological difference of the context within which Germany's strands of liberalism developed, needs to be underlined. The 'peculiarities' of German industrialisation and modernisation (Blackbourn and Eley) allowed the emergence of notions of autonomy and liberty which included both individual and collective agency, individual skill and enterprise within a self-regulating hierarchy of skill.   The principle of autonomy is thus transferred onto collective agencies within disciplined organisational hierarchies operating according to self-administered rules. This was not liberal democracy presiding over free markets, but organised bourgeois self-interest making the best of the restrictions of a biased mercantilism ('rye and iron') and limiting the disruptive effects of competition. The economic reality of the Second Empire was reflected in the particular variants of liberalism that emerged in this period.

Dahrendorf's attempt to explain the 'tragedy of liberalism' in Germany[25] rightly refers to the distinctive nature of its political economy in the last third of the nineteenth century: 1) a higher level of capital concentration within Germany's corporate sector (joint stock companies) than in Britain; 2) the unique links between German universal banks and industry, 3) the dominance of cartels and syndicates in German commercial life and 4) the contribution of a 'pre-industrial elite' in the Prussian-German state to the political management of Germany's rapid industrialisation.[26] The seemingly oligarchic nature of economic culture where Germany's industrial resources were 'under the control of a dozen men of dominant

---

[24] A recent comparative study of British and German commercial culture confirms the picture of German businessmen as considerably more risk-averse than their innovative and reckless British counterparts; Dagmar Ebster-Grosz and Derek Pugh, *Anglo-German Business Collaboration. Pitfalls and Potentials*, London (Macmillan) 1996.

[25] Ralf Dahrendorf, *Gesellschaft und Demokratie in Deutschland*, Munich (Piper) 1965, p.225

[26] Ibid. 48f

economic genius'[27] allows Dahrendorf to assert 'that the broad substratum of bourgeois entrepreneurs played a smaller role in German industrialisation right from the outset than the large economic organisations and their leaders'.[28] Dahrendorf's analysis goes as far as to conclude that German industrial society in the Wilhelmine Empire was 'not actually capitalist' (it 'remained quasi-feudal');[29] the mixture of economic concentration, state socialism (sic) and nationalism sets it apart from the archetype. This allows Dahrendorf to explain the failure of political liberalism in Germany in terms of the absence of 'liberal' entrepreneurial capitalism. His account is clearly teleological but it does help to illuminate the peculiarities of German liberalism and the dilemmas these peculiarities create for liberal intellectuals like Dahrendorf. Even if German industrialisation did not 'swallow up the liberal principle', as Dahrendorf claims,[30] it clearly sent this principle in a number of distinct directions.

The fact that the 'inauguration of the bourgeois epoch'[31] was not primarily the work of a dynamic reforming bourgeois movement but of shrewd elements within the aristocratic state, at particular stages of the 19th century, immediately sets bourgeois 'liberal' forces within the context of political subordination and 'order'. This order was in turn defined by the imperative of national unity, firstly in the Vom Stein/Hardenberg reform era at the beginning of the century, then in the aftermath of the 1848 revolution and finally in Bismarck's 'revolution from above' in 1870, as well as by economic reforms, removing feudal ties and promoting entrepreneurship. Significantly it was not the industrial bourgeoisie that was the driving force behind the 1848 revolution but intellectuals, members of the professions, students and peasants; the largest contingent in the 1848 Frankfurt parliament was drawn from various state bureaucracies of Germany's regional states.[32] Their liberalism was in part driven by the meritocratic demands of

---

[27] Thus the contemporary commentator W.H. Dawson, *The Evolution of Modern Germany*, London/New York 1908, p.122
[28] Dahrendorf, *Gesellschaft und Demokratie*, op.cit. p.49
[29] Ibid. p.53 and p.62
[30] Ibid. p. 53
[31] David Blackbourn and Geoff Eley, *The Peculiarities of German History*, Oxford (OUP) 1984, p.83
[32] Colin Mooers, *The Making of Bourgeois Europe. Absolutism, Revolution and the Rise of Capitalism in England, France and Germany*, London (Verso), 1991, p.135

career civil servants. Their interests were not identical with either those of industrialists or those of artisans, peasants and students, who made up the revolution's foot soldiers.[33] This explains the very unrevolutionary new order proposed in the Parliament's constitutional deliberations and its offer of the unified crown to the dismally reactionary Frederick William IV, who bypassed the powerless and naïve parliamentarians with relative ease.

There are a number of obvious features of middle class 'liberal politics' in the 19th century: firstly, the illiberal status quo which kept bourgeois politicians away from executive power at national level until 1918, be it through repression, constitutional constraints, bonapartist politics, willing subordination, acceptance of the sop of municipal influence; secondly, the fragmentation of liberal groupings, reflecting both regional and ideological factionalism. Krieger identifies three basic categories of liberals in the pre-March (1848) period: 1) 'Rhenish and "classical" liberals who justified the attachment to what they deemed to be the essentials of historical order' are categorised as 'moderates; 2) 'the southern liberals dominated by Rottek' combined a radical rhetoric of emancipation and liberal constitutionalism 'with a cautious acceptance of established institutions' who are (generously) dubbed 'theoretical dualists' and 3) the 'Young Hegelians in the North and the doctrinaire natural rights adherents in the South-West were representative of German radicalism after 1840'.[34] This fragmentation contributed in large measure to the failure of the national (liberal) revolution in 1848 and persisted essentially through to the Weimar Republic. There was not one liberal party as in Britain but several that espoused principles of a liberal cast and many more that appealed to particular middle class client groups, religious, regional or other ideological preferences like anti-semitism. Thirdly, the fragmentation reflected the lateness of German unification and the persistence of regional rivalries reinforced by religious differences; political alignment and voting along religious lines after the victory of the Protestant Prussian aristocracy in the unification issue increased the factionalism of bourgeois forces and with it their vulnerability to divisive Bismarckian tactics. Fourthly, non-participation in executive power and minimal influence on legislative affairs produced traditions

---

[33] See James Sheehan, *German Liberalism in the Nineteenth Century*, Chicago (Chicago U.P.), 1978, p. 146 etc.
[34] Leonard Krieger, *The German Idea of Freedom. History of a Political Tradition*, Chicago 1957, p.303

of political and economic theory which were highly abstract and untainted by the whiff of experience, but which nevertheless frequently adapted that theory to the non-liberal context within which bourgeois forces were obliged to operate. In particular the incorporation of notions of 'order' into liberal theory and the invocation of 'national freedom' as an addition to the catalogue of core liberties to be pursued can be seen as results of the fragmentation and powerlessness of German political liberalism. Bismarck succeeded in exposing the ideological contortions involved in the adaptation of already ambivalent principles to an illiberal political and economic reality. He constructed clientelist coalitions, including some middle class groups (heavy industry and big agriculture), ennobling many of their leaders, and excluding others, notably the Progressives. Conversely Bismarck united many bourgeois forces, including the National Liberals, behind his thoroughly illiberal anti-socialist laws, which removed civil rights from trade unionists and social democrats and effectively created a state of emergency for 12 years from 1878 to 1890; this in turn produced a further haemmorhage of democratic forces in a new wave of political migration.[35]

The National Liberals were the strongest liberal grouping within the Reichstag between 1871 and 1918. In 1874 they even enjoyed a majority of seats with the Progressives, in the so-called 'liberal era'. The National Liberals happily voted a further four times for the prolongation of the anti-socialist laws; the Progressives initially rejected the Law but after the merger with National Liberal 'secessionists' in 1884, forming the German Free Thinkers Party, a free vote line allowed 26 left liberals to support the prolongation, with 13 abstentions and 28 rejections.[36]

In the same year, 1878, the National Liberals acceded to the introduction of strong protectionist trade tariffs, favouring heavy industry and big agriculture, and with these facilitated a further weakening of an already flimsy form of parliamentary control over the Reich's fiscal affairs. Both National Liberals and Progressives produced principled and practical objections to Bismarck's social legislation. Bismarck's preference for state-financed welfare and pensions as an instrument of paternalistic manipulation, was

---

[35] For a closer view of the social composition and fragmentation of bourgeois political forces between 1870 and 1918, see *Langewiesche, Liberalismus in Deutschland*, op.cit. 133ff
[36] Ibid. p.191

transformed, by dint of opposition from industry and the National Liberals into a system of social insurance, with the bulk of the contributions paid by insured workers; the Progressives remained implacably opposed to the pioneering social insurance system, using arguments which were a mixture of Manchester liberalism, economic Darwinism and anti-paternalism.[37]

Together, or separately, German 'liberals' had thus foresworn several of the key principles upon which the modern democratic social liberalism of Germany's Free Democratic Party is (or was) founded: free trade, civil rights, social protection and democracy.[38] Contemporary liberals like Dahrendorf have dubbed this kind of behaviour a 'betrayal'. Eley, on the other hand, rightly warns against the retrospective condemnation of German political liberalism, by pointing out the anti-democratic and liberal imperialist values prevalent in the British Liberal Party,[39] i.e. by underscoring the general adaptability and malleability of the general 'principles' and highlighting the invidious predicament of a weak political movement trapped by its fear of Social Democracy as an alternative emancipatory ideology and its need to collaborate with autocracy to resist this danger. Perhaps the most grotesque reflection of this predicament was the fear that Bismarck and others could generate among 'liberals' by threatening to extend universal suffrage.[40] In this context it is the centrality of 'order' in German liberal ideology, together with the extension of the category 'liberty' to encompass collective agency which is of central significance.

---

[37] Ibid. p.196; the irony of this opposition can be found in the suggestion that social insurance, as a form of self-help, strengthened the principles of individualism, self-adequacy and autonomy in the German population.

[38] Another irony of Bismarckian politics was his threat of democratising the franchise throughout the Reich to persuade liberals to support his national legislation, where bourgeois interests were entrenched in Prussia and at municipal level because of privileged systems of voting.

[39] Geoff Eley, 'Liberalismus 1860–1914. Deutschland und Großbritannien im Vergleich', in: Langewiesche (ed.), *Liberalismus im 19. Jahrhundert*, op.cit. 261ff; Mooers also rejects the notion of betrayal on the grounds of the German bourgeoisie's 'entirely different' goals, op.cit. p.138.

[40] See Colin Mooers, op.cit. p.139; Grenville, *Europe Reshaped 1848–1878*, London 1986, p.161

The centrality of national unity, only just gained on Bismarck's coat-tails, pre-programmed the repressive, illiberal features of National Liberals; it made these allies of the Bismarckian state sensitive to the dangers of such a unity collapsing and of a return to economic fragmentation and thus mindful of the need to strengthen the fragile network of national markets and to defend its market agents, its national associations, its national standards. The freedom of the nation thus remained a political article of faith with which the Party could mobilize industrial interests and electoral support; this in turn was easily translated into the 'emancipation ideology of liberal imperialism',[41] as it manifested itself in the quarter century before the outbreak of the First World War.

One has to agree with Eley's assessment of the contribution made to the modernisation of the German political economy by the limited and functional interpretation of 'liberty', 'self-administration' and 'emancipation'.[42] However, it was an economic modernisation that again confounds any notion of liberal market capitalism. The political context, the lateness and speed of German industrialisation produced a high capitalism characterised by bureaucratic company structures, capital concentration and defensive collusion which, in Weber's view, was no longer compatible with the flowering of political liberalism.

This goes some way to explain the translation of the notion of legitimate autonomous agency from the single heroic economic actor to the corporation, the trade association, the nation; it helps to explain the German phenomenon of bureaucratic liberalism.[43] It didn't stop political parties of the liberal 'centre' invoking the image of the independent artisan or peasant as symbol of enterprise, skill and tenacity. Indeed this becomes all the more necessary as the intensity of capital concentration and of societal interdependence increases.

In practical terms, it illuminates the disparity between individual and bureaucratic autonomy. In theoretical terms it underlines the extreme vagueness of the liberal vocabulary of freedom, liberty, autonomy, self-determination etc. The invocation of autonomy, of liberty becomes a rhetorical or symbolic device to persuade the

---

[41] See Mommsen 'Deutscher und britischer Liberalismus. Versuch einer Bilanz', in: Langewiesche (ed.) *Liberalismus im 19. Jahrhundert*, op.cit. p.221

[42] Eley, *Liberalismus*, op.cit. p.260ff

[43] W. Mommsen, 'Deutscher und britischer Liberalismus. Versuch einer Bilanz', op.cit. p.215

powerless that their interests are best served by the operation of something else which is autonomous. That 'something' can be Röpke's 'perfect market democracy' as a ghostly 'invisible hand'; it can be the 'technical assistants' drafted in by German Social Democrats in 1918 to run ministries and organise demobilisation; it can be the non-parliamentary ministers co-opted into countless Weimar cabinets to remove the suspicion of party political favours; it can be the toothless Cartel Office which today autonomously presides over the erosion of competition, or it can be an autonomous central bank.

The theoretical difficulty about this leap from individual self-determination to autonomous bureaucratic agency is, in liberal terms, the question of when individual autonomy is over-determined by an external (autonomous) agency, when external 'autonomy' becomes 'heteronomy'.

AUTONOMY AND HETERONOMY

Of course, the transposition of the concept of autonomy from the individual human being to the individual bureaucratic agency or nation in the name of one kind of liberalism, is the object of considerable worry to other liberal philosophers who would (rightly) point to the biologism involved in ascribing a (collective) will to supra-individual 'bodies'.[44] But the problem was always and remains one of the epistemology of individualism, of rational self-interest which, in refined economic and social interaction, programmatically pools its autonomy with other self-interests. Classical liberals ascribe only instrumental value to this condition of pooling, it has a mere utility function in promoting the well-being of the rational subject. Liberal democracy is accordingly constituted to provide equal shares in this pooling process, but it is a legalistic concept of equality rather than a social one, and – as the history of liberal thinking shows – there are considerable differences over the rights of access to the group within which this equal pooling is exercised. The qualified franchise which persisted in Britain until 1918 and in Northern Ireland until the late 1960s is a clear example of this.

At the theoretical level, a philosophy based on the autonomous individual is always going to have problems when it seeks to account for collective phenomena, because it is constructed on the basis of an

---

[44] See Robert Paul Wolff, *The Poverty of Liberalism*, Boston 1968, p.165f

antinomy of self and other which is epistemologically contradictory and ultimately self-destructive: the autonomous self depends both on the 'other' and therefore on the polarity relationship of dependence for its self-definition.[45] The network of (autonomous) individuals furthermore requires the non-individual heteronomous instrument of language to express autonomy and self-determination, to demarcate oneself from the collective blur. The paradox of this antinomy is most evident in Berkeley's solipsism or Nietzsche's voluntarism which were both expounded, using the (collective) vehicle of language.[46] The epistemological contradiction of the liberal doctrine of autonomy are the core objects of Wolff's critique of the 'poverty of liberalism': the denial of the collective nature of human existence, of biology, of language, of consciousness, of discourse, of community, the hypostasis of individual reason, the acceptance of subject-predicate structures as ontological givens.[47]

One view of German liberalism up to the end of the Second World War would stress its *deviant* nature, its stretching of core principles up to and beyond breaking point (Dahrendorf's notion of 'betrayal'). Another view would be, in part, more charitable and point out that German deviancy only really highlights the inherent theoretical contradictions noted above, between the sanctity of the autonomous will and the need collectively to guarantee that autonomy by legal or social norm, between liberty and regulation, between individual and state. The dominant strand of German liberalism – National Liberalism – was strong on regulation, on the need for order and statutory guarantees, firstly because of the fragility of (bourgeois) civil rights within an autocratic state and the perceived value of the *Rechtsstaat* as independent guarantor, secondly because of the associated preparedness to adapt and to develop the *Rechtsstaat* from within. It was a *practical*

---

[45] See Frazer and Lacey, *The Politics of Community*, Toronto 1993, p.175
[46] It is a profound irony of Nietzsche's theory of an aestheticized 'will to power' was grounded in a refined and perceptive analysis of language and cognition. C.f. J. Leaman, *Nietzsche's 'Will to Power' as 'Art'*, Doctoral dissertation, Liverpool 1977
[47] Whether one begins from Nietzsche's relativistic epistemology or from Lukács' materialist epistemology of labour or indeed from 'chaos theory', the inadequacies of the liberal antinomy of self and other, subject and object, the causality of events determined by the autonomous will, are pretty clear.

accommodation with an illiberal status quo. While, in a 'liberal era', formalisation and regulation merely codify and refine the status quo as a cultural norm, in an illiberal age they tend to have a different function. Formalisation within the German *Rechtsstaat* always threatened to restrict as much as it permitted, because – for the National Liberals – it involved 'a political alliance with the authoritarian state and a social alliance with the landed aristocracy ... in exchange for protection against competition and against social democracy'.[48] Within the overall protection of bourgeois property rights by the aristocratic state – which derived revenue from indirect mass taxes rather than from direct taxation – sectional interests were protected via self-regulation and state regulation; thus sectoral trusts and cartels were administered by their respective corporate leaderships but given state approval[49] or even active encouragement (for example, in the case of the Potash Cartel).

The interpretation of statute thus became the responsibility of autonomous specialists, whether they were representatives of self-administered bodies or part of a specific branch of law/of state. As a result, the structural significance of autonomous judgement (jurisdiction) in socio-economic life increased in line with the level of juridification. *Rechstsstaat* is an abstract notion – admittedly associated with contemporary civil rights and the democracy of the Federal Republic – but at bottom vitally dependent on the substance of statutes and their interpretation. The Wilhelmine Empire was a *Rechtsstaat*, but one barely troubled by the nuances of civil rights:

'Its constitution illustrated the contour of the German political mind, which harboured such obvious contradictions as authoritarianism and liberalism, hierarchical feudalism and social radicalism, and constitutional government without parliamentary supremacy'.[50]

The notion of avoiding 'parliamentary supremacy' was in fact vigorously expounded by the National Liberal theorist, Rudolf Gneist, who developed the concept of *Rechtsstaat* to the virtual limit of illiberalism: 'Society can find the personal freedom, the moral and spiritual development of the individual only in permanent subordination

---

[48] Krieger, *The German Idea of Freedom*, op.cit. p.459

[49] On April 4th 1897 the Reichsgericht (supreme court) adjudged cartel contracts to be legal

[50] Thus J.S. Shapiro, *Liberalism, Its Meaning and History*, Princeton/London/New York 1958, p.73

to a constant higher power'.[51] As Krieger rightly points out, Gneist rejects the ideals of western constitutionalism:

'He set the state over society, made it completely independent of society, and assigned to it the decisive role in controlling the class struggle. ... The concept of *Rechtsstaat*, that barometer of 19th century liberalism, was no longer defined in terms of a state which permitted to the individuals rights apart from the state. It became now simply the kind of state whose power was articulated in legal modes of action – that is, in measures which conformed to general rules'.[52]

While the National Liberal Party itself maintained a rhetorical constitutionalism, vowing in its 1881 programme 'to combat vigorously all efforts ... which are aimed at the reduction of the constitutional rights of parliament',[53] the primacy of 'national freedom' still shines through its pragmatic politics and its public pronouncements, particularly in the run-up to the First World War: 'Steadfast loyalty to the Kaiser and the Reich. The Fatherland over the party, the common weal over all special interests. Defence and nurturing of the common goods that the nation has gained by struggle; one external representation, one army, one war fleet, one law, one transport area, equal conditions for free movement and for free labour'.[54] In contrast to Anglo-Saxon and French traditions of liberalism and indeed to the German Social Democratic Party, which stressed the sovereignty of parliament, the National Liberals emphasised the sovereignty of the state; according to Döhn, this acceptance of the 'idea of the higher state' ... 'personified by the monarch', is typical of the general tradition of German liberalism up to the end of the First World War.[55] The state is furthermore conceived as an institution that is characterised by an inherent sense of unity and harmony: 'the state is thus not conceived as value-free as in non-German, in particular Anglo-Saxon liberalism and thus subordinated to the individual and his natural rights. The state and its constitution as a 'value in itself' manifests itself in Germany in the cross-over of conservatism and liberalism with the result that liberal

---

[51] R. Gneist, *Der Rechtsstaat*, Berlin 1872, p.12
[52] Krieger, *The German Idea of Freedom*, op.cit. p.460
[53] Party Programme of the National Liberal Party, reprinted in: Wilhelm Treue (ed.), *Deutsche Parteiprogramme seit 1861*, Göttingen, Zürich, Frankfurt 1954, p.81
[54] 'Ziele und Bestrebungen der Nationalliberalen Partei', in W. Treue (ed.) (op.cit.), p.95
[55] Lothar Döhn, *'Liberalismus'*, op.cit. p.139f

democracy was only able to come into its own after the internal and external failure of the Wilhelmine state, and was then once again destroyed'.[56]

Liberal democracy in the Weimar Republic was not, however, borne by the dominant liberal grouping (the DVP as successor to the National Liberals) but by the smaller group of left liberals in the German Democratic Party (DDP) and their initial coalition partners, the Social Democrats.[57] While the Weimar Republic was 'the very model of democratic liberalism', it was governed essentially by a 'liberal regime without liberals'.[58] Furthermore, the constitution reinforced the fragmentation of both working class representation and, more markedly, of bourgeois parties.

While this fragmentation prevented the consolidation of democratic institutions and weakened the potential for constructive democratic politics, it is highly significant that the crisis of (German) society was interpreted by many liberal theorists not as the crisis of an immature democracy in need of consolidation but as a crisis of social order, exacerbated by parliamentarism. This applied in particular to the group of academics, later to be identified as ordo-liberals, who provided the central ideas of the 'social market economy'. While the ordo-liberals, like Eucken, Böhm, Röpke, Müller-Armack and Rüstow, by no means represented a dominant school of economic thinking before 1945 (indeed were generally regarded as rather eccentric), their views of democracy and of social and political 'order' were certainly more typical of bourgeois academics of the period. An examination of ordo-liberal thinking is also warranted because it helps to illuminate the difficulties which German liberalism had in reconciling the concepts of autonomy and heteronomy within a liberal democratic polity. It also illuminates some of the very real contradictions of democratic governance in post-war west Germany.

It is important to note that ordo-liberalism addresses both the crisis of (German) capitalism and economic governance and also reflects on

---

[56] Döhn, 'Liberalismus', ibid. p.140

[57] The initial surge in support for the liberal republican DDP in January 1919, when they gained 5.6 million votes (18.5 per cent) was reversed 18 months later in June 1920, and from then until 1933, the party attracted fewer votes than the German People's Party (DVP), dwindling in electoral support to just 336000 (1 per cent) in November 1932

[58] J. S. Shapiro, *Liberalism. Its Meaning and History*, Princeton/ London/ New York 1958, p.75

the specific problems of liberalism as theory and practice. The (arguably central) point of departure for ordo-liberals, in contrast to neo-liberals,[59] is the perception that capital concentration, monopolisation and market power are inimical to the operation of free markets, i.e. they proceed from the acknowledgement of market failure and the associated failure of the state to regulate competition. They do not follow Manchester liberals and neo-liberals in identifying state regulation as the primary cause of market asymmetries. Röpke, for example, criticized the failure to see 'that a market economy needs a firm moral, political and institutional framework. ... Historical liberalism (particularly the nineteenth century brand), never understood that competition is a dispensation, by no means harmless from a moral and sociological point of view; it has to be kept within bounds and watched if it is not to poison the body politic'.[60] Franz Böhm, a persistent critic of German cartels, urged that law should be 'the master, not the servant of economic interests'.[61] A strong statutory framework, policed by a strong state would, according to Eucken, operate to neutralise anti-competitive forces and structures; 'Economic policy, therefore, should not direct itself against abuse of power by existing monopolies, but rather against their very existence'.[62]

In their anti-monopolism, ordo-liberals were in an honourable minority among German economists,[63] even if they showed breathtaking naïvety in the view that economic concentration could be effectively combatted by the individual nation state in an advanced, internationalised market economy. Their anti-monopolism is not the central issue here, but the role assigned to the state and the social theory underpinning their arguments. Dieter Haselbach's painstaking account

---

[59] Anthony Nicholls breezily dismisses the distinction between ordo-liberals and neo-liberals in his study *Freedom with Responsibility. The Social Market Economy in Germany 1918–1963*, Oxford (OUP) 1994, p.12, ignoring above all the ordo-liberals' self-demarcation from neo-classical economics and the central feature of anti-monopolism in ordo-liberal theory, which is conspicuously absent from contemporary neo-liberal thinking.

[60] Wilhelm Röpke, *Social Crisis of Our Time*, op.cit. p.52

[61] Franz Böhm, *Wettbewerb und Monopolkampf*, Berlin 1933, p.323

[62] Walter Eucken, *This Unsuccessful Age (or the Pains of Economic Progress)*, London 1951, p.35

[63] C.f. Nicholls, *Freedom with Responsibility*, op.cit. chapter 1, pp.15–31

of ordo-liberal social theory[64] reveals a consistently elitist standpoint which has strong affinities to other authoritarian strands of thought prevalent in the latter days of the Weimar Republic. The term 'authoritarian liberalism' is derived from a contemporary commentary by Hermann Heller on the pre-fascist von Papen regime.[65] Von Papen headed the second of three 'presidential cabinets' in the last three years of the Weimar Republic which operated on the basis of emergency decrees which required no parliamentary approval. More ruthless than his predecessor Brüning, von Papen sought to neutralise social democracy and the labour movement and to institute a fundamental revision of the Weimar constitution in the interests of the propertied classes; this involved a *coup d'état* in Prussia, welfare cuts, inducements to cut wages and coalition talks with the Nazis. While the social composition of von Papen's administration (the 'cabinet of barons') was extraordinarily unrepresentative, this programme of the strong state enjoyed widespread support within industrial circles, the civil service, army, judiciary and academics. While different factions argued over the specific content of state policy, they were virtually all united in their hostility to parliamentarianism and their fear of working class insurrection in the chaos of depression and mass unemployment.

The ordo-liberals thus attacked not the state (as an illegitimate meddler in economic affairs) but the democratic state as the incarnation of factionalism and clientelism. Rüstow called for 'a strong state, a state above the economy, above interests, there where it belongs' ... 'a state, powerful, ... independent, ... neutral in the sense of the higher whole, superior not by dint of violence and domination but through authority and leadership *(Führertum)*'.[66] Haselbach demonstrates the proximity of Rüstow to Carl Schmitt and of Alfred Müller-Armack to fascist conceptions of the state with his espousal of actionism and the deployment of myth in state policy.[67] Müller-Armack's membership of

---

[64]   Dieter Haselbach, *Autoritärer Liberalismus und Soziale Marktwirtschaft. Gesellschaft und Politik im Ordoliberalismus*, Baden-Baden (Nomos) 1991

[65]   Hermann Heller, 'Autoritärer Liberalismus?', in: *Die neue Rundschau*, 44/1, pp.289–298, cited in Haselbach, ibid.

[66]   Alexander Rüstow, speech from 1932, reprinted in: Rüstow, *Rede und Antwort*, Ludwigsburg 1963, pp.257–8), cited in Haselbach, *Autoritärer Liberalismus*, op.cit.

[67]   Haselbach, ibid. 59f

the NSDAP and his enthusiasm for the Nazis' 'historical activism'[68] are thus no surprise: the new 'total' character of the state replaces the weak clientelist 'state interventionism', allowing 'entrepreneurial activity to become a new legitimate element of the future economic order'.[69] Rüstow advocated 'liberal interventionism' as the primary function of the strong state in contradistinction to the process-political interventionism of the weak state,[70] which was beholden to sectional interests and to the vagaries of the business cycle. In line with Eucken, Böhm, Röpke and Müller-Armack, the form of state involvement was directed towards establishing and policing a dynamic and competitive 'order', not manipulating the demand cycle *à la* Keynes or more collectivist regimes. Most clearly in ordo-liberal thinking , the principle of autonomy operates at both the entrepreneurial and at state level. This is precisely the model later described in the economic programme of the CDU in the run-up to the 1949 west German elections: 'Personal liberty is promoted by economic autonomy. Economic autonomy is based in the right to private property'; 'Competition based on performance (*Leistungswettbewerb*) is to be ensured by law. Monopolies and the bearers of market power are to be subject to an institutionally anchored autonomous monopoly control, answerable only to the law'.[71] The independent strong state body (monopoly office) ensures the independent strong competitive entrepreneur as 'master of his economic decisions'.[72] While protection from the influence of monopolies and excessive market power takes centre stage in the CDU's electoral rhetoric, ordo-liberal thinkers couched the autonomy of the strong state both in terms of combatting vested capital interests and in terms of reducing/neutralising the influence of mass democratic institutions, like parliament. Democracy is seen explicitly as antipathetic to the competitive order. Thus Walter Eucken: 'If the state ... can find the strength to free itself from the influence of the masses and once again to distance itself in one way or another from the economic *process* (my emphasis JL) ... then the way will have been

---

[68] C.f. Müller-Armack, A., *Staatsidee und Wirtschaftsordnung im neuen Reich*, Berlin 1933, p.7

[69] Müller-Armack, *Staatsidee und Wirtschaftsordnung*, op.cit. p. 48

[70] Rüstow, op.cit. p.252

[71] CDU, *Düsseldorfer Leitsätze der CDU*, July 1949, reprinted in: Huster, E-U, Kraiker, G. et. al., *Determinanten der westdeutschen Restauration 1945–1949*, Frankfurt 1975, 429ff

[72] Ibid. p.431

cleared ... for a further powerful development of capitalism in a new form'.[73] Böhm, in turn, blamed 'massification' for the ills of society and economic policy and offered conditional support to the strong Nazi state as one which would 'promote unity' and could solve the crisis of capitalism.[74] Wilhelm Röpke, while rejecting Nazism and choosing exile in Switzerland, was arguably the strongest in his critique of mass democratic society, of 'that spiritual collectivization, agglomeration, mechanization, atomization and proletarianization which have become the curse of the Western world'.[75] Against the reality of the 'termite state',[76] Röpke sets his vision of a healthy society which has strong echoes of mediaeval autocracy:

'A healthy society firmly resting on its own foundation, possesses a genuine "structure" with many intermediate stages; it exhibits a necessarily "hierarchical" composition (i.e. determined by the social importance of certain functions, services and leadership qualities), where each individual has the good fortune of knowing his position'.[77]

'... the collectivist state has its roots in the soil of unlimited democracy when that is not sufficiently balanced and diluted by "non-political spheres", "corps intermédiaires" (Montesquieu), liberalism, federalism, self-administration and aristocratism'.[78] Röpke's enthusiasm for these 'non-political' balancing features of a healthy society is developed in a later book, *Beyond Supply and Demand*, in which he stresses the overwhelming need for a 'natural nobility':

'What we need at any time and what we need all the more urgently today, when so much is crumbling and tottering, is a genuine *nobilitas naturalis* with its authority comfortingly acknowledged by the people of their own free will; an elite which derives its aristocratic title only from the most supreme achievements and from an unsurpassable moral example and which is cloaked in the natural dignity of such a life.'[79]

[73] W. Eucken, 'Staatliche Strukturwandlungen und die Krise des Kapitalismus', in: *Weltwirtschaftliches Archiv*, 36/2, pp.318–19
[74] Franz Böhm, *Die Ordnung der Wirtschaft als geschichtliche Aufgabe und rechtschöpferische Leistung*, Stuttgart 1937, p.47 etc.
[75] Wilhelm Röpke, *The Social Crisis of Our Time*, op.cit. p.103
[76] Röpke, quoted by Haselbach, op.cit. p.65
[77] Röpke, The Social Crisis of Our Time, op.cit. p.10
[78] Röpke, The Social Crisis of Our Time, op.cit. p.85
[79] Röpke, *Jenseits von Angebot und Nachfrage*, Erlenbach-Zürich/ Stuttgart 1966, p.192

Röpke's words, frequently cited – it should be said – in defence of Bundesbank autonomy,[80] correspond to Eucken's earlier fulminations about the masses, 'encroaching collectivism' and the need for 'an elite which has understood what a competitive order is, not only in itself as an economic order but also as a condition for a social order'; this is why it is necessary for the elite, 'as bearers of the order to emphasise the meaning of order'.[81] Haselbach is certainly not unfair in his judgement of ordo-liberals when he asserts that they 'sacrificed the libertarian spirit of political liberalism in favour of a concept of a market economy under the supervision of an authoritarian state'.[82]

For the purposes of this analysis, it is important to establish that the ordo-liberals constructed a view of 'order' which was both functional and normative, which operated with a duality of individual entrepreneurial autonomy and autonomous state agencies, and order which was freed from the heteronomy (external determination) of democratic influence. Röpke's substitution of market democracy for political democracy, cited at the beginning of this chapter, is the most blatant expression of this anti-democratic prejudice, in its cynical exploitation of the metaphors of political equality and opinion-formation:

'the process of the market economy is, so to speak a "plébiscite de tous les jours," where every monetary unit spent by the consumer represents a ballot, and where the producers are endeavouring by their advertising to give "election publicity" to an infinite number of parties (i.e., goods). ... The result is a market democracy, which in its silent precision surpasses the most perfect political democracy.'[83]

The metaphoricality of this and other ordo-liberal analyses of social order reveals an *aesthetic* dimension of symmetry, control and creative agency in addition to the functional and normative dimensions. This corresponds in many respects to the cultural canon of the autonomous, creative (male) individual also mentioned above. However, in line with

---

[80] C.f. Dieter Balkhausen, *Gutes Geld und schlechte Politik*, Düsseldorf 1992 p.187; Hans Tietmeyer, the current President of the Bundesbank, used the quotation in a celebratory speech for the 60th birthday of Kurt Biedkopf in January 1990

[81] Walter Eucken, *Grundsätze der Wirtschaftspolitik*, Tübingen 1960, 370f

[82] Haselbach, *Autoritärer Liberalismus*, op.cit. p.87

[83] Röpke, *The Social Crisis of Our Time*, op.cit. p.103

the National Liberal tradition, there is also a strong anthropological dimension in the exposition of autonomy and heteronomy:

'Always and everywhere the basic question is: how is the will of the state formed? And to that there are two and only two basic answers: autonomy or heteronomy, autonomous authority or extraneous authority. If we free the concept of democracy from all the verbiage entangling it and from all historical weeds, there remains as the core the autonomy of the nation'.[84]

The aesthetic and anthropological dimensions of a formalised order of autonomous individuals, operating within a complex socio-ethnic context according to rules maintained by autonomous agencies of the state complete the picture of a tradition of German liberalism which is culturally highly specific. Whereas ordo-liberals and their political counterparts in post-war Germany sought to demarcate themselves from the disastrous collectivism of both Nazism and Bolshevism on the one hand and from Manchester liberalism on the other and to establish the 'third way' of a 'social market', the affinities of ordo-liberal social philosophy to the authoritarian and oligarchic views of National Liberals and fascists underscore a strong cultural preference for autonomous authority and a strong cultural hostility to social conflict: the 'yearning for synthesis' (Dahrendorf) is thus not just a characteristic of 'collectivist' ideologies but is shared fundamentally by liberal traditions in a political and economic culture which never enjoyed the luxury of stable, organic development and had consistently sought the protection of a tight regulatory culture.[85] In such a juridified culture, the figure of the judge and adjudicator plays a central role, together with self-administered social and economic institutions which seek balanced,

---

[84] Ibid. p. 101; this and similar passages are all the more remarkable because they were written in exile in Switzerland in 1942 at the height of the war, in large measure determined by the Nazi hypostasis of 'national freedom'; c.f. Josef Goebbels: 'The limits of the concept of individual freedom are therefore the limits of the concept of the Volk's freedom. No individual human being, be he so exalted or so lowly, can possess the right to use his freedom at the expense of the concept of national freedom. For only the security of the national concept of freedom guarantees his personal freedom permanently', Speech from November 1933, in: Hofer, W (ed.), *Der Nationalsozialismus. Dokumente 1933–1945*, Frankfurt/M 1957, p.89

[85] See Dahrendorf, Gesellschaft und Demokratie in Deutschland, op.cit. chapters 10–14, 161ff.

symmetrical solutions to disputes and conflicts; in contrast, however, to the non-specialist guarantor of the fair process of law as in Britain, the judge/adjudicator in the German tradition is a specialist involved in both examination, mediation and adjudication. To this extent it was always easier to differentiate the technical expertise of the judge from any class bias of the judiciary in general.

In conclusion, therefore, it would be entirely wrong to see the autonomous central bank as an alien form imposed on Germany by victorious allies after two world wars (in 1922 and 1948). Rather, its survival and success have much to do with the fact that it was introduced into a social culture pre-programmed to the virtues of the autonomous expert agency and deeply suspicious of significant features of conflictual parliamentarianism. A further concluding observation would be that the rhetoric of autonomy, self-authorship, self-reliance, self-help, creative entrepreneurship – which lay at the core of bourgeois electoral and political propaganda in the 20th century – stands in stark contrast to the increasing interdependence of advanced industrial societies; i.e. while the complexity of the division of labour increases, the direct links to production decline and the dependency of the vast majority on delicately tuned national and international networks of cooperative human behaviour grows, we are being exhorted to aspire to the qualities of the self-sufficient frontiersman and – in the case of monetary policy – to accept a uni-causal (single agency) model of arguably the most complex network of economic relations that exists in the globalised economy.

3 Constituting autonomy – from the Reichsbank to the Bundesbank

Central banking came late to Germany for the simple reason that the modern German state itself was only established in 1871 with the subordination of the southern German monarchies to the leadership of the Prussian king as Kaiser of a united 'small Germany'.[1] With the exception of the Banca d'Italia (1893) and the Schweizerische Nationalbank (1905), all the other major European central banks were founded much earlier: the Swedish Riksbank in 1668, the Bank of England in 1694, the Banque de France in 1800, the Nederlandsche Bank in 1814 and the Belgian Banque Nationale in 1850. One of the driving motives of political unification was the desire to eradicate the commercial disadvantages of disparate systems of coinage and weights and measures. At the moment of the establishment of the Second Empire in 1871, there were no fewer than seven different systems of coinage in use by individual German states; some of the coins in circulation dated back to the 18th century,[2] many foreign coins functioned as effective tender; 20 German states had already introduced notes as legal tender and there were no fewer than 33 banks of issue,

---

[1] 'Kleindeutschland' under Prussian leadership stood in contrast to the aims of the liberal revolutionaries of 1848/49 who sought to incorporate the Austrian Hapsburg monarchy into a pan-German 'Grossdeutschland'; the exclusion of the economically backward and ethnically disparate Austrian empire was a deliberate objective of Prussia's unification wars against Denmark (1864), Austria (1866) and France (1870) under its Minister-President and later Chancellor, Bismarck.

[2] Salomon Flink calculates that 'at the time of the passage of the German Bank Act of 1875, there were no less than 140 different kinds of money in circulation', *The German Reichsbank and Economic Germany*, New York 1930, p.4

producing their own 'notes' (*Zettel*).[3] Despite the establishment in 1834 and extension of the German Currency Union (*Zollverein*), the transaction costs for traders within the multi-currency zone remained higher than in France or Britain. A key problem within the intense discussions surrounding a new common currency concerned the choice of currency system, notably between the Taler operating in Prussia and other north German states or the Gulden prevalent in the southern German states and Austria. The sensitivity associated with the establishment of Prussian political hegemony as well as doubts about the strength of any German currency led these discussions away from the choice between Taler and Gulden towards proposals for a 'Germanic Coinage Union' between the North German Federation, Britain and the USA and a more popular plan to join the gold-based and decimal Franc bloc.[4]

The draft proposal submitted to the Parliament of the North German Federation to this effect became submerged in Bismarck's machinations to provoke France into war. The spectacular defeat of the French and the rapid payment of 5 billion Gold Francs in reparations provided the political and material basis for the establishment of a national currency union based on the decimal Mark system. In two laws (the Law governing the Minting of the Reich's Own Coins of 4 December 1871 and the Coin Law of 9 July 1873) the new Mark was introduced, with the intention of gradually replacing the other currencies which remained legal tender. The unifying symbolism behind the rejection of both Taler and Gulden in favour of the Mark was weakened slightly by the conversion value of the new currency: one Taler could be exchanged for 3 Marks while the Gulden converted at the unwieldy rate of one to 1.71 Marks. The new currency was guaranteed in gold at a rate of 1395 Marks to one pound of gold. Between December 1871 and

---

[3] For further details of the so-called *Zettelbanken*, see: Knut Borchardt, 'Währung und Wirtschaft', in: Deutsche Bundesbank (ed.), *Währung und Wirtschaft in Deutschland 1876–1975*, Frankfurt am Main , 1976, 3ff

[4] Adopting the Franc was supported by the Congress of German Economists in 1868 and the German Association of Commerce (*Handelstag*) in 1869, following the World Currency Conference in Paris in 1867; see Borchardt, 'Währung und Wirtschaft', op.cit. p.5; also Harold James, 'The Reichsbank 1876–1945', in: Deutsche Bundesbank (ed.), *Fifty Years of the Deutsche Mark. Central Bank and the Currency in Germany since 1948*, Oxford, 1999, p.5.

1875 most of the parallel coinage was gradually withdrawn, but some silver coinage (notably the 1 Taler piece) remained in circulation until 1 October 1907 and only the June 1909 Coin Law established the Mark as an exclusively gold currency.

There was a significant gap between the 1871 currency reform and the establishment of the Reichsbank in 1876. The reasons for this are various. They would seem to have included the relative indifference of Bismarck's government to monetary affairs, the booming economy in the first three years of the Reich's existence (the *Gründerzeit*) and worries on both the Prussian side and on the side of the other (subordinate) states of the appearance of Prussian centralism if a new central bank based in Berlin were to replace the state central banks and the other *Zettelbanken*. The major private banks, like the Deutsche Bank, were seemingly capable of managing the transition towards a single standard currency by slowly removing rival coins and notes from circulation. Not even the wave of bankruptcies and bank liquidity crises in late 1873 nor the run on gold in 1874 convinced either the Reich or the federated states of the urgency of a central bank for the territory of the common currency. When the federal upper house (the Bundesrat) submitted a draft bank law to the Reichstag, it contained regulatory changes governing note issue but no mention of the establishment of a Reich central bank.[5] Representatives of the 'liberal' majority in the Reichstag, with few exceptions, used the debate to push the idea of a Reichsbank to the top of the agenda. Bamberger, a National Liberal, stressed the problem of a gold-based currency in the context of large-scale international movements of money and the need to maintain stable credit conditions for Germany's industrial and commercial sectors. Thus, according to James, the key function of a central bank for Bamberger and other liberals was not the maintenance of currency stability, since this was ensured by the gold standard, but the maintenance of banking liquidity via a national lender of last resort.[6] The Reichstag majority ended the first reading of the Bank Law by submitting the central bank proposals to a special parliamentary commission which in turn concluded that the law would be pointless without the incorporation of provisions for a new Reichsbank. Subsequent discussions within the Bundesrat removed the objections of the Prussian blocking majority and of Bismarck and a new draft law was submitted to the Reichstag at the end of January 1875 and, with the

---

[5] Borchardt, 'Währung und Wirtschaft', op.cit. p.13
[6] James, 'The Reichsbank 1876–1945', op.cit. p.8

approval of the Bundesrat, was enacted by the Kaiser on March 14 1875.

According to Flink, the 'Bank was more a reorganization of the Bank of Prussia than a new institution'.[7] Technically, this is quite correct, in that the property, the personnel and the branch system of the Bank of Prussia were simply taken over by the new Reichsbank; equally, the main banks of issue in the southern German states remained untouched. Nevertheless, the Prussian state was obliged to sell its stake in the Bank's capital and to surrender its privilege of taxing new issues of banknotes, leaving the ownership of the new Reichsbank entirely in private hands. It thus resembled the Bank of England or the early Banca d'Italia in its private status. There was a 'long and ardent' debate[8] about the bank's ownership structures. The final preference for private ownership reflected concerns about the politicisation of banking the very specific context of transition and development: the transition of Germany from an agrarian to an industrial and urban-based economy, from aristocratic absolutism to constitutional government, from (monetary) particularism to monetary and political unity; development from the technically and politically primitive accumulation of the grim 1840s and 1850s[9] to a dynamic capitalist trading economy capable of overtaking Britain as an industrial power. The Reichsbank was seen not so much in political terms (as part of a clearly defined executive) but rather in instrumental commercial terms; 'its primary task (was) to satisfy the demand for credit and not to attempt arbitrary regulation of the quantity of notes in circulation'.[10] While this is clearly not in tune with current doctrines of credit control and the management of the money stock, it reflected the very specific need of the business community in the context of an aristocratic state run by the representatives of agrarian interests.

---

[7] Flink, *The German Reichsbank*, op.cit. p.6

[8] Flink, ibid. p.6f

[9] Real wages continued to decline in this period, according to Jürgen Kuzcynski (*Die Bewegung der deutschen Wirtschaft von 1800 bis 1946*, Meisenheim 1948, 66ff, 81f, p.201), with levels of pauperisation reinforced by serious cyclical crises in 1846 and 1857; see Martin Kitchen, *The Political Economy of Germany 1815–1914*, London, 1978, 72ff

[10] Flink, The German Reichsbank, op.cit. p.26

The Bank was nevertheless, in formal terms, 'managed by the government'[11] apart from the Reichsbank Central Committee which represented the private shareholders, the Bank was supervised by the Federal Council of Curators (*Bankkuratorium*) which included the Chancellor, as ex officio President of the Reichsbank, and four others, one appointed by the Emperor, the other three by the Bundesrat. The day-to-day management of the Reichsbank was in the hands of the Directorate, made up of president and eight other members, all appointed by the Emperor for life. The actual influence of the Chancellor, the Curatorium or the Reich Cabinet on monetary affairs was minimal. The formal provision of executive control by the Chancellor was rarely invoked.[12] Appointing Directorate members for life indeed, according to Flink, was 'deemed necessary in order to make the Board independent of any political interference which might be detrimental to the interest of the Bank'.[13] The perception of the need for operational autonomy was reinforced in the Reichstag debates concerning the extension of the Reichsbank's charter in 1889, 1899 and 1909. Significantly, the parties representing Prussian and other landed interests (the German Conservative Party and the German Reich Party respectively) expressed a consistent preference for a state bank, because they 'hoped for a credit policy more amenable to agriculture from a Reichsbank no longer controlled by shareholders. In the eyes of the conservatives the Reichsbank was an instrument of commerce and big industry and above all, after the 1890s, of the banks as well'.[14] Their arguments were given some credence by the particular crisis of agriculture and by persistent price deflation as a result of the transition to the gold standard.[15] They were, however, opposed by both major

---

[11] Flink, ibid. p.10

[12] Holtfrerich cites the one famous instance when Bismarck urged the Reichsbank to suspend the discounting of Russian bonds in 1887, but until 1914 this was very much the exception that proved the rule: see Carl-Ludwig Holtfrerich, 'Relations between Monetary Authorities and Governmental Institutions: The Case of Germany from the 19th Century to the Present', in: Toniolo, G (ed.), *Central Banks' Independence in Historical Perspective*, Berlin/ New York, 1988, pp.105–159; Flink (*The German Reichsbank*, op.cit. p.11) asserts incorrectly that the Chancellor's 'power was never exercised'.

[13] Flink, *The German Reichsbank*, op.cit. p.11

[14] Borchardt, 'Währung und Wirtschaft', op.cit. p.16

[15] James, 'The Reichsbank 1876–1945, op.cit. p.13f

liberal parties, the National Liberals and the Progressives who underscored the fact that most of the major central banks in the world, notably the much admired Bank of England, were privately owned.[16] The Social Democrats and the Catholic Centre Party shared the suspicion that the Reichsbank was an instrument of the industrial bourgeoisie and voted in favour of a state bank in 1889 but 'later recognized that in the case of actual nationalisation it would not be their desired principles that would benefit, but rather that the big landowners of the Prussian East would exert their political influence and derive advantage from the institute'.[17] Consequently, the SPD and the Centre Party voted to renew the Bank's private charter in 1899 and 1909. The SPD's position on central bank autonomy was understandably ambivalent, given the nature of class politics in the Wilhelmine Empire; the potential for the political abuse of the central bank by an autocratic, protectionist state was soon to be demonstrated in 1914. The 1875 Bank Charter allowed some protection from that abuse under normal circumstances, even if it meant a common front with bourgeois interests. It was an ambivalence that was to remain with the party until the present day. [18]

The actual influence of the private shareholders on Bank policy is difficult to gauge. Their interests were represented by an Annual General Meeting and by the Central Committee whose fifteen members met monthly to consider reports from the Bank management; the Central Committee was empowered to determine the amounts used by the Bank to buy commercial paper and was also consulted about changes to the Discount Rate. Three members of the Central Committee participated in meetings of the Directorate. The Bank shareholders received a regular dividend on any profits earned of 4.5 per cent (Bank Act, Section VI, Article 24).[19] Borchardt argues strongly that the shareholders 'were in all seriousness unable to exert any significant influence on the Bank's conduct of business'. All that the AGMs, the monthly meetings and participation in Directorate discussions supposedly produced was 'merely a certain communication between Bank and the world of business'; this in turn allowed the Bank 'to

[16] James, 'The Reichsbank 1876–1945, op.cit. p.10
[17] Borchardt, ibid.
[18] See J. Leaman, 'Central Banking and the Crisis of Social Democracy – A Comparative Analysis of British and German Views', *German Politics*, Vol.4, No.3, 1995, pp.22–48
[19] Flink, *The German Reichsbank*, op.cit. p.13

demonstrate its autonomy towards both sides'.[20] This conveniently symmetrical view is not entirely convincing, given the intensity and substance of shareholder–Bank consultations and it would be too easy to define the shareholders' primary interests predominantly in terms of the bank's liquidity and commercial security. Profitability was clearly important and underscored by the fact that the level of salaries of senior officials at the bank was in part profit-related.[21] However, the primary function of the Bank in this period was more clearly that of lender of last resort and guarantor of sufficient levels of credit to the private economy; currency stability qua inflation control was equally clearly a less urgent task. The conduct of policy was thus much more closely linked with the maintenance of industrial and commercial expansion and thus with the business interests represented by the private shareholders. It would seem more convincing to define the 'quasi-autonomous character' or 'relative independence'[22] of the Reichsbank between 1876 and 1914 in terms of its relationship to the Reich government rather than any 'autonomy towards both sides'.

'During the first few decades of its existence, the Reichsbank considered it as its most important task to grant all credit required as long as the discounted bills conformed to the legally set standard' (Flink).[23] This essentially correct observation should be set, as suggested above, in the specific context of German economic development; questions of any theoretical underpinnings of Bank policy are interesting but secondary to its primary task of servicing the extraordinary expansion of a young, national economy. In the thirty-five years from 1875 to 1910, Germany's population grew from 42.5 million to 65 million; coal production rose from 47.8 million tons in 1876 to 222 million tons in 1910; bank deposits rose from 1.8 billion Marks in 1875 to 16.7 billions in 1910; the number of joint stock companies increased from 2143 in 1886 to 5340 in 1911, their capitalisation from 4.8 billion Marks to over 16 billion Marks. At the level of economic sectors, industrial employment overtook that of agriculture in the last decade of the 19th century, rising from 35.5 per cent in 1882 (agriculture 42.5 per cent) to 42.8 per cent in 1907 (agriculture: 28.6 per cent).[24]

---

[20] Borchardt, 'Währung und Wirtschaft', op.cit. p.16
[21] James, 'The Reichsbank 1876–1945, op.cit. p.9
[22] ibid. p.10 and p.13
[23] Flink, op.cit. p.25
[24] All figures from Flink, op.cit. p.16

Both quantitatively and qualitatively this scale of expansion was a huge challenge to the resources of the Reichsbank. The relative backwardness of the banking sector – particularly at the beginning of the period – made the need to husband the available liquidity carefully and to cultivate public trust in the private and public banks. Paragraph 12 of the Bank Law stated that the function of the Reichsbank was 'to regulate money circulation in the whole Reich territory, to facilitate the balancing out of payments and to ensure the utilisation of the available capital'. Under the normal circumstances of bank demand for cash credits against short-term securities (of up to three months), the Reichsbank was generally obliging, i.e. perfectly happy to discount bills of exchange and other securities. The major constraint on its operations was not any monetary rule designed to match the growth of credit to the growth of GDP or productive potential (as in the modern Bundesbank) but rather its rules of central bank liquidity, i.e. of reserve cover for notes in circulation. §17 of the Bank Act obliged the Reichsbank to maintain reserves of gold, currency and treasury bills equivalent to at least one third of banknotes in circulation. The other two thirds could be covered by ordinary bills. The gold cover of the Reichsbank up to 1914 was, by international comparison, relatively healthy, rising to an average of 90.4 per cent between 1891 and 1895, but falling back to around 80 per cent until 1910. Changes in the Discount Rate (and there were about 140 in the period) were designed to protect the Bank's reserve cover, not the macro-economy or the currency's internal and external value. The problems of maintaining cover when credit demand defied Discount Rate increases were eased in part by the increasing acceptance of ordinary bills of exchange as money, i.e. as the reserve category of currency. In addition, the Reichsbank and the four remaining banks of issue were permitted to issue notes beyond a total of 250 million Marks (extended to 450 million in 1899) on payment of a 5 per cent tax on the additional note issue. This was intended more as a deterrent against uncovered note issues and functioned effectively as such.[25]

Opinion about the policy performance of the Reichsbank up to 1914 is divided. Wilhelm Nölling, the recent president of the Hamburg Land Central Bank, is not particularly complimentary about their efforts, stressing the cyclical fluctuations of the economy and the neglect by the Reichsbank and contemporary observers of price developments: 'there is not a word about prices or the movements of prices. The explanation

---

[25] See James, 'The Reichsbank 1876–1945, op.cit. p.8

lies in the fact that the intrinsic value of money was left to the workings of the gold standard mechanism, but not – or not intentionally – to the influence of other factors such as the 140 changes in the Discount rate that occurred between 1876 and 1914'.[26] Contemporary observers, like Bendixen, were much more positive: 'We Germans are so lucky to have found an ideal solution to the problem of a central bank constitution, a solution which is the envy of informed people abroad'.[27] James quotes German experts in their evidence to the US National Monetary Commission in 1910, who ascribe German banking success to the Reichsbank: 'The great strength of our financial system in Germany is the Reichsbank. Under that system, the question of our own cash reserve is of secondary importance, as we can at all times convert our holdings of commercial paper into cash at the Reichsbank.'[28] In 1984, the American economic historian Paul McGouldrick, in complete contrast to Nölling, notes that the fluctuations of the business cycle in Wilhelmine Germany had been 'mild compared to those in other countries at the same time or to West Germany after 1950', ascribing some of this success to the Reichsbank albeit with a back-handed compliment that 'intentionally or not the Reichsbank thus reached a goal that has eluded modern central banks at different periods, namely avoiding procyclical movements in its money liabilities.'[29]

Judged by the pursuit of its 'major *raison d'être*' – namely 'the prevention of banking collapse' – the Reichsbank's support is deemed by James to have 'become so obviously effective that banks could use it as the basis for credit expansion, financed in part by borrowing from abroad, which corresponded to current account deficits and represented a constant threat to the Reichsbank's other major function, as keeper of Germany's gold.'[30]

The gold reserve 'problem' prefigures the developments in August 1914 and raises questions about the the nature of any functional

---

[26] Wilhelm Nölling, *Monetary Policy in Europe after Maastricht*, London (Macmillan) 1993, p.14

[27] Wilhelm Bendixen, *Geld und Kapital*, collected essays, Jena 1920, p.137

[28] Cited in James, 'The Reichsbank 1876–1945, op.cit. p.11

[29] Paul McGouldrick, 'Operations of the German Central Bank and the Rules of the Game 1879–1913', in: Michael Bordo & Anna Schwartz (eds), *A Retrospective on the Classical Gold Standard 1821–1931*, Chicago, 1984, p.312 and p.319

[30] Thus James, 'The Reichsbank 1876–1945', op.cit. p.16

autonomy that the Reichsbank enjoyed or sought. The transformation, namely, to the direct instrumentalisation of the Bank as a tool of war and generator of inflation was not as sudden as the effective suspending of the Gold Standard suggests. 'After the Agadir Crisis erupted in 1911 ... the Reichsbank directorate became increasingly preoccupied by contingency planning for war. Consequently, it took action to build up the bank's gold stocks'.[31] By 1913, the Reichsbank succeeded in virtually doubling its bullion reserves by converting much of its foreign securities into gold. The nationalisation of the Reichsbank had thus taken place surreptitiously. Havenstein, the president of the Reichsbank since 1908, had begun his fateful term of office with a pious declaration of the autonomy of monetary policy, to wit that it was 'not determined by the financial needs of the state or by the interests of politics, be they those of the government or those of the political parties, which are to be excluded even more'.[32] By 1911 at the latest, the Reichsbank Directorate under Havenstein was complicit in preparing a war chest for the specific 'financial needs of the state' and at the risk of creating a deflationary credit squeeze at home and speculative panic in world financial markets. It was a complicity that was to last through the whole war, through the transition to the Republic and, vitally important in the context of this book, through the so-called Autonomy Law of May 1922.

The surreptitious (self-) nationalisation of the Reichsbank between 1911 and 1914 underscores the *inescapability of context* in any appreciation of the function of central banking: the 'quasi'-, the 'effective', the 'operational', even the statutory autonomy of such an institution is completely worthless if the national mood, the dominant economic orthodoxy or circumstances persuade the Bank's owners and managers to make common cause, be it against the physical enemy of an invading army or the abstract enemy of depression and unemployment. Context, i.e. changing historical circumstances of the real economy, the real polity, the real global environment make any notion of a fixed, abstract autonomy for any human agency naïve in the extreme; the delusion of autonomy when the reality is at best contextually determinate and at worst clientelistic is dishonest.

---

[31] David Marsh, *The Bundesbank*, op.cit. p.94
[32] Deutscher Reichstag, *Stenographische Berichte über die Verhandlungen des Deutschen Reichstages*, Vol. 229 (12 Legislative Period, I. Session, 1907/08), 7072f

The experience of wartime and post-war inflation stretched the fiduciary dimension of the Reichsbank's function beyond breaking point, but demonstrated the extraordinary distance that a desperate public will travel with discredited institutions and utterly discredited policies before they are tempted to rebel. War is an exceptional circumstance and modern war, by definition, generates inflation for all participants. Textbooks on inflation would be incomplete if they did not note that 'there is a striking coincidence between major wars and major inflations';[33] other authors make the analogy of war when describing other exogenous shocks with inflationary consequences.[34] Both war and (hyper-) inflation are invariably traumatic experiences for societies, particularly if they repeated within a generation, as they were in the Germany of the 1920s and the 1940s. It is this trauma that is invoked in justification of the institution of central bank autonomy. One of the major lessons of two world wars for the post-war architects of German economic policy seems thus to have been that one cannot allow governments to influence the conduct of monetary policy; this should be left to a group of unimpeachable experts. There are several contradictions at play here: between the political imperative to create a stable democracy immune to militarism, nationalism and barbarous authoritarianism and the technocratic imperative of policy management; between democratic rebirth and self-doubt, therefore; of experience based on the exceptional becoming the foundation for the management of the normal; between the delusion of policy independent of sectional, elite or ideological influence and the reality of class society.

The 'quasi-autonomous' Reichsbank, with its private shareholders, became a willing instrument of war policy.[35] Immediately after the

---

[33] Thus G.L.Bach, *Inflation. Causes, Effects, Cures*, Englewood Cliffs, 1958, p.4

[34] For example, Roger Bootle, commenting on the first Oil Price shock in the 1970s states that 'for the industrial west, it was comparable, in economic terms, to the outbreak of war'. *The Death of Inflation*, op.cit. p.177

[35] Gerald Feldman describes Havenstein with the rather good pun of 'Generalgeldmarschall' to describe his contribution to the first great industrial war; G. Feldman, *The Great Disorder: Politics, Economics and Society in the German Inflation 1914–1924*, New York 1993, p.32. It is possible to compare the Reichsbank's abandonment of principle (Havenstein in 1908: 'uninfluenced ... by fiscal interests') and the acceptance by the SPD of the War Credits bill on 4 August 1914,

effective suspension of the gold standard a few days before the outbreak of war, banknote circulation doubled in just two weeks, setting in train a process in which treasury bills and private bills of exchange were discounted without question, the circulation of banknotes was allowed to rise some ninefold from 2.6 billion Marks at the end of 1913 to 22.2 billion Marks at the end of 1918 but GDP was halved in the same period. One does not need to be a strict adherent to the quantity theory of money to assert that creating such a disparity between scarce commodities and an abundant money stock would lead to higher prices. An inevitable situation was made worse by the assumptions of both the Reich government and the Reichsbank concerning the likely brevity of the war, German victory and the ability to repeat the trick of 1871 and present the defeated opponents with the bill for the war. These assumptions reduced the perceived need to finance the war from increased taxation or to limit credit to the private sector, an approach which was evident – at least in part – in British government policy during World War One.[36] While the Bank suspended its guarantee to exchange notes and money equivalents for gold, it continued to comply with its statutory obligation of providing one third cover for notes in circulation by some very fancy footwork: firstly, it allowed Treasury bills (the primary generator of excessive note issue) to function as currency reserves, alongside private bills of exchange, which was tantamount to letting the Finance Ministry have direct access to the printing presses; secondly, it sanctioned the establishment of Loan Banks (*Darlehenskassen*) which were authorised to grant credit and to issue notes (the so-called *Darlehenskassenscheine*). Loan Bank credits were secured, among other things, by tangible assets which 'from a monetary standpoint ... lacked every character of a reserve for notes in circulation.'[37] In addition, the banknotes issued by the Loan Banks were given the same legal status as Imperial notes and could therefore be used as part of the Reichsbank's reserve cover. 'In other words the Reichsbank could now use these notes issued by the Loan Banks as the

---

having hitherto adhered to the party vow of giving 'not a man, not a groschen to this system'.

[36] Robert Knauss estimated that Britain covered 20 per cent of its war costs by tax revenue, compared to just 6 per cent in Germany, *Die deutsche, englische und französische Kriegsfinanzierung*, Berlin 1923, p.175

[37] Flink, *The German Reichsbank*, op.cit. p.41

basis for issue of three times as many Reichsbanknotes. The inflating influence of such a note issuing policy is obvious.'[38]

During the first half of the war, Treasury bills were only discounted if they were covered by equivalent volumes of government bonds. Nine issues of war bonds were sold by the Reichsbank on behalf of the government at six-monthly intervals, raising a total of 98.5 billion Marks. The attractiveness of the bonds, as well as their repayment, was still dependent on German victory. As the war persisted, and the likelihood of victory receded, so the preparedness of the German population to commit what was left of their savings to funding the war evaporated.[39] From the autumn bond issue of 1916 onwards, bond placements were increasingly unsuccessful; in practice, treasury bills remained uncovered by bond sales, leaving almost a third of total war costs (estimates vary between 150 and 165 billion Marks) financed by just Reichsbank credits to the government, i.e. by the printing press.

None of the Reichsbank's assumptions about the length of the war, German victory or reparations proved correct. Apart from the brief mirage of Russian reparations, following the Treaty of Brest-Litovsk,[40] the German state was confronted with enormous domestic financial liabilities, the indirect costs of sustaining the victims of war and an as yet unspecified sum in reparations to the victorious Entente. All-in-all, the costs of the First World War for the nations involved are estimated at around 1,350 billion Marks (750 billion in direct costs and 600 billion in indirect costs). Set against this, German pre-war net GNP of 48 billions and Reich expenditure of 3.5 billions appear staggeringly small.[41] Defeat aside, the state of the Reich's finances was the worst

---

[38] Ibid.

[39] See C-L Holtfrerich, *Die deutsche Inflation 1914–1923*, Berlin 1980, 111f

[40] The bulk of Russia's gold reserves were transferred to the vaults of the Reichsbank just four days before the abdication of the Kaiser on 9 November 1918.

[41] One should also not forget the long-term cost of the interruption of European and global economic development between 1914 and 1945 which is evident from any graphical illustration of production and trade growth in this period. For example, Werner Abelshauser, *Wirtschaftsgeschichte der Bundesrepublik Deutschland 1945 bis 1980*, (Frankfurt am Main, 1983) shows an absolute growth trajectory of industrial production for Germany which stops abruptly in 1914 and is only reached again around 1960 (p.93).

possible burden bequeathed to the new democratic republic. Whether one takes Stolper's 'purchasing power Mark' or the standard Gold Mark measure, coverage of Reich expenditure by Reich revenue declined to insignificant proportions by 1918 and, despite some improvement, never reached more than 35 per cent (Stolper: 43.7 per cent) in the pre-stabilisation period:

Table 3.1   Ratio of Reich Expenditure Covered by Reich Revenue, 1913–1923 in per cent

	1916	1918	1919	1920	1921	1922	1923
Nussbaum Goldmark Basis	5	8	15	32	19	35	20
Stolper 'Purchasing Power Mark' Basis				36	43.7	36.5	19.5

Source: Nussbaum, *Wirtschaft und Staat in der Weimarer Republik*, op.cit.; Stolper, *Deutsche Wirtschaft seit 1870*, op.cit. p.96

By the end of December 1918 Reich indebtedness had risen to 156.1 Billion Marks, of which 40 per cent was short-term. Falls in industrial production of 43 per cent between 1913 and 1918 and of agricultural production of 25–30 per cent in the same period, together with the effects of losing colonies, most of the merchant fleet and large amounts of German railway stock as a result of the armistice, had reduced both absolute levels of national product and the productive capacity of the German economy with which such a massive debt could have been serviced. If one compares the average borrowing requirement of the Reich for the five years 1919–23 of 75.8 per cent with the Maastricht ceiling of 3 per cent, the scale of the problem becomes evident. The virtual impossibility of covering state borrowing with bond sales left the revolutionary government of SPD and USPD, as well as its successors, with no other option than to present the Reichsbank with more and more Treasury bills for conversion into cash, to 'borrow' money from the Reichsbank. Within six months, the Reich debt rose to 175 Billion Marks, with interest due of 9 Billion (2½ times Reich expenditure in 1913 in nominal terms); the Reich's borrowing requirement rose constantly from month to month and from year-end to year-end.

Table 3.2   Reich Debt from Discounted Treasury Bills,
                     1918–1923 (Year End) in Billion Marks

1918	1919	1920	1921	1922	1923
55.2	86.4	152.8	247.1	1495.2	191580465422.1

Source: Holtfrerich, *Die deutsche Inflation*, op.cit. 64f

The Reichsbank's willingness to provide the state with unlimited funds and at low (negative) rates of interest was informed by the acknowledgement of the immediate inescapability of debt-financing and further reinforced by the terms of the Versailles Treaty of June 1919 and the London Schedule of Payments of May 1921, which fixed Germany's reparation debt at 132 Billion Goldmarks. It justified the maintenance of a low Discount Rate with the convincing argument that any repression of credit demand would damage both the macro-economy and increase still further the pressure on state finances.[42] The Reichsbank's views on the course of currency devaluation and domestic inflation were nevertheless interestingly contradictory and indicate strongly the degree to which it continued to be firmly rooted in the national cause of resistance. During the War, the Reichsbank in its annual reports consistently blamed Germany's foreign economic position of trade and payments for both the external weakening of the Mark and for domestic price rises, placing itself four-square behind the so-called Balance of Payments Theory of Inflation; this theory asserts that deficits in the balance of trade and payments exert downward pressure on the exchange rate of a national currency, reducing export earnings and increasing the cost of imports, obliging the state to attract capital via higher interest rates; inflation is thus imported directly through commodity prices and indirectly through increased corporate costs. The Reichsbank's public stance continued in post-war reports and statements. However, parallel to the annual reports, the Bank also submitted confidential reports to the Reich President via the Chancellor in which views were expressed which 'for overwhelming reasons could

---

[42] See James, 'The Reichsbank 1876–1945', op.cit. p.19f

not be well accommodated in the administrative report aimed at the public'.[43] These private views of the Directorate placed the Bank much more clearly in the ranks of quantity theorists; the 'continuing increase in paper means of payment' was a primary cause of inflation; an 'essential precondition' for an improvement in general economic conditions was a reform of Reich finance policies and an end to Reichsbank credits to the government.[44] Even after the signing of the Versailles Treaty, consistently dubbed as 'unfulfillable' by the Bank, confidential communications from the Directorate stressed the fiscal source of inflation; in July 1919 the reports even included threats to halt the open and cheap discounting of Treasury bills.[45] The contradiction is understandable. The balance of payments theory suited the political purposes of both government and Bank: it deflected blame from the German state for the misery, hunger and chaos created by war and inflation, it provided justification for inflationary fiscal policy as a *faute de mieux* and it provided 'scientific' grounds for pressurising the Entente into moderating reparations demands. But 'Havenstein new perfectly well how questionable his public explanations of the causes of inflation were, which referred to foreign or reparations policy'.[46] The confidential reports and other private utterances reflected the Reichsbank's perceptions of the truth, that there was an inescapable link between an excessive supply of money and a very limited supply of goods. The threats of an end to the discounting of Treasury bills, on the other hand, are less easy to explain. Both Holtfrerich and Marsh are

---

[43] Letter from the Reichsbank Directorate to Reich Chancellor Scheidemann on 30 March 1919, quoted in Holtfrerich, *Die deutsche Inflation*, op.cit. p.163f.
[44] Ibid. p.164; the views were not just for the consumption of government. Havenstein stated clearly in a secret meeting of the Directorate in December 1920: 'All experts here and in other countries are agreed that the first precondition for the recovery of our monetary and fiscal systems is the shutting-down of the printing press'; Zentrales Staatsarchiv, Nl Havenstein, Nr. 3, Havenstein in the Reichsbank Directorate, 16 December 1920
[45] Letters from the Reichsbank Directorate to the Finance Minister on 1 1 and 14 July 1919, quoted in Holtfrerich, *Die deutsche Inflation*, op.cit. p.164
[46] Claus-Dieter Krohn, *Die große Inflation in Deutschland 1918–1923*, Cologne 1977, p.24

clear about their lack of seriousness but provide no explanation.[47] One
obvious explanation, however, is firstly the need to ensure that the
Reich government was aware of its exclusive blame for monetary
conditions but secondly that the Weimar Coalition led by the Social
Democrat Bauer would have been eyed with at least suspicion by both
the Directors and the private shareholders of the Reichsbank, in relation
both to the taxation of income and property proposed in Erzberger's
reforms and to the promise of generous social welfare.[48] The fact that
there was a clear 'shift of emphasis' in the Reichsbank's confidential
reports to the government after 1920, when the SPD-led coalition had
been replaced by a straightforward bourgeois coalition may certainly
have something to do with the worsening of German foreign economic
and political conditions,[49] but the change in the domestic constellation
of political forces involving the inclusion of the strongly capitalist DVP
in government will not have gone unnoticed in the Bank Directorate.
Havenstein conceded that the July 1919 threats had been a 'bluff' in a
letter to Montagu Norman in December 1921.[50] Given the later hostility
of the Reichsbank to the SPD-led grand coalition of 1928–30, the
suspicion of a class-political dimension to the 'bluff' is not
unreasonable. It is also significant that the apparent theoretical
contradiction of private and public pronouncements (in confidential and
published reports) was resolved by the simple absorption of quantity
theory into the balance of payments theory: yes, domestic inflation was
being driven by excessive note issue but this was unavoidable in the
circumstances of a punitive reparations regime: the 'extremely
damaging method of financing' (unconsolidated note issue JL) could
only be abandoned if 'the reparations commitments are reduced to a
level which corresponds to the tax potential of the population'.[51]

The fact remains that the Reichsbank continued to discount state and
private bills without compunction until November 1923. But there are
strong indications that it did not simply do so because it was somehow

[47] See Holtfrerich, *Die deutsche Inflation*, op.cit. p.164; Marsh, *The Bundesbank*, op.cit.p.97
[48] Holtfrerich deals at length with the opposition of banking and industrial interests to the Erzberger taxation reforms (op.cit. p.131ff) but does not seek to establish a link to Reichsbank attitudes to the Bauer government.
[49] Thus Holtfrerich, *Die deutsche Inflation*, op.cit. p.165
[50] Quoted in Marsh, *The Bundesbank*, op.cit. p.287, n.44
[51] Reichsbank, *Verwaltungsbericht*, April 1921, p.5

resigned to the inevitability of inflation,[52] or was complicit in a politics of catastrophe aimed at the Entente. Just as important is the *perception of both economic and political advantages which it shared with elements of Germany's traditional elites.* It is important to repeat that the Reichsbank from its inception clearly pursued a policy designed to aid national economic development, in particular that of industry and trade; James defines it accurately as a 'policy of production'. This role was transformed into a thoroughgoing commitment to the national cause of wartime production and victory (whether one interprets that cause as defensive or expansionist). Defeat did not alter that commitment; if anything it reinforced it.

'The Reichsbank in fact took from the pre-war world a concern for financing production – any kind of production. This approach fitted perfectly with the predominant tendency of viewing the inflation as originating with the balance of payments. According to this diagnosis of the German malaise, Germany needed to produce more in order to export more, and in this way help to tackle the balance of payments problem. This *Produktionspolitik* fitted perfectly with the social-psychological analysis that had been created by German elites in the aftermath of the Russian revolution: that producing and creating work was essential in order to preserve Germany's fragile political stability'.[53]

The Hamburg Banker, Friedrich Bendixen was an open and thus honest proponent of 'inflation as a means of salvation'.[54] His views expressed both economic and political preferences: a) 'For Germany after the war ...nothing is so bitterly necessary as the straining of all economic forces towards comprehensive production';[55] inflation was an evil 'but it is the only means of preventing a even greater evil'.[56] Maintaining production and employment would ease the transition to a peacetime economy and run a lower risk of provoking social discontent. b) The avoidance of revolution through a deliberate policy of reflation/inflation was linked to a contempt for the new 'social republic' and its plans to introduce progressive taxation of income and wealth

---

[52] Marsh speaks of resignation, *The Bundesbank* op.cit. p.98

[53] James, 'The Reichsbank 1876–1945', op.cit. p.21

[54] Thus the title of an article by Bendixen in the *Bank-Archiv*, Vol.19 (1919/20), p.54 (1 December 1919): 'Die Inflation als Rettungsmittel'.

[55] Friedrich Bendixen, 'Die Parität und ihre Wiederherstellung', in: *Bank-Archiv*, Vol.18 (1918/19), p.13 (15 October 1918)

[56] Bendixen, '*Die Inflation als Rettungsmittel*', op.cit. p.48

into Germany for the first time in its history; inflation was an irregular but preferable alternative to regular income tax: better 'exploit to the full the opportunities that generating money presents than to paralyse the strength to work and the entrepreneurial spirit through a confiscatory system of taxation'.[57] Finally, inflation was also an effective lever for achieving changes in 'the deep blackness of the Versailles Peace Treaty'.[58] Bendixen's published views of the economic advantages of inflation were clearly shared by both the Reichsbank and by the series of governments that presided over the period.[59]

The notion of inflation as an easy form of taxation was persuasive, even if one still sees Erzberger's 1919–20 reforms as a genuine attempt both to raise reliable state revenue and to establish a degree of fairness in Germany's tax regime. In the event, all German governments in the period proved too weak to persuade the tax-shy bourgeoisie to accept income and wealth taxation, and chose inflation as the path of least resistance later described by Keynes as the 'form of taxation which the public find hardest to evade and even the weakest government can enforce when it can enforce nothing else'[60] The vehicle of this irregular form of taxation was the manipulation of short-term debt and required the complicity of the Reichsbank in maintaining negative rates of real interest.

To cover its domestic expenditure commitments, the Reich Finance Ministry exchanged three-month treasury bills for cash from the Reichsbank, repaying this 'credit' three months later with cash raised in a similar way, but in the sure knowledge that a small or large part of the original capital value of the first credit would have been eroded by inflation.

---

[57] Bendixen, *Kriegsanleihen und Finanznot. Zwei finanzpolitische Vorschläge*, Jena 1919, p.19

[58] Bendixen, *Die Inflation als Rettungsmittel*, op.cit. p.56

[59] Holtfrerich, *Die deutsche Inflation*, op.cit. p.131, cites the discussions and proposals of both the Reich government and the Reich civil service in 1919

[60] John Maynard Keynes, *A Tract on Monetary Reform*, London 1971, (first edition: 1923), p.37

Table 3.3   Domestic Inflation (Wholesale Price Index) and Reichsbank Discount Rate 1918–1923

	1918	1919	1920	1921	1922	Jan–July 1923	July–Oct 1923
Discount Rate %	5	5	5	5	5	30	90
Price Rises Average in %	18	384	12.5	154	7488	2585	9359815

Source: Gustav Stolper, *Deutsche Wirtschaft seit 1870*

As Table 3.3 suggests, the price exacted for discounting bills on this merry-go-round – the Discount Rate – was not designed to deter but to encourage the demand for credit; it created a debtor's paradise. Borrowing 100 000 Marks at 5 per cent and repaying it three months later with a new credit but after annualised inflation of 154 per cent or 7488 per cent represents a saving in the first instance of 36599 Marks in the first instance or 99955.7 Mark in the second. The Reich effectively paid 54.3 Marks for a 100000 Mark credit in 1922.

The history of the May 1922 Autonomy Act is a strange one. The disquiet among the Entente powers about German monetary and fiscal policy grew steadily from the end of the war. Poincaré was convinced that the German authorities were pursuing a deliberate policy of inflation. Sir John Bradbury, the British delegate to the Reparations Commission, spoke of the 'gross mismanagement of Germany's public finances' and Lord d'Abernon, British Ambassador in Berlin, described German fiscal policy as 'extraordinarily bad'.[61] The Reparations Commission criticized 'the rather passive attitude of the Reichsbank towards the discount of treasury debentures'[62] but ascribed this to the provisions of the 1875 Bank Act whereby the 'Reich Chancellor is the President of the Reichsbank' and 'issues the regulations and working

---

[61] Both cited in Stephen Schuker, 'Finance Policy in the Era of the German Inflation: British, French and German Strategies for Economic Reconstruction after the First World War', in: Büsch, O. and Feldman, G. (eds), *Historische Prozesse der deutschen Inflation 1914 bis 1924, Berlin 1978*, p.352

[62] Thus Flink, *The Reichsbank*, op.cit. p.63

orders to the Directorate'. On the recommendation of the Reparations Commission, the Allied governments (of France, Britain and the United States) demanded of the German government that the Reichsbank Law be amended to free it from the control of the Reich Chancellor. The idea was first floated at the intergovernmental conference in Cannes in January 1922 and then, after a formal note by the Reparations Commission from 21 March 1922, the special economic conference held in Genoa between 10 April and 19 May directed a formal demand for the autonomisation of the Reichsbank and made the fulfilment or the measure a condition for the granting of a reparations moratorium. Dutifully, the Reich government presented the Reichstag with appropriate amendments to the Bank Law which was passed on 20 May 1922. There was no effective debate in the Reichstag. There was only one speaker in the second reading of the bill, Jakob Riesser, whose German People's Party (DVP) was not part of the Wirth government, and none in the third reading which followed immediately after the second. Riesser stressed that the Entente was 'completely wrong' in its assumptions about the relationship between inflation and a dependent central bank, repeating the view that reparations were primarily to blame and that the Reichsbank had 'no other option' than to discount Treasury bills.[63] No government spokesmen felt obliged to support the bill. The amendments to the Bank Bill included the introduction of life-long tenure of all members of the Directorate (Article 27) and the omission of the words rendering the decisions of the Directorate 'subject to the prescriptions and instructions of the Reich Chancellor'. The continuity of Directorate membership was clearly devised as a counterweight to the brevity of electoral cycles (4 years in the Weimar Republic) and the even shorter survival periods of most Weimar governments (8.1 months on average); it was driven by the assumption that the different time perspective would produce a different policy perspective from that of a government dependent on the short-term whim of both electorate and parliament. The wording of the amendments describes the Bank as 'a completely independent legal entity', its autonomy 'raises the reputation and the credit of the institute'.[64] However, there is a resignative tone to the actual bill when its authors state '(b)ecause of the circumstances, it seems appropriate to

---

[63] Thus Riesser (DVP), in: Stenographische Berichte des deutschen Reichstags, Vol. 355, 215 Session, Saturday 20 May 1922, 7454f
[64] *Stenographische Berichte des deutschen Reichstags*, Vol. 372, Appendix N3863, p.4116 and p.4118

grant the Reichsbank an autonomous position.'[65] Furthermore, it was a strange kind of autonomy, where six of the nine members of the Directorate were still to be nominated by other parts of the Weimar state covered directly or indirectly by electoral answerability: three by the Federal Economics Ministry and three by the Federal Council (Bundesrat). Supervision of the Bank was broadened but also remained defined by the state executive. Article 25 stated that '(t)he right to supervise the Reichsbank, formerly exercised by the government, is now exercised by the Curatorium which consists of the Chancellor as Chairman, the Finance Minister and the Economics Minister as vice-chairman and of six other members, three of whom are appointed by the Reich President after consulting with the Federal Economics Ministry and the other three designated by the Federal Council.' The link to government was thus not broken in the way that subsequent autonomy laws have achieved. In particular, no provision was made for Allied/Entente supervision of the Reichsbank's activities. This was remarkable, given the effective abandonment by the Reichsbank under Havenstein of the standard principles of cover and the contrasting efforts by both the Bank of England and the Banque de France to achieve monetary stability in the aftermath of the Great War.

All the more remarkable is the fact, that having taken the dramatic step of insisting on the formal autonomy of the Reichsbank in exchange for which a partial moratorium on reparations payments was granted in 1922, the Reparations Commission sat back and watched the Bank continue as if nothing had happened. Indeed, according to several authors the 1922 Autonomy Law coincided with an escalation of the Bank's 'policy of catastrophe'; 'the Autonomy Law of May 1922 changed nothing' ...indeed only after the Law 'did the printing of banknotes take on that uncontrollable excess that led to the collapse of the financial system in 1923'.[66] The truth is, as Krohn stresses, that the Reich Chancellor had never had to put pressure on the Reichsbank to do his or the government's will;[67] it was a willing conspirator in a national cause.

---

[65] Ibid. p. 4116

[66] Thus Krohn, *Die große Inflation*, op.cit. p.19; see also Kurt Gossweiler, *Großbanken, Industriemonopole, Staat.Ökonomie und Politik des staatsmonopolistischen Kapitalismus in Deutschland 1914–1932*, Berlin (E), 1971, 145f

[67] Krohn, *Die große Inflation*, ibid.p.19

'After the Autonomy Law of May 26 1922 ... had strengthened the position of the Reichsbank in relation to the Reich government and, theoretically at least, placed it in a position to put a stop to the expansion of the money supply even against the will of the Reich, it made absolutely no use of this opportunity. Instead, it increasingly accepted private bills of exchange in its portfolio as well as Reich treasury bills and thus opened the flood gates of monetary expansion still wider in favour of its traditional customer, private business.'[68]

The *acceleration of the Bank's discounting of bills* in the second half of 1922 is unmistakable, as the Table below demonstrates. The Bank started the year with just 1.1 billion Marks of commercial bills in its portfolio, but started openly advocating their use as a means of payment in July 1922 and then announced that it was prepared to discount such bills directly to industrial and other companies.

Table 3.4   Bills Discounted by the Reichsbank June–December 1922 in Millions (M)

June	July	Aug	Sept	Oct	Nov	Dec
4751	8122	21704	50234	101155	246943	423235

Source: Flink, *The German Reichsbank and Economic Germany*, op.cit. p.65

This could have been construed as a defiant provocation of the Entente, particularly in the context of a brief reparations moratorium granted in exchange for a different Reichsbank with supposedly different policies. Equally the Bank's agreement to the licensing of emergency note issue by some banks and credit institutions the same year flew in the face of 'the most important change in the Bank Act concern(ing) the right of note issue'.[69] Instead, no action was taken to enforce compliance with the spirit of the Autonomy Law. It was left, rather, to the French to take

---

[68] Holtfrerich, *Die deutsche Inflation*, op.cit. p.167; even Gustav Stolper, an exponent of the Balance of Payments theory and the primacy of reparations in the generation of German hyperinflation, concedes that the Reichsbank's extension of discounting to commercial bills 'increased the inflationary effect of its credits to the Reich by no less than one third', *Deutsche Wirtschaft seit 1870*, op.cit. p.101
[69] Thus Flink, The German Reichsbank, op.cit. p.64

direct action occupying the Ruhr area in February 1923 to ensure compliance with the agreement on payment in kind (part payment of reparations in kind was another concession of the Entente powers which damaged the interests of French, British and Belgian producers of the goods used). To view the Ruhr Occupation as a gratuitous act of a malevolent power on a flimsy pretext,[70] is to ignore the wider context of a thoroughly dishonest policy of fulfilment. Britain's refusal to sanction the occupation is taken as sweet reasonableness compared to Poincaré's vengeful nationalism. If one judges the action in terms of British passivity over the non-fulfilment of autonomous, anti-inflationary monetary policy after May 1922 and the double standards revealed by German cabinet papers of the period,[71] Poincaré's actions seem at least understandable, even if they did trigger a worsening of the inflationary spiral.

The policy of open-house discounting continued undisturbed by the economic catastrophe which unfolded in the second half of 1923. Under the new chancellor, Cuno, and in the context of the occupation of the Ruhr and the so-called 'passive resistance' to French occupation.[72] there was a barely concealed consensus which has been summarized by some commentators as the 'politics of catastrophe',[73] namely of doing

---

[70] This is typical of conservative German historians like Michael Freund, *Deutsche Geschichte*, Munich 1969, 150f or Helmut Heiber, *Die Republik von Weimar*, Munich 1977 (10th edition), 118f

[71] Both Chancellor Wirth and his Foreign Minister Rathenau talked about the 'honour' of Germany's pledge to fulfil the London Schedule of Payments of May 1921 (quoted in Ernst Laubach, *Die Politik der Kabinette Wirth 1921/22*, Lübeck/Hamburg 1968, pp.30 and 41 etc), but Wirth scotched the proposals by Hirsch, Secretary of State in the Reich Finance Ministry, to introduce an effective wealth tax as a means of fulfilling reparations payments: 'The aim of our whole policy must be the dismantling of the London Ultimatum. It is therefore wrong if at the present moment, by means of a tax on capital, we declare the Ultimatum to be 80 per cent sustainable' (Wirth, quoted by Stephen Schuker, 'Finance and Foreign Policy...', op.cit. p.355)

[72] Rosenberg is scathing about the contradictions of passive resistance in *Geschichte der Weimarer Republik*, Frankfurt am Main 1977, 125ff

[73] E.g. Gossweiler, *Großbanken, Industriemonopole, Staat*, op.cit.; Manfred Weißbecker, *Macht und Ohnmacht der Weimarer Republik*, Freiburg/ Berlin 1990, p.85 etc.; the 'politics of catastrophe' are frequently set in contrast to the supposed 'politics of fulfilment' under

nothing 'until the fundamental cause of Germany's plight is removed, i.e. not before we have been offered a satisfactory moratorium and a tolerable solution of the reparations problem'.[74] The madness of negative interest rates, of paying for daily goods with wheelbarrows full of money, and of non-action by the Reichsbank was never criticized by the Cuno cabinet; indeed even when the exchange rate had slumped to 5 million Marks to the Dollar, the Central Committee of Property Owners was still happy to express its support for and trust in Havenstein.[75]

Stabilisation, when it came, had nothing to do with Reichsbank autonomy. Its timing and its conditions were decided within the political arena, the very sphere from whose influence the May 1922 act had supposedly removed the Bank. The mythology of stabilisation, however, contributed in no small way to the subsequent popularisation of the   principle of autonomy after the Second World War. Contemporary observers, not least the direct participants in the state's monetary and fiscal affairs, created some very effective legends surrounding the reasons for, and above all the main architects of the seemingly miraculous process. The reasons for the need for such legends are perhaps as significant as the legends themselves; they centred around both the current views of the nature of money and monetary policy and also the domestic and foreign political requirements of the statesmen involved. To have admitted the truth, namely that the currency became stable simply because the Reichsbank stopped discounting Treasury and other bills, would have been tantamount to a confession of responsibility for the original policy of inflation and would have undermined the already weakened legitimacy of the Weimar state. It would also have increased the chances of successful litigation over the revaluation of old (devalued) debts. The stabilisation had therefore to be presented rather as the genial achievement of great statesmen struggling against the odds, against a 'higher power',[76] so that the economic and political sacrifices

---

Wirth but, as the above suggests, 'fulfilment' was clearly only the rhetorical cover to an equally deliberate policy of proving German inability to pay.
[74] Reichsbank proceedings from 22 October 1922 and 25 August 1923, cited in Krohn, *Die große Inflation*, op.cit. p.23
[75] Quoted in: G.Büscher, *Die Inflation und ihre Lehren*, Zürich 1926, p.140
[76] Thus O. Pfleiderer, in his article on the problem of revaluation, 'Das Prinzip "Mark=Mark" in der deutschen Inflation 1914 bis 1924', in:

demanded of the mass of the German population as the price of stabilisation could be justified more readily and borne more willingly. Mixed in with the conscious cynicism behind the politics of liquidating inflation were the particular vanities of men like Schacht and Luther who subsequently sought to claim the lion's share of the credit.

The liquidation of hyper-inflation was thus more than a technical problem of monetary and fiscal policy, of regulating the money supply and balancing budgets; the nature and timing of stabilisation reflected more strongly the domestic and foreign political priorities of Germany's economic elites and the need to roll back the social and economic concessions of the revolution of 1918–19. The process and its presentation illustrate the instrumentality of the state in relation to dominant economic interests as well as the meaninglessness of central bank autonomy in the context of such domestic and foreign political turmoil. There was never any doubt that stabilisation would be decided at Reich cabinet level. The many proposals for its realisation reflected a common preoccupation with the concept of 'real' cover for the national currency as a precondition for the restoration of national and international 'confidence' in Germany's monetary affairs. In the absence of the cover of gold and foreign currency reserves, a number of alternatives were proposed in the course of 1923 as transitional forms of cover before a full return to gold could be effected. In August 1923, Karl Helfferich of the German Nationalist Party (DNVP) proposed a new currency based on the price of rye (the '*Roggenmark*'),[77] guaranteed by security claims on private capital, one half on agriculture, the other on industry and commerce. The centrality of agriculture to this strange scheme, taken quite seriously by the Stresemann governments, was driven in part by the argument that the agricultural community needed to be persuaded to bring their new

---

Büsch, O. & Feldman, G. (eds), *Historische Prozesse der deutschen Inflation*, Berlin 1978, p.78; Cuno's Economics Minister Becker talked about inflation as an unavoidable 'natural event' (*Akten der Reichskanzlei, Regierung Cuno*, Boppard am Rhein, 1971 et.seq., p.569); similarly specious arguments are to be found in popularised histories of the Great Inflation like Adam Ferguson's *When Money Dies: The Nightmare of the Weimar Collapse*, London 1975
[77] In 1922 the Land of Oldenburg had issued inflation-proof 'rye-debentures'; see Pfleiderer 'Das Prinzip "Mark=Mark"', op.cit. p.75

harvest to market to prevent serious shortages in the winter months.[78]
In early September Hilferding, the Social Democratic Finance Minister
in Stresemann's first cabinet (13 August – 4 October 1923) proposed a
new gold-based currency but guaranteed not by gold or currency
reserves but by interest-bearing, inflation-proof 'gold bonds' based, like
Helfferich's plan, on a mortgage-type claim on the whole German
economy. The Reichsbank rejected Hilferding's plan, expressing
preference for the 'Rye-Mark' and a new 'Rye-Bank' as a parallel
central bank to the Reichsbank, but altering Helfferich's proposal by
suggesting an end to the Reichsbank's function as credit-bank to the
Reich and its replacement by the 'Rye-Bank'. Luther, the Food
Minister, then proceeded to propose a 'Land Mark' ('Bodenmark'),
whose value would be defined in parity ot the Goldmark and
guaranteed by 'gold bonds' as in Hilferding's plan but based, as in
Helfferich's 'Rye-Mark' proposal, on capital represented half by
agriculture and half by the other sectors of the economy. A further
compromise proposal by Hilferding for a 'New Mark' incorporated the
main features of the 'Land Mark' and was accepted both by Cabinet
and by the Reichsrat, but failed to reach the Reichstag because of the
collapse of Stresemann's first cabinet on 4 October 1923. His second
(Grand) coalition still included the SPD put placed both the Finance
and Economics portfolios in the hands of non-party ministers, namely
Hans Luther and Josef Koeth respectively. Stresemann had wanted to
offer the Finance Ministry to 'his long-standing confidant', Hjalmar
Schacht,[79] but was prevented by strong opposition within the Finance
Ministry.

Luther renamed the 'New Mark' the 'Rentenmark'[80] but with
virtually identical terms of reference and, on the basis of the Enabling
Act of 13 October 1923, a decree governing the establishment of a
'Rentenbank' was promulgated on 15 October and on 15 November the
Rentenmark was introduced. It was subordinate to the Reichsbank and
could conduct its affairs only with the Reich, the Reichsbank and the

---

[78] The problem of food supplies appears frequently in the cabinet papers
of the time, e.g. Food Minister Luther to Stresemann, 22 August 1923,
Akten der Reichskanzler, Kabinett Stresemann, R431/2436
[79] Thus Gerd Hardach, *Weltmarktorientierung und relative Stagnation:
Währungspolitik in Deutschland 1924–1931*, Berlin 1976, 21f
[80] 'Rente' in this context means an 'annuity' or yield from financial
securities; it has become a common term for fixed interest securities in
Germany, not to be confused with 'Rente' as 'pension'.

issuing banks, not with private corporations. However, as credit bank to the Reich it provided the essential basis for the control of fiscal policy. The new Rentenmark, which existed parallel to the old Mark, was introduced at a rate of 1 Rentenmark to 1000000000000 Mark (1 'Billmark') and at parity to the Goldmark. The exchange rate was fixed at 4.2 Rentenmark/Goldmark (4.2 Billmarks) to the Dollar, i.e. at its pre-war level. The Rentenbank was permitted to circulate 2.4 billion Rentenmark, half allotted to the Reich, the other half through the Reichsbank to private enterprises. The Rentenmark was not general legal tender; nor could it be employed outside the Reich. Rather the old Mark remained the chief means of exchange, but pegged by the new Rentenmark to a fixed parity.

The effective date of currency stabilisation was 20 November 1923, coinciding with the fixing of the Dollar exchange rate at 4.2 Billmarks, the abrupt ending of automatic discounting by the Reichsbank, the shutting down of the printing presses and, ironically, with the death of the long-standing president of the Reichsbank, Rudolf Havenstein, whom Stresemann had been wanting to replace on grounds of old age for some weeks. The 'Rentenmark-miracle' was, in some measure, an exercise in public relations and obfuscation, even though it reflected the notion of real cover for the currency; given that the Rentenmark had no external value and that the external stabilisation of the currency was a major condition of internal stabilisation, it was the old paper Mark, hedged now by a new probity in Reichsbank policy, that carried the actual stabilisation through.[81] The idea of the Rentenmark restoring trust in a way which the old Mark could not is thus misleading,[82]

---

[81]Viz Gerd Hardach, *Weltmarktorientierung und relative Stagnation*, op.cit. p.23; Wilhelm Hankel poured cold water on the notion of the new Rentenmark's cover, by pointing out very convincingly that 'it had practically no value, because it was totally non-liquid', *Währungspolitik, Geldwertstabilisierung, Währungsintegration und Sparerschutz*, Stuttgart 1972, p.238

[82] The concept of trust is central to many discussions of market economics in general and the German stabilisation in particular; Dietmar Petzina uses it in relation to the discredited paper Mark and, although he acknowledges that the new 'cover' could never have been rendered liquid, he asserts the the Rentenmark 'completely fulfilled its psychological function', *Deutsche Wirtschaft in der Zwischenkriegszeit*, Wiesbaden 1977, p.84; it is very difficult to believe that the mere introduction of a new exotically covered currency would have induced

particularly in relation to international capital markets. Luther's subsequent claim to the laurels for the 'Rentenmark-miracle'[83] does not stand up to examination, given that the groundwork had been done by Helfferich, Hilferding and others. Schacht's claim is supported more by the mythology of subsequent histories, as his nickname 'the old wizard' implied, but is no less specious.[84] The date for the introduction of the Rentenmark and the conditions for stabilisation, notably the halting of Reichsbank open-house discounting, were fixed on 15 October, a month before Schacht's appointment as advisory Currency Commissioner on 13 November. His various self-eulogies also fail to mention that he opposed the Reichsbank Directorate when it decided to fix the Dollar rate at 4.2 Billmarks, proposing a further devaluation instead.[85]

---

the required portion of 'trust' among the baffled observers of German financial affairs at home and abroad without the concrete measures which closed down the engine of inflation, namely rigorous monetary controls which attempted to marry money supply to the supply of commodities; see, in particular, Krohn, *Stabilisierung und ökonomische Interessen. Die Finanzpolitik des deutschen Reiches 1923–1927*, Düsseldorf 1974, p.26

[83] This is the tenor of Luther's memoirs, *Politiker ohne Partei*, Stuttgart 1960, and of Netzband and Widmaier's account of Luther's period of office, *Währungs- und Finanzpolitik der Ära Luther 1923–1925*, Tübingen 1964.

[84] Viz in particular Schacht, H., *Die Stabilisierung der Mark*, Stuttgart/Berlin/ Leipzig 1927 and chapter XXII of his later autobiography, *Confessions of the 'Old Wizard'*, Boston 1956. Schacht's conceit was prodigious: of Luther he wrote that he 'did not feel able to cope with the task of reforming the national currency and looked about for a specialist in that line', (ibid. p.164) inviting Schacht to become Currency Commissioner. 'Next morning, November 13 1923, I entered upon my duties as Commissioner for National Currency. ... I realized that Germany was in danger of succumbing to communism and felt it was my duty not to shirk a task which, as I hoped, lay within my power to fulfil'. (ibid. 166f)

[85] Letter from the Reichsbank Directorate to Secretary of State Bracht, 17 December 1923, Bundesarchiv R43 I/962, in which it vigorously opposed Schacht's appointment to the vacant presidency of the Reichsbank; viz also Gerd Hardach, *Weltmarktorientierung*, op.cit. 24ff

Schacht is a key figure in the development of the mythology of central bank autonomy. It was he who personally exploited the later Bank Act of August 1924 by generating the false polarity between government extravagance and Reichsbank probity, which underpins the today's ideology of central bankism. By linking his appointment with the timing and substance of stabilisation, and underscoring Schacht's single-handed struggle against an irresponsible fiscal state, the myth-makers distort the reality of a stabilisation process, which was in fact driven by the Reich cabinet and implemented (willingly) by the Reichsbank and its new parallel central banks, the Rentenbank and the Golddiskontbank. Neither the conditions nor the operational arrangements of stabilisation originated from an autonomous central bank. The whole process was masterminded and monitored by the Reich and served the primary interests of the Reich, as the details on the liquidation of the Reich's debt in Table 3.5 demonstrate. Despite the apparently new restrictive monetary regime, which imposed an effective rediscount quota on the Reich, stabilisation politics in the following months continued to be dominated by the fiscal interests of the state.

Table 3.5   Liquidation of the Reich's Debt in 1923

	Discounted Treasury Bills in Mill. Marks	Goldmark: Mark conversion rate	Reich Debt in Mill. Goldmark
31 Aug. 1923	1196	2.4 million: 1	50250
30 Sept. 1923	46700	38 million: 1	1230
31 Oct. 1923	6907500	17.3 billion: 1	400
11 Nov. 1923	191580500	600 billion: 1	320
20 Nov. 1923	191580500	1 trillion: 1	191.6

Source: C-D. Krohn, *Die große Inflation* op.cit.

The cynical expunging (devaluation) of the Reich's domestic debt was predicated on the assumption that no debts, but particularly state debts, would be revalued after stabilisation. This assumption was set in doubt temporarily by a Reichsgericht appeal judgement on 28 November 1923, which overturned the earlier negative ruling by the Berlin Supreme Court on the revaluation of a mortgage debt on property in South West Africa, employing the argument of 'good faith' as laid out in the civil code (Article 242).[86] It is understandable why this judgement, particularly with regard to the notion of 'good faith', would have been 'a bombshell' to the incoming Marx government and would have led to rapid moves to prevent the judgement becoming a precedent; the first draft of Finance Minister Luther's Third Emergency Tax Decree thus contained a general exclusion of revaluation in all cases where it had not been agreed beforehand between the contracting parties.[87] This would make the application of any notion of 'good faith' impossible. Ironically, the same draft decree includes proposals for the taxing of the inflationary 'profits' from mortgage debts and private bond obligations,[88] whereby Luther stressed the vital importance of such taxes for the Reich's budgetary position,[89] a noteworthy case of having one's cake and eating it. Debates within the Cabinet over the revaluation problem were not unanimous, some opposition coming from Justice Minister Emminger who spoke of the 'expropriation of creditors',[90] while Food Minister Kanitz opposed any taxation of mortgage profits on the grounds that agriculture would be made even less creditworthy if their incomes were further hit.[91] Economics Minister Hamm argued against the revaluation of industrial obligations, since the profits from inflation had already been (well) spent on new investment and any redistributed monies from a partial revaluation would only fuel consumption and hence inflation.[92] In its final published version the Third Emergency Tax Decree did contain the possibility of a 15 per cent revaluation of private obligations dating from the period of inflation as well as a number of 'inflation taxes', but public debts were specifically exempted.[93]

---

[86] Krohn, C.-D., *Stabilisierung und ökonomische Interessen*, op.cit. p.27

[87] Viz Pfleiderer, 'Das Prinzip "Mark=Mark"', op.cit. p. 79

[88] The draft text of the Third Emergency Tax Decree is contained in a memorandum from Luther to the Cabinet of 16 December 1923 (R43 I/2394); see Article I Paras 1–6; viz also Luther, H. *Politiker ohne Partei*, Stuttgart 1970, p. 229ff

[89] Luther in Meeting of the Cabinet's Economic Committee, 15 December 1923, BA R43 I/1390

[90] Ibid.

[91] Letter from Kanitz to Chancellor of 8 January 1924, BA R 43 I/2454

[92] Hamm to Chancellor, 6 January 1924, BA R43 I/2454

[93] Decree promulgated on 14 February 1924; viz Cabinet Meeting of 29 January 1924, R43 I/1391

A key parallel factor in facilitating the stabilisation of German currency affairs was the American-led initiative to resolve the reparations issue, begun in October 1923 by President Coolidge and his Secretary of State Hughes. On 30 November 1923 the Reparations Commission appointed two specialist committees, the most important of which was headed by Charles Dawes, the American banker and later vice-president of the US. The Dawes Committee report of 9 April 1924, apart from providing a new payments timetable for reparations and the basis of US funding support, insisted on specific conditions of foreign control over German state affairs to encourage such support. These included the effective internationalisation of the Reich railways via an 11 billion Reichsmark bond issue and the appointment of foreign representatives to its managerial board; furthermore the Reichsbank Law was to be amended, strengthening its autonomy from government influence but placing foreign supervisors in key positions within the Bank; in addition Dawes proposed an Office for a Reparations Agent to be located in Berlin. The new Bank Law, like the May 1922 'Autonomy' Law was introduced dutifully by the Reichstag with no major amendments to the Dawes conditions; it was accepted by the majority of members as a necessary inconvenience:

'We have no other choice other than to approve the opportunities afforded by foreign aid and, yes, unfortunately foreign tutelage. ... If Germany were free, if we had the option to change things in the bill which we have agreed with the Entente powers, we would have many requests for changes'.[94]

The issue of central bank independence played an insignificant role in the debate. Rather, the dominant concern – in particular of the vocal opposition minorities – was about foreign control of the Bank and Germany's dependence on foreign capital. Schacht, who had been appointed Reichsbank president on 22 December 1923, was strongly opposed to any foreign influence within the Bank.[95] As Flink points out, the 'main reason for the introduction of foreign control upon the

---

[94] Thus Wilhelm Keil, an SPD monetary affairs spokesman, in the Bank Law debate, *Stenographische Berichte des deutschen Reichstags*, Vol.; 381, 11th Legislative Period 1924, 24th session, Tuesday 26 August 1924, p.884; Keil earlier acknowledges that the 'roots of the destruction of the German Mark' lay in 'the finance policy of imperial Germany', ibid. p.883

[95] See Schacht, Hjalmar, *Die Stabilisierung der Mark*, Stuttgart (DVA) 1927, p.167 etc.

management of the Reichsbank was the desire ... to render impossible
the recurrence of a new inflation caused by excessive issue of notes' as
well as 'the necessity to reestablish international confidence in the
stability of Germany's currency'.[96]

Under the new law, the Bank's General Council consisted of seven
German and seven foreign representatives. The approval of the General
Council was needed for the appointment of Directorate members,
including the Bank President; the formal powers of the Reich President
concerning the appointment of the Bank President were also reduced. In
addition, one of the foreign members of the General Council was the
Commissar for Note Issue who was empowered to halt the issue of
notes if this was considered to jeopardise currency stability or its gold
convertibility. Overall, therefore, the autonomy of the Reichsbank was
considerably reduced by the August 1924 Law in terms of the external
influence introduced. There is no doubt that this was informed by the
exasperation of the Reparations Commission over the ineffectiveness of
the May 1922 autonomy provisions. It nevertheless established a de
facto separation of monetary and fiscal policy-making in Germany
which lasted at least until early 1930 when foreign representatives were
removed from the Reichsbank General Council as well as from the
Reich railways as a result of the Young Plan. The foreign monitoring of
the Reichsbank arguably strengthened Schacht's hand not just in his
very public demarcation of Reichsbank activity from the Reich's fiscal
institutions but also in his ability to influence or alter fiscal policy.
Schacht cultivated his personal links with Parker Gilbert, the
Reparations Agent, and with Montagu Norman, governor of the Bank
of England to increase his domestic freedom of manoeuvre and his
institutional power base. Certainly, the much vaunted 'central bank cooperation' of the late 1920s proceeded from the assumption that central
banks should be immune from governmental influence, but Schacht
remained dependent on his foreign allies, be they ideological or
political; furthermore the maintenance of the gold standard demanded
strict adherence to international standards, which obliged the
Reichsbank to hold its short-term interests higher than other members
of the central bank family.

Schacht's use (and abuse) of power was autocratic and wilful, but it
was the style of the brutish subaltern, confident of the protection of his
seniors in the hierarchy of international power relations and not that of
a sovereign bully. The attacks by Schacht and the Reichsbank on the

---

[96] Flink, *The Reichsbank* op.cit. p.139 and p.140

(democratic) constitution of the Weimar Republic are well documented.[97] They reflected, in the main, a strong partisanship for the interests of capital against the claims of both the state and of labour. The most severe attacks were directed against the 'extravagance' and foreign borrowing of German municipalities but Schacht and von Dreyse, his vice-president, extended their criticism to other key areas of fiscal policy (taxation, social transfers, subsidies and Reich borrowing) and to 'wage relations under the Marxist (sic) system'.[98] Municipal borrowing to finance infrastructure and housing projects was deemed to be 'unproductive'[99] and to crowd out productive private investment. The Reichsbank succeeded in influencing the extent of long term state foreign loans, firstly through its role in the Advisory Office for Foreign Credits (*Beratungsstelle für Auslandskredite*), established in 1924, and secondly through an extraordinary campaign of international lobbying to dissuade potential creditors from buying regional, municipal and Reichsbahn bonds,[100] even though these, in contrast to foreign loans for German agriculture which Schacht approved,[101] were generally regarded as very sound financial investments; more recently location theorists have identified infrastructural investments as significant 'hard factors' for attracting inward private investment.[102] The campaign reached almost obsessive and absurd proportions when Schacht contacted a number of American banks personally in 1925 to prevent a modest long-term loan to the town of Stettin and an even more modest loan to the tiny coastal town of Küstrin.[103]

---

[97] In particular, see: Böhret, *Aktionen gegen die 'kalte Sozialisierung' 1926–1930. Ein Beitrag zum Wirken ökonomischer Einflußverbände in der Weimarer Republik*, Berlin (Duncker & Humblot), 1966, 173ff and James, *The Reichsbank*, op.cit. 19ff and 95ff

[98] Thus Schacht, *The End of Reparations*, op.cit. p.197f

[99] See Hjalmar Schacht,'Selbstkontrolle', *Der deutsche Volkswirt*, Vol.2. (1927), Nr.7; also Böhret, *Aktionen*, op.cit. p.174 etc.

[100] See James, *The Reichsbank*, op.cit. 45ff

[101] See James, *The Reichsbank*, op.cit. p.75

[102] See, e.g. Douglas North, 'International Capital Movements in Historical Perspective', in: Raymond Mikesell (ed.), *US Private and Government Investment Abroad*, Eugene, 1962, quoted in Gerd Hardach, 'Reichsbankpolitik ...', op.cit. p. 578

[103] See Müller, *Die Zentralbank*, op.cit. p. 67; James, The Reichsbank, op.cit. p.50

The campaign was not without contradictions. The weakness of German capital markets after 1924 has been well described, deriving in large measure from the destruction of savings and thus of the important class of rentier savers in the Great Inflation. Private and state borrowing in Germany was always going to be reliant on foreign sources, and this was a common assumption of all those involved in the Dawes Plan arrangements, including Schacht. However, by preventing local authorities from taking out long-term loans at relatively low rates of interest, the Reichsbank forced town treasurers to tap both domestic and foreign short-term markets at higher rates of interest, compounding any crowding-out effects and increasing the fiscal insecurity of local authorities.

Even if one acknowledges that German capital market rates and thus central bank discount rates had to be higher than in France, Britain and the US, and that German creditworthiness had to be demonstrated internationally by both central bank discipline and attractive real returns, there is good evidence that Schacht's 'credit dictatorship'[104] and his bad-mouthing of municipalities was both exaggeratedly zealous and served to strengthen the hand of foreign lenders in negotiating lucrative borrowing rates.[105] The excessively restrictive domestic capital market, which was heavily dependent on expensive Reichsbank discounting,[106] arguably contributed to the process of capital concentration, given that small producers, traders and farmers were reliant on expensive domestic credit, while the large oligopolies enjoyed better domestic credit conditions anyway through the Universal Bank system and by dint of higher asset security, and furthermore had access to foreign sources of cheaper credit.[107] Both Müller and Nussbaum assert that Schacht pursued a deliberate policy which

---

[104] Thus Müller, *Die Zentralbank*, op.cit. p. 54
[105] See Theo Balderston, *The Origins and Course of the German Economic Crisis*, November 1923 to May 1932, Berlin (Haude & Spener), 1993, p. 211
[106] See Nussbaum, *Wirtschaft und Staat*, op.cit. 206ff
[107] Thus Willi Prion, Kreditpolitik, Berlin (Springer) 1926, p.169. This is also the   finding of Reinhard Kohler in relation to the effects of Bundesbank interest rate policy in the 1970s, 'Die Bremspolitik der Bundesbank hat nie richtig funktioniert', *Frankfurter Rundschau*, 27 June 1979

favoured big capital, notably in the period of credit rationing from 1924.[108]

The dominance of the Reichsbank as an independent agency of German state economic policy thus derived from its power to define the framework conditions and the credit costs for the other (elected) agencies of the German state which were unable to survive without borrowing and whose legitimacy relied in part on delivering a minimum level of social support in the area of unemployment, basic utilities and housing. The Reichsbank's power was compounded by the relative permanence and continuity of its top personnel, compared with the inconstancy of Reich governments – there were eight changes of administration in Schacht's first seven years as Reichsbank president; some of these changes can be in part ascribed to Schacht's influence.

In his preface to the English translation of Hjalmar Schacht's 'The End of Reparations', George Glasgow concedes that Schacht is guilty of some analytical weaknesses but commends 'in particular, Chapter XIII, on the "Socialist System"', which 'contains a warning for Great Britain which can hardly fail to make a profound impression'.[109] The chapter in question is in fact a pretty typical conflation of authoritarian German nationalist prejudices about 'the Marxist system which the Social Democracy (sic) conferred on us after the War';[110] not only does Schacht apply the blanket category 'Marxist' to all variants of socialist economic management, but he also extends his critique to most forms of bourgeois state economic activity which involve the ownership of natural monopolies (like water, gas and electricity), state wage arbitration, welfare transfers and progressive taxation.[111] For Schacht, the 'Allies, particularly the French government, have used their entire

---

[108] Müller, *Die Zentralbank*, op.cit. p.59; Nussbaum, *Wirtschaft und Staat*, op.cit. p.211

[109] Schacht, *End of Reparations*, op.cit. p.13

[110] Schacht, *End of Reparations*, ibid. p.193

[111] Schacht, *End of Reparations*, ibid. p.195 and p.203; this is in line with the general right-wing attack on "municipal socialism" in the Weimar Republic which, as often as not, was conducted by bourgeois mayors with bourgeois council majorities; see J. Leaman, 'The "Gemeinden" as Agents of Fiscal and Social Policy in Twentieth Century Germany', in: Robert Lee & Eve Rosenhaft (eds*), State and Social Change in Germany*, New York/Oxford/Munich (Berg) 1990, pp.260–9

(sic) influence to encourage the Marxist political system in Germany'[112] as a cynical lever to optimise the extraction of reparations. The 'socialist system' – as perceived by Schacht – functions to undermine both individual responsibility and the 'marvellous sense of order of the German people'.[113] The sanctity of private property is thus linked to a strong defensive nationalism within Schacht's ideology; the claims of Social Democracy (or even bourgeois municipal councils) to German private property are thus also linked to potential foreign claims to reparations.[114]

Schacht's prejudices were doubtless reinforced by the Reparations Agent, Parker Gilbert, who decried the 'socialist' system of Weimar finance,[115] and by the patrician Montagu Norman. He arguably reserved his fiercest political opposition for the Grand Coalition of 1928 to 1930 under the Social Democrat, Herman Müller, and its Social Democrat Finance Minister, Hilferding. Both before and after the October Crash of 1929, Hilferding was obliged to scuttle round a variety of European and American private banks to secure short-term funding to cover temporary short-falls in the Reich budget,[116] because Schacht refused to support any application for foreign loans to cover the recurrent budget

---

[112] Schacht *The End of Reparations*, op.cit. p.205

[113] Schacht, *The End of Reparations*, ibid. p.204

[114] In the Weimar Republic the argument was frequently expressed that socialisation measures would simply increase the Reich's asset security which could be claimed by Entente powers if Germany defaulted on reparations payments. This applied even to Social Democrats like August Müller, see e.g. Jörg Berlin (ed.) *Die Deutsche Revolution 1918/19*, Cologne, 1979, p.258

[115] James, *The Reichsbank*, op.cit. p.99

[116] See the memoirs of the Swiss banker, Felix Somary, *Erinnerungen aus meinem Leben*, Zürich, 1959, pp.208–9, on Hilferding's request for 100 Million Francs to pay Reich salaries in May/June 1929; see also *Akten der Reichskanzlei Weimarer Republik* Boppard (Harald Boldt) (hereafter AR) *Kabinett Müller* II/2, Documents 390 (Meeting of parliamentary party leaders of 16 December 1929, File R 43 I/2362) and 392 (Ministerial Discussion of 19 December 1929, File R 43 I/1440) for the background to the Dillon/Read loan which finally broke Hilferding's resistance and caused his resignation (Document No. 397 R 43 I/1306). C.f. also Schacht's own account of the Dillon/Read episode in *End of Reparations*, op.cit. 169ff. For a fairer account, c.f. Balderston *Origins*, op.cit. 266ff.

without a matching programme of budget cuts.[117] Schacht's sniffiness about the 'irresponsible and amateur financial policy pursued by the Cabinet of Hermann Müller', its 'helplessness and spinelessness' and the pride with which he described the Reichsbank's need 'to fight constantly against mistaken socialistic financial policies'[118] was matched by the anti-socialist offensives of German industry and agriculture[119] and in particular of the 'League for the Renewal of the Reich' which was headed by Schacht's successor at the Reichsbank, Hans Luther. Luther's avowed intent – to 'get the Social Democrats by the throat'[120] and to remove Prussia from the political map – was entirely consistent with the posture of the Reichsbank from 1924 onwards and with the shift towards aggressive autocratic politics throughout bourgeois political and commercial circles.

Schacht was an ardent defender of the Reichsbank's autonomy throughout his period of office, but his association with the extreme right-wing fringe of Weimar politics, which induced his resignation in March 1930 over the Young Plan, and his later willing self-subordination to the fiscal demands of the Nazis, when he returned as both Reichsbank President and Economics Minister, suggest that he was concerned primarily with the autonomy and immunity of the Bank from democratic politics. While the statutory independence of the Reichsbank was only ended in February 1937, Schacht willingly undermined the restrictive provisions of the 1924 law with a variety of ruses, notably discounting 12 Billion Marks worth of bills from the essentially fictitious front company, the *Metallurgische Forschungsgemeinschaft* (Mefo), which had asset security of only 100000 marks. This willingness went hand in hand with Schacht's other role as plenipotentiary for war preparations to which he was appointed on 1 May 1935. Schacht even welcomed the end of Reichsbank independence in 1937 and its subordination to the Führer as 'the best possible guarantee of maintaining monetary stability'.[121] While this

---

[117] See Schacht's rebuttal of appeals in the meeting of parliamentary party leaders on 16 December 1929, AR *Kabinett Müller* II/2, no.390, pp.1273–1276

[118] Schacht, *End of Reparations*, op.cit. p.107, p.169 and p.168.

[119] See Ulrike Hörster-Philipps, 'Großkapital, Weimarer Republik und Faschismus', in: R.Kühnl and G. Hardach (eds), *Die Zerstörung der Weimarer Republik*, Cologne 1979, 59ff

[120] Cited in Hörster-Philipps, 'Großkapital', op.cit. p.61

[121] Quoted in Marsh, *The Bundesbank*, op.cit. p.117

posture contrasts grotesquely with Schacht's fierce advocacy of Reichsbank independence between 1924 and 1930, it does reinforce the suspicion that Schacht did not seek central bank autonomy as such but rather its independence from democratic control; this is further demonstrated by his campaign to subordinate state fiscal policy to the direct control of the Reichsbank.[122]

Germany's second war of expansion was, like the first, financed by unconsoldiated borrowing by the state, discounted by a central bank, essentially renationalised since Schacht's resumption of the presidency in 1933. The monetary overhang was concealed by the very nature of wartime production, where liquidity was locked into the state-military-industrial circuit of investment, production, destruction and replacement, where wages and key prices were controlled and where consumption was constrained politically in favour of the war effort. As soon as defeat paralysed the system of war production, the overhang was 'liberated' from the circuit: money flooded into private households or freed from dormant savings accounts, only to be confronted by severely limited supplies of goods, compounded by Allied restrictions on production (as well as prices) and a badly disrupted transport system.[123] The result was a predictable devaluation of the Reichsmark and a widespread use of either barter or alternative currencies, notably American cigarettes. Mendershausen estimated that over half of all business transaction before the currency reform involved barter.[124]

The virtual collapse of the money economy rendered its regulation by central bank institutions largely irrelevant. While the Allies failed to establish a co-ordinating monetary institution for the whole of Germany, the local and regional Reichsbank branches which survived the chaos of defeat and zonal division, restored some of the former information networks, but they were deployed in the main as either a banking police (blocking the accounts of known war criminals) or as managers of the physical stock of banknotes. The collapse of German capital markets and of the state bond system of the defeated Reich

---

[122] See Harold James, *The Reichsbank*, op.cit. p.22 etc.

[123] Further, see: Karl-Heinrich Hansmeyer & Rolf Caesar, 'Kriegswirtschaft und Inflation (1936–1948)', in: Deutsche Bundesbank (ed.), *Währung und Wirtschaft in Deutschland 1876–1975*, op.cit. 418ff

[124] Horst Mendershausen, 'Prices, Money and the Distribution of Goods in Postwar Germany', in: *The American Economic Review*, Vol.39, 1949, 652ff

rendered these residual German monetary agencies insignificant in policy terms. In some instances – in both the French and British zones – the Reichsbank provided bridging loans for the zonal fiscal authorities in a manner not dissimilar to practice after the First World War, but it 'no longer regulated the currency in circulation. ... In view of the tremendous excess liquidity, it is no surprise that there was little demand for credit from the private sector and commercial banks. ... A mark of the lack of a true monetary policy was that, at 3.5 and 4.5 per cent respectively, the discount and Lombard rates in western Germany remained unchanged until 1948'.[125]

Table 3.6   Money Stock and Gross National Product in Germany, 1913–1946 (in Billion Reichsmark)

	1913	1932	1938	1945	1946
Notes and Coins	6.6	5.6	10.4	73.0*	–
Sight Deposits	12.3	12.7	18.7	100.0*	–
Time Deposits	24.5	15.3	27.3	125.0*	–
Money Stock	43.5	33.6	56.4	298.0*	–
GNP at Factor Costs	49.5	42.6	79.8	–	40.0*
* approximate figures					

Source: G. Stolper, *Deutsche Wirtschaft seit 1870*, Tübingen 1966

What distinguished this post-war situation from that following the First World War was the powerlessness of German authorities in influencing the conduct and institutions of monetary and other economic policies. Hans Möller records the dismay of German experts that 'the opportunities of German agencies for cooperating in the Military Government law on the Bank deutscher Länder ... had been lamentably few'.[126] The reconstitution of central bank autonomy after World War

---

[125] Thus Christoph Buchheim, 'The Establishment of the Bank deutscher Länder and the West German Currency Reform', in: Deutsche Bundesbank (ed.), *Fifty Years of the Deutsche Mark*, Oxford 1998, p.66

[126] Möller, 'Die westdeutsche Währungsreform von 1948', in: Deutsche Bundesbank (ed.), *Währung und Wirtschaft in Deutschland 1876–1975*, op.cit. p.446; Möller also notes that earlier attempts to influence monetary affairs from the German side had fallen on deaf ears; ibid. 441f

Two was thus dictated by the occupation authorities in the context of
zonal (later East-West) division and against the background of the
Entente's previous experience in relation to the total or partial failure of
the Autonomy Laws of 1922 and 1924, both of which were established
at Allied insistence. The path of least resistance for the western Allies
would have been to have restored central bank institutions in the
western zones under the umbrella of a relocated Reichsbank and
provide for a currency reform under strict Allied supervision. This
option was deliberately ignored. Above all the Americans, in contrast to
the British, 'wanted to prevent a unified national central bank
organisation for Germany',[127] both out of a concern to avoid a
repetition of abuse by German authorities and a preference for the
structures of the US Federal Reserve System with its 12 constituent
Federal Reserve banks. The delay in establishing viable central
banking structures was due in large measure to the 'two years of
acrimonious argument between the US and British governments'.[128]
The British, in part as a result of successful pre-war links between Sir
Montagu Norman and Hjalmar Schacht and their respective staffs, saw
no reason to adopt new structures and identified serious risks in
decentralisation.[129] The eventual 'compromise', leading to the

---

[127] Buchheim, 'Establishment of the Bank deutscher Länder', op.cit.
p.67
[128] Thus David Marsh, *The Bundesbank*, op.cit. p.144f; OMGUS
(Office of Military Government for Germany, United States)
established separate Land Central Banks in their zone by decree at the
end of 1946, transferring Reichsbank assets to a trustee agency; the
French followed suit in February 1947, while the British maintained the
Reichsbank network until February 1948 when they yielded to US
pressure to establish a common central banking system in the Trizone
and created Land Central Banks in North-Rhine Westphalia, Lower
Saxony, Schleswig-Holstein and Hamburg. The closure of the
Reichsbank central branch in Hamburg at the end of March 1948
represented the official end of the old centralised central bank. Further
details, see Buchheim, 'Bank deutscher Länder', op.cit. 74f
[129] Charles Gunston of the Bank of England described American
proposals as 'lunatic', containing the risk of renewed financial disasters
and a return to dictatorial politics; the Americans, on the other hand,
saw decentralisation (of both the central bank and the commercial
banks) as a means of preventing the accumulation of politico-economic
power. See Marsh, *The Bundesbank*, op.cit.148ff

establishment of the Bank deutscher Länder on 1 March 1948, bore the hallmarks of US influence on German political institutions in the post-war period: the bank was a federal institution, owned by the constituent Land Central Banks of the Trizone, banks established at different stages in the previous two years in the eleven newly created regions (Länder) in the western zones, but not including Berlin.[130] The shape of the bank differed little from that outlined by Joseph Dodge, head of the OMGUS Finance Division, in 1946: 'the suggested bank is not a government-owned institution; it is not an individually owned institution; it is not a central financial department, although it can act in some respects as a substitute for one; and it is not, as is customary, an institution created at the national level and spreading downward, but one created from the bottom upward, with its roots in the banks of the Länder, but which can serve Germany as a whole'.[131]

The BdL was based in the old Reichsbank branch headquarters in Frankfurt am Main. The bottom-up structure was reflected firstly in the joint ownership of the BdL's capital stock by the Land Central Banks, secondly in the composition of the Bank Council which, in addition to the eleven Land Central Bank Presidents, included only the President of the Council and the President of the Bank's permanent Directorate, both of whom were elected by the LCB presidents. Thus, while the top personnel of the LCBs were nominated either by the Land Minister-President or the Land Finance Minister, the BdL had no direct linkage to elected German authorities. Thirdly, members of the Directorate were allowed to attend Council meetings but had no vote, in contrast to constitution of the Bundesbank. Like the LCBs, however, the BdL was designed to be free from the political influence of either Land governments or other agencies of the German state. Article 3 of the BdL Law (promulgated in three parallel decrees in the three western zones) states that the Bank 'shall not be subject to the instructions of any political body or public non-judicial agency'. This newly constituted autonomy was, however, quite clearly in relation to German

---

[130] The eleven included the three Länder – Württemberg-Baden, Württemberg und Hohenzollern and Baden, later merged into one, as well as Bavaria, Bremen, Hamburg, Hesse, Lower Saxony, North-Rhine Westphalia, Rhineland-Palatinate, Schleswig-Holstein, but not including Saarland which only became part of the Federal Republic in 1960, nor Berlin.

[131] Memorandum from Joseph Dodge, 5 April 1946, quoted in D. Marsh, *The Bundesbank*, op.cit. p.148

authorities. The Allied Bank Commission, which was established at the same time as the BdL, had as one of its main functions the supervision of monetary policy and was empowered both to give instructions to the Bank and to veto its decisions. This corresponded to many other elements of policy making under the Occupation Statute. The Commission had its offices at the BdL headquarters in Frankfurt and in the first four years of the Bank's operations, Commission members took part in the BdL Council meetings. While in practice the Allies used their controls over monetary affairs very sparingly, the hierarchy of power and the subordination of German policy-making to occupation objectives are vitally important to understand the particular nature of the 'autonomy' established in 1948. It was based in the very particular distrust of German representative political institutions, engendered by the abuse of central banking on the part of administrations in the Wilhelmine Empire, the Weimar Republic and the 'Third Reich'. Yes, the relationship to other national authorities mirrored that of the Federal Reserve System, but the Allied veto made the BdL essentially less free than other dependent central banks, like the Bank of England, nationalised in 1946. This is unsurprising in view of the utter dependence of west Germany's political economy on the emerging western bloc in relation to basic supplies, reconstruction aid, trading and payments relations, foreign and security policy etc.[132] The hierarchy of power is evident in the remit of the Allied Bank Commission, namely 'of exercising general supervision over the policies of the Bank deutscher Länder to the end that the objective of military government law establishing the bank shall be carried out'.[133]

The powers of the Bank deutscher Länder only came into their own after the Currency Reform of 1948 and the establishment of a proper monetary economy. While the potential for political abuse was reduced by strict limits on bridging loans to the state and discounting state paper, the BdL's scope for controlling credit was increased by the introduction of minimum reserve requirements covering bank deposits, a measure imported from the US. This meant that all commercial banks were obliged to maintain a specified ratio of its sight deposits or time

---

[132] Further details see: J. Leaman, *The Political Economy of West Germany 1945–1985*, London (Macmillan) 1988, 18ff and 81ff; also Werner Abelshauser, *Wirtschaftsgeschichte der Bundesrepublik 1945–1980*, Frankfurt/M (Suhrkamp), 147ff

[133] OMGUS statement, 15 February 1948, cited in Marsh, op.cit. p.307, n.14

deposits interest free with the BdL; by raising or lowering the reserve ratios, the BdL – like the Bundesbank after it – was able directly to influence the level of liquidity in the economy; when liquidity levels are high, the indirect levers of discount and Lombard rates on their own are less effective. The BdL, together with the Land Central Banks, was not allowed to lend money directly to private customers, in contrast to the Reichsbank before it. On the other hand, after the Currency Reform, it had the monopoly on issuing bank notes. It also acted as a clearing house for the LCBs, dealt with the state's foreign transactions and operated the country's commercial and private payments system with foreign partners while German currency remained unconvertible.

The Currency Reform of June 1948 clearly reflected a somewhat greater German input into monetary affairs than previously allowed, even though it was a joint operation of the occupying powers and the BdL 'was not directly involved in the process'.[134] The Allies brought German experts together in Rothwesten near Kassel for 49 days, starting in late April 1948, where Allied plans (and German counter-proposals) were discussed. Möller, who took part in this so-called 'conclave', arguably exaggerates German influence on the outcome of these discussions in an attempt to bask in the reflected success of the later reform; he argues that the Allies reduced their initial per capita provision of new currency to 40DM in response to German concerns of the inflationary consequences of a higher quota.[135] However, as Buchheim points out, German proposals (contained in the so-called Homburg Plan) for converting savings were more generous and involved greater inflationary hostages to fortune than the Allied Plans. Likewise, the Homburg Plan proposal to convert debt at a 1:1 ratio would have proved a significant hindrance to recovery.[136] The final shape of the west German Currency Reform incorporated virtually none of the Homburg Plan suggestions and differed little from the Colm-Dodge-Goldsmith-Plan of 1946, which envisaged a severe limitation of liquidity and the establishment of a separate system for cushioning the effects of hardship under the heading of the 'equalization of burdens'. The contribution of the German authorities lay in the implementation of Allied policy, the handing-out of banknotes already printed by the Allies in 1947 and the subsequent administration of the new money stock. A qualitative change in the role of Germany's monetary

---

[134] Marsh, *The Bundesbank*, op.cit. p.154
[135] Möller, 'Die westdeutsche Währungsreform', op.cit. 448ff
[136] Buchheim, 'Bank deutscher Länder', op.cit. 81ff

'autonomy' occurred gradually but momentously in the first few years
of the Federal Republic. Here monetary policy practice showed an
increasing divergence from the rhetoric of Allied supervision and veto
rights and paved the way for the radical recasting of autonomy in the
Bundesbank Law of 1957.

The Central Bank Council remained dependent on instructions from
the Allied Bank Commission until August 1951, when its statutes were
renewed under German law. It inherited an exchange rate, set in April
of 1948, of 3.33 Marks to the Dollar, but after the devaluation of
Sterling by 30 per cent on 18 September 1949 and shortly thereafter of
the French Franc by 22.5 per cent, the Federal Cabinet – ostensibly
responsible for external currency affairs – proposed a DM devaluation
of 25 per cent. The western occupation powers instead chose a
devaluation rate of 20 per cent, bringing the Dollar exchange rate to its
1914 and November 1923 level of 4.2: 1. This imposed rate had much
to do with (justifiable) French concern over German export
competitiveness. In other respects, however, the ABC chose not to
intervene when, after the Currency Reform, the BdL cut the discount
rate by three percentage points to 5 per cent against the ABC's advice.
David Marsh describes the early years of the BdL in terms of a 'battle
for independence',[137] firstly in relation to the occupation powers and
subsequently in relation to the new Federal Government. The first and
most obvious demonstration of this battle was in the choice of the
Bank's leading personnel which was subject to approval by the ABC.
Despite the fact that an initial list of 30 names for president of the Bank
Council and President and Vice-President of the Directorate had
illicited negative responses on several from the ABC, the council
meeting on 2 April 1948 chose to ignore allied objections, electing Otto
Schniewind president of the Council and Hermann Josef Abs president
of the Directorate. The choice of Abs, who had been on an American
wanted list for complicity in economic crimes in eastern Europe during
the war,[138] stunned the ABC members present at the meeting who
proceeded to produce dossiers on both men for the next CBC meeting
on 14 April. In the meantime Abs and Schniewind chose to demand an
alteration to the Bank deutscher Länder Law, strengthening its powers
over fiscal authorities as a condition of their acceptance. The CBC, in

[137] Marsh, *The Bundesbank*, op.cit. 164ff
[138] See in particular Tom Bower, *Blind Eye to Murder*, London 1981,
17ff; Abs was even sentenced to death in absentia by a Yugoslav court,
ibid. p.408

apparent acceptance of the proposals, sought permission from the ABC members at the next meeting on 21 April to alter the Bank law, a request that was unsurprisingly rejected. Marsh describes the proposals as 'a face-saving exercise of Byzantine complexity'.[139] Alternatively, the CBC's behaviour can be explained in terms of a spirit of resistance, compounded by Allied neglect of German expertise in the framing of central bank institutions and representing a strong element of continuity between the personnel of the old Reichsbank and the post-war establishment. Marsh is in fact one of the few historians of the Bundesbank who draws attention to the fact that within a few years many of 'the old guard' returned to posts within the new central bank; in 1948 Karl Mürdel was the only ex-Nazi in the CBC, but by 1958 five of the nineteen members were former NSDAP members, eight out of twenty in 1968. Taking all the central bank's leading executives, including those of the LCBs, Marsh notes that by 1968 53 per cent (18 from 34) were former NSDAP cardholders.

After some to-ing and fro-ing, the post of CBC president went to Karl Bernard, who had worked in the Economics Ministry under Brüning but was unsullied by Nazi associations, and of president of the Directorate to Wilhelm Vocke, a member of the Reichsbank Directorate for twenty years from 1919 to 1939 but not an NSDAP member;[140] Vocke was nevertheless well known as a strong supporter of centralized structures of monetary policy. Despite this, both appointments were approved by the Bank Commission. Vocke and the Directorate, with the clear support of the centralisers in the CBC, proceeded to develop the practice of the Band deutscher Länder away from the two-tier decentralised system envisaged by the US towards an effectively one-tier system in which the Land Central Banks made no use of their legal autonomy. The success of this strategy was built in large measure on the performance of the Bank in the first four years of its existence where the conditions for stable policy-making were very unfavourable: the massive challenges of post-war reconstruction were compounded by

---

[139] Marsh, *The Bundesbank*, op. cit. p.152; Buchheim (op.cit.78f) takes the move by Abs and Schniewind at face value, i.e. merely as a manifestation of their 'strong inclination towards centralization'.

[140] Vocke was dismissed as one of the signatories of the famous letter to Hitler in January 1939 which had expressed the Reichsbank's concern over the inflationary effects of state expenditure; a facsimile of the letter is reproduced in: Deutsche Bundesbank, *Währung und Wirtschaft*, op.cit. pp.381–3

a large and steady influx of German refugees from the East, by high
unemployment and – as a result of division and cold war – the need to
construct new and more intense trading relations in an environment not
fully freed from suspicion and hostility. The exchange rate crises of
1949 highlighted the vulnerability of all post-war European societies to
trade and payment fluctuations and in part pre-programmed the major
balance of payments crisis of 1950–51. In the summer of 1950 West
Germany's balance of payments moved sharply into deficit largely as a
result of imports associated with reconstruction. The deficit rose rapidly
to a cumulative total of $457 million in February 1951. While the
European Payments Union (EPU) helped to cushion some of the initial
effects, Germany had already exceeded its agreed credit quota of $320
million by November 1950, raising the very real threat of state
bankruptcy.[141] The Bank deutscher Länder proved to be the key policy-
making institution in countering this threat. Its 'extraordinarily drastic'
measures,[142] aimed at reducing import demand and boosting exports,
included raising the two minimum reserve ratios by 50 per cent and
100 per cent respectively and increasing the discount rate from 4 per
cent to 6per cent and the Lombard rate from 5 per cent to 7 per cent on
26 October 1950; it had also already reintroduced the 50 per cent cash
deposit requirement for foreign currencies associated with applications
for import licences and imposed a rediscount quota on bank bills. While
the increase in the discount rate had the approval of Economics
Minister Erhard, it was vigorously opposed by both Chancellor
Adenauer and his Finance Minister Fritz Schäffer.[143]   By putting
pressure on domestic demand for both imports and indirectly on
production for the home market, it was hoped to encourage German
producers to direct their attention towards export markets; the BdL
assisted them in this latter respect by allowing export drafts to be
bought 'at the lower discount rate of the target country'.[144] The success
of BdL policy was evident in the reversal of the trade balance from
DM–2 314 000 in 1950 to DM+1 493 000 in 1951, such that it was able
to declare that the crisis was over in the summer of 1951. West

---

[141] See Jens Hölscher, *Entwicklungsmodell Westdeutschland. Aspekte
der Akkumulation in der Geldwirtschaft*, Berlin 1994 29ff

[142] Hölscher ibid. p.36

[143] See both Hölscher, ibid. p.36 and Holtfrerich, 'Monetary Policy und
Fixed Exchange Rates (1948–1972), in: Deutsche Bundesbank (ed.)
Fifty Years of the Deutsche Mark, op.cit. 337f

[144] Holtfrerich, 'Monetary Policy', op.cit. p.339

Germany was in a position to repay the EPU's special credit of DM 120 million in May 1951. However, while the government removed the cash deposit requirements on imports in September 1951, the BdL kept its short-term rates unaltered until May 1952 and lowered them to their pre-crisis level only on 8 January 1953.

The 1950–51 crisis had significant consequences for the future of Germany's central bank institutions. First of all, it represented a victory for Vocke and the BdL Directorate over sceptical views within the CBC regarding the efficacy of a severe credit policy in the circumstances of reconstruction and in the absence of a fiscal squeeze. Vocke is known to have been frustrated by the attitude of the LCB presidents and ascribed the initial weakness of the BdL in relation to the balance of payments crisis to the decision-making structures of the Bank; he was supported by the Board of Directors of the EPU in early 1950 who urged the German government to strengthen the powers of the central bank.[145] Vocke had also been concerned about the apparent plans of the Federal Government to recast the bank's statutes such that the Federation (Bund) became the exclusive shareholder in a new central bank or that the power of the ABC to instruct the BdL would be replaced by similar powers vested either in the Finance Ministry or in a parliamentary committee. Both Adenauer and Fritz Schäffer were convinced advocates of a dependent central bank. However, as the first phase of the occupation statutes came to an end in 1951 and the BdL Law was reconstituted, Vocke's views held sway. The new law of 8 August 1951 which phased out the executive role of the Allied Bank Commission essentially secured a new quality of independence by not replacing the ABC with a German supervisory body. The federal government could hold up BdL decisions for eight days on the basis of a suspensive veto, but in practice made no use of this facility. The two-tier structure, together with LCB ownership of the BdL remained untouched, but, after the vindication of Vocke's political and policy strategy, the CBC deferred increasingly to the views of the Directorate; Vocke became the main addressee of advice, requests and complaints. The practice of BdL policy prefigured more and more the eventual shape of the Bundesbank.

The constellation of political and institutional forces in the early 1950s had little of the certainties we now readily associate with German political culture. Re-establishing 'creditworthiness' was a key buzzword of the 1950s, frequently used by Adenauer, and it applied to

---

[145] Holtfrerich, 'Monetary Policy', op.cit. 337ff

all sorts of institutions, those of the private economy, of Germany abroad, of political parties and of the different agencies of a federal state with an extreme separation of powers. This separation of powers was both vertical in nature, with strictly defined competencies and resources allocated to central, regional and local authorities, and horizontal, with governmental responsibilities – for, say, fiscal and education policy – separated from the responsibilities of autonomous agencies for competition policy, labour markets and monetary policy, all subject to the supervision of an (autonomous) Constitutional Court. The separation was also symbolised by the geographical location of government in Bonn, Cartel Office in Berlin, Labour Institute in Nuremberg, Central Bank in Frankfurt and Constitutional Court in Karlsruhe. While the governing Christian Democrats had performed remarkably well as a new party in the 1949 August elections with 31 per cent of the popular vote, the party system remained volatile for most of the 1950s, with 'other parties' (apart from CDU/CSU, SPD and FDP) gaining 27.8 per cent (1949), 16.5 per cent (1953) and 10.3 per cent (1957). With four-year legislative periods and regular regional elections, electoral perspectives played a key role in partys' strategic calculations. In the context of unemployment, goods and housing shortages and inflationary scares, the relationship between separated agencies of economic policy was potentially explosive. The CDU's economic policy manifesto, the *Düsseldorf Principles* of July 1949 made no mention of central bank autonomy, but rather of the need to conduct coordinated economic policy 'in a sensible combination' of monetary, fiscal and other policy elements.[146] Both Adenauer and Schäffer (CDU) were worried about the implications of the separation of monetary and fiscal policy, in particular about the electoral effects of the 1950/51 credit squeeze,[147] fears cited by Vocke himself in correspondence with Schäffer who had apparently stated his concern about the possibility that 'the central bank can topple the government'.[148] Early on, Erhard also had reservations about central bank independence in relation to fiscal policy when, in February 1950,

---

[146] 'Die Düsseldorfer Leitsätze der CDU' (15 July 1949), reprinted in: Huster, E. et.al. *Determinanten der westdeutschen Restauration*, Frankfurt am Main, 1975, 429ff

[147] Viz Holtfrerich, 'Monetary Policy' op.cit. p.338; Marsh, *The Bundesbank*, op.cit. 168f

[148] Quoted in a letter from Vocke to Schäffer from March 1950, cited in Marsh, ibid. p.169

he stated that BdL refusal to provide financing for combatting unemployment would mean that 'we will have a very hard time in the government and in the Bundestag in supporting the notion of an independent central bank'.[149] While Erhard's views on central bank autonomy moderated in the light of economic (policy) success, and Schäffer chose increasingly to side with Erhard, Adenauer persisted in his scepticism during the preparatory work for the Bundesbank Law, expressing his 'great regret' that the central bank (the BdL at the time) was not responsible to anyone.[150]

Adenauer's electoral concerns re-emerged in August 1955 after discount and Lombard rates had been raised by 1/2 per cent. After lobbying by German industry, Adenauer wrote to Vocke asking him 'not to propose or implement incisive measures in the field of credit policy without prior consultation with the Federal Government'.[151] Vocke's immediate reply drew implicit attention to Article 3 of the BdL Law, which frees the Bank from 'the instructions of any political body', by stating pithily that 'incisive policy measures are part of the responsibility of the Central Bank Council'.[152] There ensued a running battle in which Adenauer and the Federation of German Industry (BDI) faced the united front of Vocke, Ludwig Erhard and Fritz Schäffer, both of whom agreed that the overheating German economy needed slowing down. The affair achieved a farcical dimension when, at the Central Bank meeting in March 1956, Erhard and Schäffer, under instructions from Adenauer attempted to impose a suspensory veto on further rate rises, even though they were in full agreement with the CBC. The BdL nevertheless felt justified in ignoring the veto, on the grounds that Schäffer had already asked for a postponement two weeks before by telephone and the time had elapsed. Both discount and Lombard rates were raised accordingly by a full percentage point on 8 March to 4½ per cent and 5½ per cent respectively. Vocke then proceeded to establish an informal 'Conjunctural Council', involving himself,

---

[149] Transcript of the CBC meeting of the BdL on 22–23 February 1950, quoted in: Manfred Neumann, 'Monetary Stability: Threat and Proven Response' in: Deutsche Bundesbank (ed.) *Fifty Years of the Deutsche Mark*, op.cit. p.276

[150] Adenauer, quoted in H. Köhler, *Adenauer*, Munich (Ullstein) 1994, p.926

[151] Adenauer to Vocke, 7 November 1955, Bundesbank Historical Archives B 330/2011

[152] Vocke to Adenauer, 8 November 1955, ibid.

Finance Minister Schäffer and Economics Minister Erhard to discuss appropriate stabilization measures. This was a tactical masterstroke by Vocke, because it conceded the request for 'prior consultation' with key cabinet players but reaffirmed the Bank's freedom from instructions. A surprised cabinet was informed of the consultations on 17 May and of the ministers' suipport for further measures to limit credit. The central bank raised the discount rate to 5½ per cent and the Lombard rate to 6½ per cent on 19 May and lowered the rediscount quota. Despite the fact that the BdL decision had been made in the presence and with the approval of both Erhard and Schäffer, Adenauer proceeded to berate the Bank for dealing 'a heavy blow to the German economy' at a meeting of the BDI in Gürzenich on 23 May; Adenauer was strongly supported by Fritz Berg, the President of the BDI. Köhler describes Adenauer's speech rightly as a political 'sensation'.[153]

While Adenauer's position cannot be faulted in terms of democratic logic and consistency, it was tactically naïve and became – ironically – a legislative hostage to fortune. In a cabinet meeting in June 1956, discussing the the draft Bundesbank Act, Adenauer raised the possibility of moving the central bank from Frankfurt to Cologne, i.e. closer to Bonn: 'in choosing the location, it should be borne in mind that the activity of the bank should be guided by the correct spirit. The present location of the Bank means that the Bank deutscher Länder leads a very separate life. The federal central bank should be susceptible to the political atmosphere as, more than most other institutions, it had to take this into account'.[154] The majority opinion within the Cabinet seems to have been with Erhard in his support of the BdL and its continued location in Frankfurt. The ultimate resolution to the issue in the Bundesbank Law of July 1957 was no more than a sop to Adenauer, designating the Bank's location the same as that of the federal government, but only when that location was Berlin; until then it would remain Frankfurt. More significantly for Adenauer's immediate fortunes, press reaction to his criticism of the Bank was consistently negative; furthermore the Federation of German Trade Unions (DGB) had lined up with the BdL against the BDI[155] and were supported within the Bundestag by the Social Democrats. The SPD was

[153] Köhler, *Adenauer*, op.cit. p.928
[154] Bundesarchiv (ed.), *Die Kabinettsprotokolle der Bundesregierung*, Vol.9, Boppard am Rhein, p.19
[155] See H.P.Schwartz, *Die Ära Adenauer. Gründerjahre der Republik 1949–1957*, Stuttgart 1981, p.323

above all keen to exploit the contradictions evident within the Cabinet between Adenauer and his Economics and Finance Ministers. With an emerging timetable of final readings for the Bundesbank Act in the Summer of 1957, followed by federal elections in September 1957, the role of the SPD in easing the passage of German central bank autonomy – while not decisive – is nevertheless indicative of the dilemma within which elected politicians found themselves in relation to their own and their state's credibility. It is therefore worth looking at briefly.

Like the CDU, the SPD underscored the need for co-ordinated economic policy in its 1949 electoral material. In the 'Policy Guidelines for the Bundestag', agreed by the party executive in August 1949, Point 2 talks categorically of the 'planning and management of credits and raw materials for the satisfaction of the needs of the economy'.[156] The view was reinforced by the party's monetary policy specialist, Ernst Nölting, who talked of broad agreement within the SPD 'that crisis management cannot be achieved with the mere use of Discount Rate policy, the instrument of classical liberalism ... We advocate planning in the spheres of production and of credit'.[157] In its 'Action Programme' of 1952, the SPD presented its ideas on central bank organisation: 'In this (Law) the Federal Bank of Issue is to be bound to the basic principles of the overall national economic budget in its monetary, credit and interest rate policies'.[158] This subordination of central bank policy to the policy priorities of democratic national governments remained fixed in SPD policy documents until 1956 and the Bundestag deliberations on a replacement for the BdL. In the debate on Friday 30 November the SPD vice-chairman of the Bundestag Committee for Money and Credit, Walter Seuffert, produced an extraordinarily radical statement in favour of central bank autonomy:

'Ladies and Gentlemen, it is ... the view of the Social Democratic opposition that the bank of issue must be independent at all costs, independent of every political influence, independent of the government, independent, I would like to say, of every government, independent also of regional policy and regional interests, independent

---

[156] 'Richtlinien der Politik im Bundestag (Dürkheimer 16 Punkte)', reprinted in: O. Flechtheim (ed.), *Dokumente zur parteipolitischen Entwicklung in Deutschland seit 1945*, Vol. III, pp.34–36
[157] 'Die wirtschaftspolitischen Vorschläge der SPD', reprinted in: Flechtheim, ibid. pp.48–58
[158] 'Aktionsprogramm von 1952', in: Flechtheitm, ibid. pp.64–87

in all its parts and all its divisions and in this complete state also independent of the private economy. It should therefore be strong.'[159]

In the same debate, other SPD speakers even criticized the CDU-government for its proposal to index pensions to price rises, because this implicitly acknowledged the possibility of inflation![160] The SPD's *volte face* on central bank autonomy can certainly be explained in terms of the party's general conversion to the so-called 'social market' model so successfully propagated by Ludwig Erhard, but the electoral opportunism is also unmistakeable. Equally clearly, the fear of the electoral abuse of monetary stimuli to growth and incomes had strong empirical foundations both in Germany and in other countries[161] and the SPD's bitterness over the catastrophic consequences of hyperinflation for Weimar Democracy cannot be underplayed. Nevertheless, there were several SPD MPs who would have remembered the abuse of autonomous Reichsbank power and influence under Schacht and the the particular fate of Müller's Grand Coalition in 1929 and 1930 and could have made appropriate conclusions. In the circumstances of the SPD's electoral doldrums, however, the solid support given by the SPD to the Bundesbank Law of July 1957 is understandable. Furthermore, the fact that the Central Bank Council in 1957 contained a significant majority of SPD Land Central Bank presidents (with some 64 per cent of the votes) would have convinced many party members that the Bank was a valuable counterweight to the frequently quixotic and authoritarian features of Adenauer's 'chancellor democracy'.

As a result of Vocke's campaign to popularise the notion of central bank independence and a one-tier decision-making structure and perceptions of the Bank's success within broad sections of the population, including above all the labour movement, the final passage of the Bundesbank Act through both Committee and parliamentary stages was unproblematic. This contrasts with the other major piece of legislation of July 1957, the Law on Restraints on Competition, which had been rendered essentially toothless by a concerted campaign orchestrated by the BDI, to the regret of Erhard and other ordo-liberals

---

[159] *Verhandlungen des deutschen Bundestags (Stenographische Berichte)*, Second Legislative Period 1953, 175th Session, Bonn, Friday 30 November 1956, p.9716

[160] Ibid. pp. 8363, 8375, 8376 etc.

[161] See notably William D. Nordhaus, 'The Political Business Cycle', in: *Review of Economic Studies*, Vol 42, pp.169–90

within the CDU.[162] With comparative price stability in the context of the continuing economic boom, the arguments for continuity were overwhelming.

The Bundesbank Law of 26 July 1957 is generally perceived as a political compromise,[163] i.e. as a 'hybrid' (Marsh), incorporating features of federalism and autonomy, favoured by the Americans as well as centralism and macro-political integration, and thus accommodating a variety of preferences expressed in the extended debate between the promulgation of the Basic Law on 23 May 1949 and the Law's final reading by the Bundestag. There is something rather obvious about any democratically determined law being the result of compromise; more significant is perhaps assessing the relative weighting of one preference over another in the final shape. Notwithstanding the continuing debate about the degree of independence enjoyed by the Bundesbank,[164] there is a widespread view that the Bundesbank has arguably the highest degree of autonomy accorded any national central bank this century; it may yet be eclipsed by the European Central Bank, but that remains to be seen. On the scale of independence developed by Cukierman, Webb and Neyapti, ranging from 0.00 for zero independence to 1.00 for absolute independence, the

---

[162] Further details, see J. Leaman, *Political Economy of West Germany*, op.cit. 58ff; Jörg Huffschmid, *Die Politik des Kapitals*, Frankfurt 1972, 143ff

[163] Thus Ellen Kennedy, *The Bundesbank. Germany's Central Bank in the International Monetary System*, London 1991, p.13; Volker Hentschel, 'Die Entstehungsgeschichte des Bundesbankgesetzes 1949–1957' (Part I), *Bankhistorisches Archiv*, Vol.14 (1988), p.4 (Nölling p.32)

[164] See, for example, Roland Sturm, 'How Independent is the Bundesbank?', *German Politics*, Vol.4 (1995), pp.27–41; Konrad von Bonin, *Zentralbanken zwischen funktioneller Abhängigkeit und politischer Autonomie*, Baden-Baden 1979; Rolf H. Kaiser, *Bundesbankautonomie, Möglichkeiten und Grenzen einer unabhängigen Politik*, Frankfurt am Main 1980; Klaus Stern, 'The Central Bank in the Constitutional and Financial Set-Up of the Federal Republic of Germany', in: Deutsche Bundesbank (ed.), *Fifty Years of the Deutsche Mark*, op.cit. pp.103–164

Bundesbank had the highest score of 0.69.[165] The legal framework and the policy practice of the Bank indicate that it also operates in a highly centralised manner with regard to major policy issues. Victory therefore seems clearly to have gone to the autonomous centralisers in 1957.

Article 12 of the Bundesbank Law (BBL) typically gives the appearance of compromise, stating that the Bank is obliged (*verpflichtet*) 'to support the general economic policy of the government' but with the rider 'without prejudice to the fulfilment of its duty' (*unter Wahrung ihrer Aufgabe*). The following sentence then states categorically that the Bank 'is independent of instructions from the Federal Government' when it is employing its various powers in pursuit of its main duty, namely 'safeguarding the currency' (§3). The article thus suggests a legal commitment of the central bank to government policy guidelines but immediately frees it of that obligation in principle (freedom from instruction) and in practice ('without prejudice' to the fulfilment of its primary duty: securing currency stability). The former CBC member and president of the Hamburg Land Central Bank, Wilhelm Nölling, formulates the relationship in a slightly less obtuse way: 'The Bundesbank is certainly supposed (*soll zwar*) to support the general economic policy of the federal government, but in the process has always to observe its actual duty. ... Naturally the Bank was not supposed to operate in a vacuum and accordingly rules concerning cooperation – albeit weak rules – were formulated.'[166] Nölling is here referring to Article 13 of the BBL, in which firstly the Bank is obliged to advise and inform the Federal Government on matters relating to monetary policy and secondly Federal Ministers are able to take part in Central Bank Council meetings, table motions and impose a suspensive veto of two weeks on Council decisions. In legal terms the political leverage provided by Article 13 is minimal; in terms of the political practice of ministers in CBC meetings there has been only one case of a minister tabling a formal motion for easing credit policy (duly ignored) and no cases of a suspensive veto being applied,[167] despite a history of government-bank

---

[165] Alex Cukierman, Steven B. Webb and Bilin Neyapti, 'Measuring the Independence of Central Banks and Its Effect on Policy Outcomes'' in: *World Bank Economic Review*, Vol.6, no.3, pp.353–98
[166] Nölling, *Unser Geld*, op.cit. p.33
[167] Nölling, ibid. p.34

relations littered with hidden and open conflicts.[168] Compared to the obligation of the Federal Reserve Board in the US to make regular reports to and respond to the questions of Congress, the 'advice and information' rules in the Bundesbank Law are weak indeed. There is certainly no trace of any role for the Bundestag Committee for Monetary and Economic Policy Questions in even supervising Bundesbank behaviour, let alone instructing it, as envisaged by the first Adenauer government.

Ownership of the Bank was nevertheless vested in the Federation (§2 BBL), despite Vocke's claim that this would be 'totally unworldly and impractical'.[169] However, ownership confers none of the voting rights normally associated with commercial equity; the Bundesbank's operating surpluses are nevertheless transferred annually to the federal government, such that they are effectively incorporated into the Finance Ministry's forward planning calculations. The Bundesbank also fulfils a number of standard central bank duties from which it cannot escape: it is the sole bank of issue (§14) and is thus responsible for the physical distribution of notes and coin (M0), for the increase in legal tender and for the regular replacement and destruction of worn tender; it functions as the bank of banks, i.e. as source of credit and clearing transactions for credit institutions (§19); it is also the house bank of the federal government and (through the Land central banks) of regional governments as well as of other public authorities (§19.1 and §20.1); the Bundesbank is also obliged to issue and manage all government securities (e.g. bonds) on the open market (§20.2).

As sole owner, the Federation is directly involved in the appointment of the President, Vice-President and other Directorate members, although the process involves the formal obligation to consult with the Central Bank Council on such appointments, there are relatively strict qualification criteria applying to the candidates and the CBC has the right to object to nominees. Nominations for the posts of Land Central Bank President operate at regional level but with similar consultation rights conferred on the CBC and the formal appointment made the Bundesrat; the CBC has made regular objections to some nominations. The ability of any government to influence central bank policy through its nomination rights is minimised firstly by the long periods of tenure accorded to Directorate and CBC members – eight

---

[168] In particular, see: Marsh, *The Bundesbank*, op.cit. Chapter 7 (168ff) etc.
[169] Vocke in a letter to Adenauer in 1949, quoted in: Marsh, ibid. p.166

years with the right to one renewal;   this is clearly intended 'to decouple the timing of the selection of top officials of the Bundesbank from the calendar of parliamentary elections'.[170]   Secondly, the staggering of nominations over time prevents a significant number of CBC members being replaced in any given period.   Neumann calculates that between 1960 and 1996, there were only four years when four members were replaced; in most other years it was fewer and usually only one.[171]   Renewal of appointments is standard practice, with the average tenure for the CBC members who left or died between 1972 and 1995 being 14 years.   Finally, the age of each member on appointment has tended to mean that it is the last full-time post held, ensuring – for a number of observers – the so-called 'Becket-effect', which alludes to Thomas-a-Becket's defiant defence of the Church against the English King Henry II.[172]   A number of analyses have attempted to show that the Bundesbank is nevertheless prone to policy swings which can be correlated to the political allegiance of CBC majorities.[173]   Manfred Neumann demonstrates convincingly that Vaubel's hypotheses about the partisan voting behaviour of CBC members in the run-up to federal elections in Germany are difficult if

---

[170] Thus Roland Sturm, 'The Role of the Bundesbank in German Politics', *West European Politics*, Vol 12 (1989), no.2, p.2

[171] Neumann, 'Monetary Stability', op.cit. p.279

[172] See Neumann, M. 'Precommitment by Central Bank Independence', in: Open Economies Review, Vol. 2, 1991, p.103;   Otmar Issing, member of the Directorate of the Bundesbank until 1998 and currently member of the Executive Board of the ECB, was wont to use the Becket metaphor with its obviously tragic associations of principled self-sacrifice (Becket was murdered by the King) as part of a culture of Bundesbank self-stylisation, see: Issing, Perspektiven der Europäischen Währungsunion', in: Deutsche Bundesbank (ed.), *Auszüge aus Presseartikeln*, 1992 no.18

[173] For example, Roland Vaubel, 'The Bureaucratic and Partisan Behaviour of Independent Central Banks: German and International Evidence', Manuscript December 1995; or Vaubel, 'Eine Public-Choice-Analyse der Deutschen Bundesbank und ihre Implikationenen für die Europäische Währungsunion', in: Duwendag, Dieter et.al. (eds), *Europa vor dem Eintritt in die Wirtschafts- und Währungsunion*, Berlin 1993, pp.23–80; or Susanne Lohmann, 'Federalism and Central Bank Autonomy: The Politics of German Monetary Policy', Manuscript, Los Angeles 1994

not impossible to substantiate.[174] There is much stronger evidence for an absence of party political bias in Bundesbank decision-making, where the narrow primary task of the Bank of safeguarding the currency is automatically internalised by all new appointments, along with the theoretical underpinnings of the essentially monetarist institution. As Roland Sturm asserts,

'(E)very appointee is rapidly socialised into the corporate culture of the Bundesbank. On a theoretical level the importance of the intra-institutional logic of decision-making for policy outcomes is stressed today by the theories of neo-institutionalism. The Bundesbank provides a good example for the reorientation of individuals when entering their new organisational environment where they are confronted with an elaborate set of rules and expectations derived from the Bundesbank's organisational culture'.[175]

Some defenders of Bundesbank autonomy, including those who would wish to strengthen its independence, stress that its freedom from instructions is legally but not constitutionally guaranteed. This means that the Bundesbank Law of 1957 could be revised in the direction of dependence or more strongly defined guidelines (e.g. specific inflation targets) on the basis of a simple Bundestag majority. It would not require a constitutional amendment, involving two thirds majorities in both the Bundestag and the Bundesrat. Certainly, Article 88 of the Basic Law makes no mention of the (future) Bundesbank's organizational and operational autonomy; at some critical points in the relationship between federal government and federal bank, there have been veiled hints – notably by Helmut Schmidt in the 1970s – that parliament could be called on to revise the Bank's statutes, but it has never come to this kind of test of strength. Forty-one years of Bundesbank practice (fifty-one if one includes the effective independence of the Bank deutscher Länder) nevertheless established an autonomous status for the German central bank which is inextricably embedded in the country's political economy, so much so that the ceding of monetary sovereignty to the European Central Bank following the Treaty of Maastricht was only permitted on the basis that this embeddedness be transferred to the European level and its foundations be approved by Germany's Federal Constitutional Court. It is not constitutional autonomy, but an arguably stronger ideological-

---

[174] Manfred J.M. Neumann, 'Monetary Stability: Threat and Proven Response', op.cit. 280ff.

[175] Roland Sturm, 'How Independent is the Bundesbank?', op.cit. 33f

cultural autonomy anchored in majority opinion in Germany and now beyond.

Despite the original efforts of the US, the statutes of the Bundesbank ensure that a high degree of centralisation in policy-making is achieved. Regional interests are represented inasmuch as the Presidents of the Land Central Banks, who sit on the CBC, are normally drawn from their respective region and officially nominated by the Bundesrat as a collective body of all German regions; secondly, the LCB presidents have a guaranteed majority over the members of the Directorate within the Central Bank Council: in 1957 there were eleven LCB presidents and a maximum of ten members of the Directorate eligible to sit on the CBC (§7.2 BBL); after unification, in February 1991, several of the Land Central Banks were conflated, reducing the total number to nine, but at the same time the maximum representation of the Directorate was reduced from ten to eight. Given the narrow definition of the Bundesbank's task of 'safeguarding the currency' and its freedom from instructions, the numerical majority of regional representatives is essentially cosmetic; it conveys a sense of decentralised legitimacy but does not affect the monopoly of the centre on key decisions. Article 6.1 of the Bundesbank Law lays down that the Central Bank Council 'can in specific instances give instructions to both the Directorate and the executive boards of the Land Central Banks.' In any event, the Land Central Banks have even fewer powers than their predecessors in the Wilhelmine Empire or in the Weimar Republic and function as subordinate regional agencies of the Bundesbank, fulfilling vital administrative duties but without policy discretion.[176] Kennedy rightly underscores the value of the Land Central Banks as 'listening posts' which pick up sectional, regional and local perspectives through their Advisory Boards, in which representatives of the local business and banking community, farmers and labour organisations provide expert views, but also stresses that the effectiveness of these advisory boards as political barometers and/or

---

[176] These functions include a) administering credit policy and supervising the implementation of the centrally agreed interest rate changes by the Land branches, b) supervising the operations of commercial banks and compliance with minimum reserve requirements, c) monitoring monetary and general economic trends within the region, d) collecting and interpreting regional economic data, e) monitoring foreign currency transactions, f) supervising bond transactions, g) administering central bank's personnel affairs at regional level

safety valves much depends on the skill of the particular LCB president who chairs their meetings.[177]

The devolved nature of the Bundesbank's administration meant that historically the bulk of its personnel was concentrated in LCBs and their respective branch offices. In 1982, the staff at the Frankfurt Directorate numbered 2713 (18 per cent) with the remainder (12389 = 82 per cent) operating either at the 11 LCBs or the 306 branch offices. The 1980s saw a process of rationalisation, closing over a third of branch offices, such that after unification and the addition of fifteen subsidiaries in the five new Länder, the total of branch offices had fallen to 193, while the Bank's total staff establishment had risen to 18237 by early 1992 (2973 at the Directorate, the rest at regional or branch level). In the wake of the revision of the Bundesbank Law and the reduction of the number of LCBs to just nine, staff rationalisation reduced total numbers to just 15891, equivalent to 14458 full-time posts, when part-time employees are taken into consideration.

Even if one concedes that the LCB presidents' guaranteed majority on the Central Bank Council reflects the survival of a federal principle in the Bundesbank's organizational structure, the Frankfurt Directorate – like the Bank deutscher Länder before it – is responsible for the day-to-day conduct of central bank policy. The Directorate's role was undoubtedly reinforced by the abandonment of fixed exchange rates and the floating of all major world currencies between 1971 and 1973; not only did this remove the effective determination of the Deutschmark exchange rate from the control of the Federal Government, it increasedthe significance of open market operations within the armoury of central bank weapons for 'safeguarding the currency'. Since central bank interventions in the open market represent very short-term reactions to currency market fluctuations, policy discretion lies in large measure in the hands of the Directorate. The Central Bank Council can clearly define the parameters for such interventions at its fortnightly meetings and it still controls both the rates at which such transactions are conducted and the key discount and Lombard rates, but the gradual sidelining of minimum reserve ratios since the early 1980s certainly shifted the balance of policy responsibility onto the Directorate and, in the view of some commentators, increased the potential for either conflict orfor a more brutal rationalisation of the regional dimension of German central banking (i.e. even greater centralisation). The arrival of the ECB should certainly accelerate this process.

---

[177] Kennedy, *The Bundesbank*, op.cit. p.18f

With the passage of the Bundesbank Law in July 1957, the Bundestag confirmed a defensive preference for the separation of monetary from other state economic powers. Its roots, as Chapter Two sought to elaborate, were in part determined by a very specific economic culture and a very specific variant of authoritarian liberalism. The historical process of constituting the Bundesbank's now firmly embedded independence was more haphazard than the continuities of economic and ideological history and fraught with more contradictions than its architects would be willing to concede. Few mention the fact that monetary policy in the final stages of the great inflation, during the subversion of the Weimar Democracy and the early years of the Third Reich was presided over by an autonomous central bank, a fact which raises many question marks about the very principle of incorruptible autonomy in real politics. The following chapter will examine the operation of central bank autonomy in the context of Germany's complex and increasingly troubled political economy.

Box 1

LAW ON THE GERMAN BUNDESBANK (26 July 1957)

Extracts

§ 2 Legal Form, Share Capital and Location
The German Bundesbank is a federal juridical person under public law. Its share capital of two hundred and ninety million Deutsche Mark belongs to the Federation (Bund). The Bank has its location at the location of the Federal Government; as long as the latter is not in Berlin, the location of the Bank is Frankfurt am Main.

§3 Task
The German Bundesbank regulates the circulation of money and the provision of credit to the economy with the help of the powers of currency policy invested in it according to this Law, with the aim of safeguarding the currency; and it provides for the bank-related conduct of payments within the country and with foreign countries.

§5 Organisational Bodies
The organisational bodies of the German Federal Bank are the Central Bank Council (§6), the Directorate (§7) and the Managerial Boards of the Land Central Banks (§8).

§6 Central Bank Council
The Central Bank Council determines the monetary and credit policy of the Bank ... In individual cases it can also give instructions to the Directorate and to the Managerial Boards of the Land Central Banks.
The Central Bank Council consists of the President and Vice-President of the German Federal Bank, the other members of the Directorate and the Presidents of the Land Central Banks.

§12 Relationship of the Bank to the Federal Government
The German Federal Bank is obliged to support the general economic policy of the government without prejudice to the fulfilment of its duty. In the employment of the powers, vested in it according to this Law, it is independent of instructions from the Federal Government.

---

4 Exercising Autonomy From the 'Miracle' Years to the End of Bretton Woods (1958–1972)

The reputation of the Bundesbank and its predecessor, the Bank deutscher Länder, is rooted in the remarkable record of the secular German economy in the 1950s and early 1960s – the so-called 'miracle years' – during which the elusive magic square of stable high growth, low inflation, full employment and healthy external balances was achieved and maintained, seemingly defying the normal pattern of the classic business cycle. The lowest rate of real GDP growth in the 1950s was 3.5 per cent in 1958, the year that the Bundesbank Act came into force, while the average for the decade was 8 per cent and for the sixteen years 1951–1966 it was still an impressive 6.8 per cent; inflation averaged less than 2 per cent in the 50s; the rate of unemployment fell from 11 per cent in 1950 to just 1.3 per cent in 1960, despite significant increases in the working population due to refugee immigration. After the brief balance of payments crisis of 1950/51, the current account surplus rose steadily from 2485 million DM in 1951 to 5612 million DM in 1960 and with it the country's gold and foreign currency reserves (1951: 1.08 billion DM; 1960: 33.34 billion DM). It is unsurprising that this degree of success bolstered the reputation of Germany's political economy, in particular of its key political agencies, the central bank and the Federal ministries of Economics and Finance.[1] It is appropriate in this context to take a

---

[1] In its 1957 Report, the Academic Sub-Committee of the Federal Economics Ministry ascribed the international strength of the German economy to the success of 'monetary, credit and fiscal policies which were able to maintain stable domestic price levels in a system of fixed exchange rates and thus strengthened considerably the competitive position of German industry in world markets', quoted in Herbert Ehrenberg, *Die Erhard-Saga*, op.cit. p.51

closer look at the conditions under which this perceived success and the associated reputation were achieved.

It was noted in the previous chapter that the Bank deutscher Länder pursued a strongly pragmatic policy orientated not exclusively towards domestic monetary conditions but including a primary consideration of external economic relations. This 'monetary protectionism', as it was dubbed at the time,[2] was driven above all by west Germany's marked new export dependency after partition had severed important intra-German trade links, and by associated balance of payments problems in 1950/51 before the country was able to adapt to the new international circumstances. Despite Erhard's fundamental rejection of dirigiste methods, both the federal government and the federal bank adopted essentially mercantilist methods to reduce import demand and direct the attention of German manufacturers towards increasing exports. This included support for DM-devaluation, rediscount quotas and relatively high interest rates, particularly in the first three years of the Republic's life; on the fiscal side, import licences, a cleverly gradated set of import tariffs[3] and tax exemptions helped to re-direct economic flows towards boosting exports. There is also no doubt that the outbreak of the Korean War in June 1950 contributed immensely to the dynamisation of global trade in general and to the surge in demand for German goods in particular. More importantly in this context is the continuation of a mercantilist monetary policy beyond the 50/51 crisis, i.e. BdL-President Vocke's dictum of 'keeping domestic affairs tight in order to strengthen exports' remained in place up to the hand-over to the Bundesbank.[4] This involved maintaining discount rates significantly above those of the United States until 1958, aimed above all at deterring enterprises

---

[2] The Annual Report of the German Savings Banks and Giro Association for 1959 called for the abandonment of 'monetary protectionism' to ease domestic monetary conditions and to ease pressure in the revaluation turmoil.

[3] The Customs Tariff Law of October 1951 strategically discriminated against finished goods, with tariff rates of between 20 and 35 per cent. Semi-finished goods were subject to intermediate tariff rates of between 10 and 20 per cent, while raw materials and other primary goods were generally tariff-free. This corresponded to a barely concealed strategy in production and trade of buying cheap and selling dear, a strategy which became the hallmark of west German economic success.

[4] Vocke's remarks to the Central Bank Council in October 1949 are quoted by Holtfrerich, 'Monetary Policy', op.cit. p.344

from awarding excessive wage awards. 'Raising exports is vital for us, and this in turn depends on maintaining a relatively low price and wage level' (Vocke).[5] At the same time fiscal policy deliberately promoted capital formation through a variety of relief measures; these included very high assessments of corporate assets in the Law on the Opening Balance in Deutschmarks' (August 1949) which gave firms considerable scope for exploiting depreciation allowances. The use of degressive and accelerated depreciation also promoted self-financed investments via retained profits and helped both corporations and simple trading companies to avoid paying the very high rates of Income and Corporation tax imposed by the Allies for the period of the Occupation Statute.[6] Capital formation via savings was encouraged by exempting the first 15 per cent of savings income from taxation (§ 10 Income Tax Law) until 1954, after which the allowance was gradually reduced to zero. However, the self-financing opportunities provided by generous tax allowances were only of use to those companies that generated sufficient profits on turnover, notably in sectors where capacities had not been particularly affected by bombing or dismantling, but did not apply to key infrastructural and industrial branches like energy production, waterworks, coalmines, railways and the merchant fleet. Energy, water and transport were affected not just by damaged capacities but also by price controls, which led the first Adenauer government to introduce the Investment Aid Law of December 1951. This involved extracting a mandatory loan of DM 1 billion from more prosperous manufacturing companies to the primary industrial and infrastructural sectors, channeled through an Industrial Credit Bank and secured by low-interest bonds. In addition the Law provided special depreciation facilities which allowed 50 per cent and 30 per cent write-offs for moveable and immovable assets for firms in the targeted branches over three years. Shipping was arguably the most pampered of all economic sectors, with tax breaks allowing bond-holding creditors to channel huge tranches of capital to shipyards, yielding very high profits at little tax cost.[7] While manufactured imports were discouraged by high tariffs, exports were encouraged by

---

[5] Thus Vocke in a speech on 17 May 1951, quoted in Holtfrerich, ibid., p.345
[6] Further details, see J. Leaman, *Political Economy of West Germany*, op.cit. 116ff
[7] See in particular, Alan Kramer, *The West German Economy 1945–1955*, New York/Oxford 1991, 203f

the Export Promotion Bill of 1951 which included tax allowances for manufactured exports, exemption of export-related bills of exchange from the Bills Tax (*Wechselsteuer*) and of export insurance from Insurance Tax, as well as the repayment of Turnover Tax on exports. In addition, generous export credit guarantees were provided by the state-funded Hermes agency.

The primacy of capital formation in both fiscal and monetary policy and of balance of payments stability was understandable,[8] given the weak state of the capital market, the urgency to become a successful exporting economy and to fulfil post-war obligations to both the Allies (reparations and occupation costs) and to the state of Israel. The apparent success of the policy can be measured by a number of indicators: between 1950 and 1960 the investment ratio rose from 22.6 per cent of GNP to 26.3 per cent, while the consumption ratio fell from 64.2 per cent of GNP to 57.3 per cent in the same period, considerably below levels in competitor countries like France (1960: 63.9 per cent), the USA (64.0 per cent) and Britain (65.4 per cent).

However, the degree to which a clear causal link between policy measures in the 1950s (of a fiscal or monetary nature) and key economic variables like wage, price and capital formation can be deduced is rendered problematic by a number of other influences. The determination of wages was arguably strongly influenced by labour market conditions, where – until the late 1950s – supply exceeded demand and was regularly topped up by net inward migration;[9] until August 1961 and the erection of the Berlin Wall, the migration of highly skilled engineers, scientists, doctors and craft workers also prevented the operation of particular skill scarcities in wage and salary

---

[8] Thus also Rudolf Richter, 'German Monetary Policy as Reflected in the Academic Debate', in: Deutsche Bundesbank (ed.), *Fifty Years of the Deutsche Mark*, op.cit. p.527

[9] Between 1949 an average of 316 000 people migrated from east to west Germany each year; this was on top of over 7 million refugees in the western zones registered for the period 1945–49; in addition an irregular flow of ethnic Germans from Poland, Rumania, Czechoslovakia and the Soviet Union continued through the 1950s; over 100 000 in both 1957 and 1958 arrived in the west, mostly from Poland. See: R. Münz and R. Ulrich, 'Changing Patterns of Immigration to Germany 1945–1995', in Klaus Bade and Myron Weiner (eds), *Migration Past, Migration Future*, Providence/ Oxford 1997, pp.65–119

formation in many sectors[10]; there were alarmist reports of labour shortages in 1956,[11] notably in the mines and in construction; however, very soon after the Suez Crisis subsided, the opposite problem of over-manning in the coal industry was revealed, reflecting poor planning in Erhard's energy policy and costing later administrations millions in severance pay.[12] Only a small number of sectors experienced real labour bottlenecks, like the booming construction sector, where workers were reported to be working seventy hours a week or in motoring services, where in 1956 there were 10 vacancies for every qualified worker available; housing shortages not only created a vast demand backlog and bulging order books for housebuilders, but they also did affect labour mobility in the early post-war years to some degree; 1956 saw the first targetted recruitment of migrant workers from Italy to fill specific gaps, even though aggregate unemployment was still quite high. The total number of registered unemployed did fall from 1.87 million in 1950 to 876 000 in 1956, but still stood at 764 000 in 1958, providing a large pool of reserve labour which at this stage did not enjoy the levels of social provision which later characterised the German 'social state', despite the introduction in 1957 of a generous scheme of indexed pensions. Most significant in this context is the fact that high and continuous rates of real economic growth allowed real incomes to rise year on year throughout the 1950s, providing marked leaps in the standard of living of individual households, even though income growth was consistently below levels of productivity growth.[13] The cost of living was further cushioned by the retention of strict price controls on household rents until 1960; average household expenditure on housing as a proportion of total outgoings thus remained exceptionally low at between 7.2 per cent (1950) and 7.6 per cent (1960), but subsequently 'normalised' at around double that level

---

[10]   Abelshauser (*Wirtschaftsgeschichte der Bundesrepublik*, op.cit. p.96) records that from 1952 to 1963 more than '20 000 engineers and technicians, 4 500 doctors and 1 000 university teachers' from the GDR sought asylum in West Germany.

[11]   See, for example, 'Germany faces a Labour Shortage', *The Economist*, 18 February 1956

[12]   See J. Leaman, *Political Economy of West Germany*, op.cit. p.97 and p.120

[13]   See W.Glastetter, G. Högemann and R. Marquardt, *Die wirtschaftliche Entwicklung in der Bundesrepublik Deutschland 1950–1989*, Frankfurt am Main 1991, p.117 etc.

(1970: 12.6 per cent; 1980: 16.4 per cent) after rent controls were removed.[14] Wage settlements were furthermore moderated by new and effective institutions of worker participation, notably in the form of Works Councils which every enterprise with more than 5 employees had to establish and which ensured actual dialogue within workplaces in contrast to the conflictual culture of the Weimar Republic and the autocracy of the Third Reich. This is not to say that there were sporadic demonstrations of labour unrest, among shipyard workers, public sector workers and even textile workers. Overall, however, on the supply side both the material conditions and the culture of the labour market still predisposed the economy to a process of accumulation which favoured capital and, with very modest unit cost growth, to wage rises that could be easily accommodated within the context of healthy corporate cash flows.

The favouring of capital is most clearly evident in the development of the distribution of national income; the adjusted gross wages ratio (which accounts for changes in the size of the labour force and the self-employed) fell from 59 per cent of national income in 1950 to 54 per cent in 1960. The development of net incomes demonstrates the growing disparity between labour and capital in the 1950s even more eloquently: while net income from labour grew 100.3 per cent between 1950 and 1960, net profit from capital grew by 250 per cent.[15]

On the demand side of the labour market, i.e. at enterprise level, the scope of monetary policy to influence business decisions on either wages or investments was constrained by a number of significant factors. The process of reconstruction and growth in the 1950s did not see simply a continuously healthy development of revenues in the expanding manufacturing sector but, uniquely almost in the 20th century, a steady increase in capital productivity, i.e. in output per unit of capital, and with it increases in the rate of return. Whereas the modernisation and increased mechanisation of production generally produces a higher ratio of capital to labour (increased capital intensity), the capacity surpluses following the investment boom of the late 1930s and the war years produced a situation where a progressive improvement in capacity utilisation was possible, right through to

---

[14] Figures from Werner Abelshauser, *Wirtschaftsgeschichte der Bundesrepublik Deutschland*, op.cit. p.131
[15] See J. Leaman, *Political Economy of West Germany*, op.cit.,126ff and Glastetter et.al., *Die wirtschaftliche Entwicklung*, op.cit. pp.100–110

around 1961; more machines were run for longer, producing more goods. Enterprises thus expanded their production into existing capacities, such that both capital and labour productivity increased in the first crucial decade; they were certainly assisted by generous depreciation allowances which concealed the real value of a firm's capital stock, but the trend of increasing capital intensity accompanied by a rising rate of profit is undeniable. The combination of strong cash flows, improving returns and growing corporate reserves over an extended period produces a culture of expectations which is arguably immune from short-term changes to central bank rates or other monetary levers, especially when investment decisions are driven by medium- to long-term perspectives, as in Germany's rapidly expanding investment goods sector with its strong export profile.

Monetary leverage was reduced still further by the rapidly increasing liquidity of the banks, as well as of corporate reserves; a report in *The Economist* from February 1956 notes the fear of some German banks of 'being sidetracked by firms (i.e. non-banks) which act as money lenders' with their cash reserves.[16] These leverage problems were compounded by an unending inflow of foreign currency buying DM-nominated securities, indeed the interest-rate lever had arguably a dysfunctional effect on liquidity, such that a high discount or Lombard rate, intended to reduce domestic demand for cash, would attract foreign investors to buy German paper, thus increasing liquidity through increased foreign reserve holdings. The influx of hot money thus revealed a core problem of a thriving German economy in a system of fixed exchange rates, where monetary stability was the responsibility of a single agency, but it also revealed problems of the Bank's operational assumptions.

Independent central banking, implicitly by the nature of the standard instruments at its disposal but mostly explicitly in terms of published principles, ascribes central importance to the control of the money stock. As was observed in the introductory chapter, the definition of the money stock (broad money, narrow money etc) has changed at regular intervals in Germany and in other countries. Accordingly the Bank deutscher Länder employed a narrow measure of the money stock up until 1958, namely the so-called Central Bank Money Stock, a measure retained subsequently by the Bundesbank until 1988. The CBMS was defined as the currency in circulation plus bank deposits which can be withdrawn within 30 days, the so-called sight deposits. The growth of

---

[16] *The Economist*, 11 February 1956, 419f

the CBMS was considered by both the BdL and the Bundesbank to be the most reliable indicator of liquidity trends which would signal the need for appropriate modifications of monetary policy. The CBMS was chosen in preference to M2 or M3, which include various categories of time deposits, because the latter were deemed not simply to be illiquid but 'were thought to have a contractive influence on the money stock and therefore on total money demand'.[17] Thus the consistently higher growth in M3 in the 1950s was not considered alarming. Indeed, as Holtfrerich notes in relation to 1953, high bank lending was tolerated because there was a correspondingly high increase in time deposits.[18] If the current operational rules of central banking had applied in the 1950s, M3 growth way in excess of nominal GDP growth would have provoked severe deflationary responses from the central bank.[19]

Furthermore, Chart 4.1 below indicates that even the pattern of growth in the central bank money stock did not match that of nominal GDP, i.e. there was no correlation between this money stock indicator and inflation, even if one adjusts the graph lines to a variety of the standard time lags. Indeed inflation, after 1951, posed no obvious danger both in domestic historical comparison or in relation to other countries.

However, it is obvious that liquidity in the German economy was growing faster than the BdL or Bundesbank was prepared to admit and that, far from exerting a contracting influence on credit flows, the growth of total balances in German banks increased both their security and their willingness to lend money. Indeed the steady improvement and maintenance of bank liquidity ratios, of their free liquid reserves, made them, like the majority of manufacturing and trading enterprises, increasingly impervious to the manipulation of short-term interest rates.

---

[17] Thus Holtfrerich, 'Monetary Policy', op.cit. p320

[18] Holtfrerich, ibid.

[19] This should not be interpreted as criticism of BdL pragmatism in prioritising production and exports, but rather as evidence of the humbug reflected in the rhetoric of Bundesbank mythology, of monetary/ monetarist purism and imperviousness to lobbying. Yes, the German economy was growing at an astonishing speed, but it needed to. There is therefore something slightly prissy about Holtfrerich's critique of the BdL in 1955 where he regrets the Bank's 'subordinating the recognized needs of proper monetary policy' to 'production-related aspects and interests' (ibid. p.354)

This was reflected in the relationship between money market rates
and central bank discount rates, such that the former in some years were
lower than the latter (see Chart 4.3). Whatever the BdL or Bundesbank
asserted in relation to money stock changes in the 1950s it is clear that
its interest rate decisions bore little relation to such changes. Strong
growth of the CBMS in 1951, 1952 and 1957 illicited rate reductions
while the trend decline between 1958 and 1960 was accompanied by a
rate rise between 1959 and 1960.

Chart 4.1   CBMS, M3 and GDP, 1950-1960

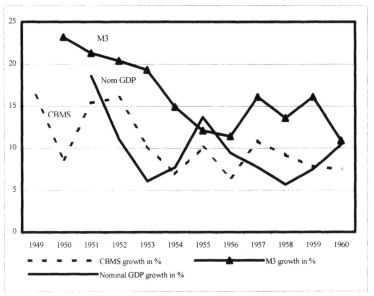

*Source:*Bank   deutscher   Länder,   *Monthly   Reports*   (various);
Bundesbank, *Monthly Reports* (various).

There was a brief interest rate squeeze from March 1956 to January
1957, following CBMS growth in 1955, but reports of Central Bank
Council discussions and other deliberations reveal that the Bank's
decisions were driven by other indicators, namely bank lending,
investment and wages growth,[20] i.e. by broader indicators of
overheating and not by inflation (See Chart 4.2)! This allows Helmut
Schlesinger, later Vice-President and President of the Bundesbank, to

---

[20]   See Holtfrerich, 'Monetary Policy', op.cit. 349ff

describe monetary policy in the years 1950 to 1958 as 'anticyclical policy', albeit with a very strange analysis of the causal linkages, involving 'time-lags' between changing cyclical trends and the deployment of monetary measures. 'The reasons for these time-lags and the absence of any prophylactic measures (sic) are obviously not primarily and certainly not solely to be found in the fact that the "true" cyclical position had not been so precisely accessible to analysis at the time, such as later refinements in cyclical analysis and the very advantage of hindsight allow. It is decisive rather that apart from the anticyclical objective other aims of monetary policy played an equal – and occasionally dominant – role'.[21] This gobbledygook (was it anti-cyclical policy or wasn't it?) is a rather undignified attempt to reconcile BdL pragmatism with an orthodox view of monetary theory and ignores the complexity of politico-economic conditions in this period (see below).

The core problem of constructing a monetary policy which was both consistent with the implied principles of autonomous central banking and the actual politico-economic conditions of the period lay in the country's external economic relations. Defeat, partition and integration into the western bloc obliged west Germany to adapt to a new set of imperatives: regaining international trust and 'creditworthiness' (in both political and economic terms) arguably determined the country's behaviour in a fundamental (and fundamentally different) way. Formally this meant compliance with the rules of international institutions, like the European Recovery Programme (Marshall Plan 1948), the OEEC (1949) (later OECD), the European Payments Union (1950), GATT (1951), the Coal and Steel Community (1951), the World Bank and the IMF (1952); this involved the long-term ceding of sovereignty beyond the restrictions of the Occupation Statute. Ideologically, it meant the abandonment not just of autarkic ambitions much loved by traditional economic élites before 1945, but also of the free-rider position preferred by many representatives of German industry in the post-war period. In practice, it meant the development and cultivation of intense trading links with the USA, Europe and other nations; Germany's export ratio rose from an average of 6 per cent of Net Social Product in 1935–38 to 9.3 per cent in 1950, 17.2 per cent in 1960 and 23.8 per cent in 1970, where the post-war figures do not

---

[21]   Thus Helmut Schlesinger, 'Geldpolitik in der Phase des Wiederaufbaus', in: Deutsche Bundesbank (ed.), *Währung und Wirtschaft in Deutschland*, op.cit. p.588f

include trade with East Germany.[22] This was driven both by west
Germany's unaccustomed lack of raw materials and the wealth-creation
advantage of finished goods production. From 1951 to 1973, west
Germany's terms of trade – the exchange relationship between export
and import prices – rose year by year; while real export prices rose by
some 50 per cent in this period, real import prices fell by around 10 per
cent, until the oil crisis of 1973/74 partly reduced the disparity.[23] The
export dependency of individual (key) industrial sectors in 1954 was
already considerably higher than the economy as a whole: chemicals
(27.2 per cent), iron and steel (37.2 per cent), engineering (31.4 per
cent) and electricals (28.7 per cent) were already vital earners of foreign
currency whose interests (as investors, taxpayers and employers) had to
be carefully cultivated. Most importantly, however, export ratios of this
magnitude meant that large and increasing proportions of demand were
outside the effective realm of influence of either monetary or fiscal
authorities; the manipulation of interest rates, bank reserve ratios and
rediscount quotas by the German central bank does not affect the
strategic investment or consumption decisions of customers in other
countries, particularly in a system of fixed exchange rates. West
Germany's own location within the Bretton Woods system was also
proving extremely advantageous. A low exchange rate against the US
Dollar, Sterling and the French Franc meant, *ceteris paribus*, that
comparable German products were cheaper on world markets, an
advantage that was reinforced by lower (hourly and unit) wage costs.
The potential disadvantage of higher import costs was neutralised by
Germany's rising terms of trade and the direction and quality of its
trade, with high-grade production and consumer goods going to other
industrialised countries and raw materials and semi-finished goods
coming (not exclusively but in higher proportion) from less developed
countries with weaker currencies. West Germany's trading advantages
were reflected in its structural surpluses with industrialised countries
like Britain and France in this period which more than compensated for
the temporary structural deficit with the USA.

At an early stage in the 1950s, these structural surpluses began to
create tensions within the exchange rate system. Adenauer's comments
to the Federation of German Industry in May 1956 reflect the dangers

---

[22] The inclusion of 'intra-German trade' would have increased the
export ratio to 25.2 per cent in 1970.
[23] See Glastetter, W. et al. *Die wirtschaftliche Entwicklung in der
Bundesrepublik 1950–1980*, Frankfurt am Main 1983

inherent in the country's trading success: 'Our economic rise frightens other nations far more than it would be looked on with affection by them'.[24] The unequal development of economies whose currencies are linked by fixed rates of exchange demands above all that timely adjustments to those rates are made to absorb the shock of BOP deficits/surpluses. The problem with both the fiscal and monetary authorities in west Germany is that between 1949 and 1961 they resisted such adjustments, attempting to compensate for the BOP disparities in other ways, but also compounding those disparities with the measures adopted.

There is no need in this context to examine in detail the lengthy debate about revaluation in Germany in the 1950s and early 1960s. It is sufficient to illuminate firstly the contradiction between the mythology and the reality of central bank influence in this connection and secondly the politico-economic damage caused by the institutional competition between autonomous central bank and other governmental authorities. As was observed above, monetary leverage (of a deflationary nature) was constrained by the removal of increasing proportions of demand from the influence of German authorities, by high and increasing bank liquidity within Germany, by high levels of corporate self-financing on the part of German firms which, once induced by fiscal measures, became self-perpetuating, in turn generating high cash-reserves, by rising rates of return and thus a culture of expectations which could ignore short-term squeezes because the medium-term perspective for investments remained favourable. As a result, the traditional use of interest rates as (indirect) weapons against the demand for money was supplemented by more dirigiste methods: by a) the manipulation of minimum reserve ratios (an innovation to German central banking borrowed from the Americans) on all (or selected) bank deposits, b) by open market transactions, selling illiquid securities in exchange for cash and c) by the imposition of refinancing or rediscount quotas. In both the BOP crisis of 1950/51 and the 'overheating'-crisis of 1955–57, there was extensive use of rediscounting restrictions, such that the BdL/Bundesbank would refuse to discount bills of exchange offered by banks for cash after monthly ceilings had been reached. The main targets of the 1950/51 squeeze were imports, such that – in addition to hefty increases of minimum reserves on both sight and time deposits – special cash deposits of foreign currencies were imposed by the BdL

---

[24] Adenauer, quoted in Hallgarten/Radkau, *Deutsche Industrie und Politik*, op.cit. p.469

for all import transactions, while the government halted the OEEC liberalisation process temporarily. In contrast, the later crisis produced a general squeeze with accompanying efforts to promote commodity imports and deter speculative capital inflows; in May 1956 the BdL suspended its preferential treatment of foreign bills and the new Bundesbank increased the minimum reserve ratio for foreign deposits in German banks to 30 per cent in August 1957, contrasting with just 12 per cent for the deposits of German residents. What is interesting about the 55–57 squeeze is that the use of the discount rate was abandoned in favour of seemingly more brutal controls of liquidity and capital inflows; from a maximum of 5½ per cent in May 1956, the central bank began lowering the discount rate in September (down to 5 per cent), followed by further reductions in January 1957 (to 4½ per cent), the following September (4 per cent) and January 1958 (3½ per cent). This said, the effectiveness of rediscount restrictions was at most symbolic of a deflationary stance on the part of the BdL. The ample liquidity of German banks meant that at the very most, 45 per cent of central bank rediscount quotas were actually used up, namely during the winter of 1955/56.[25]

At the same time, the US, Britain and France were raising their discount rates, in part as a result of the Suez crisis but – in the particular case of Britain – because of growing balance of payments difficulties and the need to attract funds via the capital account to finance its deficit. German rate reductions were informed by the (implicit) recognition that a domestic squeeze, using predominantly the manipulation of short-term central bank rediscounting conditions, was counterproductive, as any minor advantage gained from restricting German market actors from borrowing was more than neutralised by the fact that such interest rate rises made German bank deposits and other securities more attractive to foreign investors. This was particularly the case where all the major European currencies were moving towards formal convertibility and where the desirability of a revaluation of the German DM was being widely discussed, both at home and abroad. As early as July 1956, the Academic Advisory Committee to the Bonn Economics Ministry formally proposed revaluation as a means of combatting the country's structural payments surplus; the British press, suddenly made aware of the vulnerability of colonial post-war states by the Suez fiasco and the vision of Germany

---

[25] Thus Holtfrerich, 'Monetary Policy', op.cit., p.352

'winning the peace', gives active support to such proposals.[26] In October 1956, the strengthening of the DM to 11.69¾: £1.00 in the narrow fluctuation bands of the Bretton Woods system increased rumours of an imminent revaluation of the Mark.

The revaluation debate, once started, was difficult to suppress and was set to rumble on until 1969, or indeed until the floating of the DM in 1971. The key opponents of revaluation were Germany's increasingly influential industrial lobby, headed by the BDI under Fritz Berg, and the farmers whose German Farmers Federation still numbered about 1 million members at the end of the 1950s; both organisations were closely linked to the ruling CDU/CSU parties and deployed the full weight of their lobbying against revaluation, essentially on the grounds that it would make German exports more expensive on world markets and endanger turnover, investments and employment. Röpke, one of Erhard's ordo-liberal allies, described the 1961 campaign by the BDI as 'almost terroristic'.[27] While Erhard was not dogmatic about revaluation, Adenauer remained strongly influenced by Berg and the BDI. The anti-revaluation camp also had the support of Vocke, president of the BdL until 1957, and subsequently of Karl Blessing, president of the Bundesbank; the latter even threatened to resign should a revaluation be forced upon him.[28] There was thus a strong consensus within Germany's economic elite which saw revaluation as the least acceptable option.

In consequence, both political and economic agencies sought to deploy a wide variety of alternative measures to reduce the pressure on both the DM and on the BdL/Bundesbank as guardians of the currency. These included:

• The removal of all import restrictions on (in particular high-grade) goods in three stages between March 1955 and June 1956; this

---

[26] See, for example, *The Economist*, 7 July and 18 August 1956, also 31 August 1957, where revaluation is seen as Germany's 'easiest way out'.

[27] Wilhelm Röpke, quoted in Hallgarten and Radkau, *Deutsche Industrie und Politik,* op.cit. p.505

[28] Thus Ehrenberg, *Die Erhard-Saga*, op.cit. p.60; Blessing and the Bundesbank were subsequently criticized by Hjalmar Schacht in a retrospective commentary for having allowed exports to rip and to have resisted revaluation, in: *Die Politik der Bundesbank*, ms from around 1970, quoted in Hallgarten & Radkau, *Deutsche Industrie und Politik*, p. 470

was rendered in part problematic by the later signing of the Rome Treaties in March 1957 which signalled both the establishment of a customs-free zone for member states and the reintroduction of selective customs tariffs and discriminatory trade relations with third countries.

• The removal of significant capital transfer controls; in December 1955, absolute mobility for foreign assets and associated earnings is established; in January 1957 permission is granted to German residents to establish bank accounts abroad and at the end of December 1958 full convertibility for the D-Mark and most other west European currencies is introduced (the DM had been effectively convertible in October 1957).

• The active discouragement of foreign bank deposits and other securities with discriminatory reserve ratios, raised to 20 per cent in April and 30 per cent in September 1957.

• The increasing use of open market transactions by the BdL/ Bundesbank, whereby the 1955 ceiling of 2 billion DM for such dealings was raised to 7 billion in 1957; up to the end of October 1957 5.6 billion DM worth of mobilisation paper had actually been placed in the hands of the banks in exchange for cash.

• The deliberate generation of federal budget surpluses by Finance Minister Schäffer (the so-called 'Julius Tower' of strategic reserves) aimed initially at both removing liquidity from circulation via taxation and establishing a reserve fund for future deployment in German rearmament.

The federal government posted budget surpluses for four years from 1953 to 1956, the public sector as a whole for six years from 1951 to 1956; the overall state surplus averaged 1.5 per cent of GDP between 1953 and 1956 and amounted to 11 billion DM, with a federal share of 5.5 billion DM. The Bank deutscher Länder was at odds with the federal government over the effectiveness of these budget surpluses, both because it conflicted with the self-image of the central bank as the primary controller of the money stock and also because it revealed weaknesses in its own armoury.[29] Such budget surpluses were arguably double-edged: yes, they withdrew money from circulation but they also removed pressure from capital markets, because the state was reducing

---

[29] Holtfrerich cites discussions within the Central Bank Council where one member, Eduard Wolf, bemoaned the fact that 'the proper task of credit policy is being performed not by credit policy itself but by fiscal policy on the basis of very different considerations', 'Monetary Policy', op.cit. p.353

its borrowing and 'crowding in' private borrowers; secondly, the non-use of tax revenues to satisfy the immediate need for public goods (housing, transport, education, training) compounded structural economic weaknesses which would revisit the state later and with serious effect; thirdly, revenues could have been deployed to boost imports and thus to remove the pressure of the BOP surpluses. The 'Julius Tower' thus compounded the overall dilemma of deflationary policies which could only affect domestic demand, increasing the disparity between dynamic earnings abroad and dampened economic activity at home. According to Kitterer, the 'Julius Tower' was a marked failure as fiscal policy, essentially because it was driven not by economic policy but by military policy considerations, but he sees no serious clash with monetary policy.[30] Holtfrerich implies a strong contradiction in Germany's institutional arrangements when he notes that the 'Julius Tower', which at its height contained 7.5 billion DM, 'tied up more liquidity than the Bank deutscher Länder managed from the end of 1950 to the end of 1956', i.e. the Finance Ministry was doing the central bank's job for it, a central bank that 'was virtually helpless in the face of the growth of the money stock'.[31]

The speedy emptying of the 'Julius Tower' from 1957 to 1959 followed the advice of informed opinion at home and abroad and used the funds in an attempt to neutralise BOP surpluses via the capital account: through the accelerated repayment of post-war loans, through a series of loans to the IMF, totalling $348 million (1.46 billion DM) up to the end of 1958, through direct development aid and by purchases of military equipment (including the luckless Starfighter) from other NATO countries.

---

[30] Wolfgang Kitterer, 'Public Finance and the Central Bank', in: Deutsche Bundesbank (ed.), *Fifty Years of the Deutsche Mark*, op.cit. p.170; the view of the primacy of military consideration over any anti-cyclical objectives is shared by Schlesinger, 'Geldpolitik in der Phase des Wiederaufbaus', op.cit. p.593ff; Abelshauser, while asserting that Erhard manifested an aversion for anti-cyclical intervention, suggests that the Julius Tower was the exception that proved the rule, i.e. that it had a specific anti-cyclical thrust, in: *Wirtschaftsgeschichte der Bundesrepublik*, op.cit. p.109

[31] Holtfrerich, 'Monetary Policy', op.cit. p.392

The alternative of allowing more price inflation, which was being urged on the German authorities from some quarters abroad,[32] was rejected by both fiscal and monetary authorities. With the relaxation of interest rates by the BdL and (after August 1957) by the Bundesbank, direct appeals were made to workers and to enterprises not to force prices up by demanding/conceding excessive wage rises or reductions in the working week. Having regularly asked firms to cut prices and workers to moderate wage claims,[33] Ludwig Erhard in 1958 was even asking 'the German people' whether it should not be prepared 'instead of working less than 45 hours a week, to work an hour extra', thereby reducing pressure on the labour market and on wage costs.[34] For their part enterprises sought to prevent a deflationary squeeze (increased costs and lower demand) by making public pronouncements on prices. For example, in April 1956, 58 consumer goods manufacturers placed a ¾-page advertisement in major newspapers and magazines, promising not to raise prices for the rest of the year, while department stores sent telegrams to the Economics Ministry with similar assurances.[35]

There were occasional signs that the combination of countervailing measures and the rhetoric of domestic and external stability were reducing pressure on the DM: at the end of October 1957, after reductions in the discount rate and increases in reserve ratios for foreigners' deposits made German securities less attractive, the DM actually slipped against Sterling,[36] boosted by a joint German-British statement that exchange rate parities would not be changed and by

---

[32] 'It is curious that the world outside Germany should be discussing how to get the Germans to misbehave, how to teach them to inflate, to invest less'; thus an (anonymous) article in *The Economist*, 'The German Surplus', 1 February 1958, p.383

[33] Ludwig Erhard, Bundestag Debate October 19 1955, in: Erhard, *Deutsche Wirtschaftspolitik*, Düsseldorf 1962, 291ff

[34] Erhard, 'Nicht alles zur gleichen Zeit', Radio Broadcast 13 January 1958, in: *Deutsche Wirtschaftspolitik*, op.cit. p.383; this echoed the demand by the industrialist Hugo Stinnes in the early 1920s that German workers should work an extra hour for the benefit of the German economy.

[35] See: *The Economist*, 27 April 1956

[36] Bank of England rates remained consistently above the German discount rate from 1956, reflecting British BOP problems; however, the drop in the DM:£ rate to 11.76:1 was temporary.

devaluation of the French Franc in August, but this represented only a temporary respite.

1958 saw a dip in Germany's growth rate to only 3.5 per cent; the unemployment rate stopped falling and remained on 3.7 per cent and the investment ratio was still a full percentage point below 1956 levels at 22.7 per cent. The main determinants of the slowdown were problems in other industrial economies, notably in the US, France and Britain and a consequent drop in global production and trade. Nevertheless, money stock growth (M3: +13.6 per cent) was still buoyant, bank lending grew by 12.4 per cent and the banks' free liquid reserves grew to 16.1 billion DM. 1959 and 1960 saw a further acceleration of global trade and with it a significant boost to German growth (1959: +7.4 per cent, 1960: +9.0 per cent); bank lending grew dramatically by 18.6 per cent in 1959 and 23.3 per cent in 1960 and the investment ratio began an impressive period of growth, rising to 24 per cent in 1959 and reaching a high point of 26.6 per cent in 1964. Even if one concedes the exceptional context of post-war reconstruction, and even though German inflation was minimal at 1.0 per cent in 1959 and 1.4 per cent in 1960, most indicators pointed to the dangers of overheating and disequilibrium in the medium term. Given that most other OECD economies were growing more slowly and that many had structural trade deficits with Germany, the problem of inappropriate exchange rate parities reappeared with a vengeance. Karl Blessing, still strongly opposed to revaluation, urged the federal government to reduce both its borrowing and its capital expenditure, notably on construction projects, to dampen demand but without endangering the maintenance of strong growth in the secular economy. It would also obviate the need for tighter credit policy. The request epitomised the Bundesbank's dilemma: ostensibly it was the institution charged with the duty of independently controlling domestic liquidity but forced to acknowledge the inadequacy of its instruments simultaneously to control domestic and inward flows of capital, and the need for a close coordination of fiscal and monetary policy; the Bundesbank's duty was to safeguard the currency, but the Federal Government was still in charge of exchange rate questions. In the absence of moves by the Federal Government to comply with his request, Blessing and the CBC proceeded to reverse the January 1959 reduction of both discount rate (to 2¾ per cent) and Lombard rate (to 3¾ per cent) with three successive increases of both rates, in September to 3 per cent and 4 per cent , in October to 4 per cent and 5 per cent and in June 1960 to 5 per cent and 6 per cent respectively. This was done in the full knowledge that it would make

DM-securities more attractive to foreign investors, in both yield terms and in terms of exchange rate speculation. With the permission of the federal government, the Bundesbank imposed a short-term freeze on interest on foreign-held deposit accounts in German banks. As Holtfrerich points out, this 'amounted to a reversal of the trend towards economic liberalization and a renewed discrimination against international capital movements which ... had only just been liberalized.'[37] Minimum reserve ratios were increased and open market operations intensified, selling paper not just to the banks but also to the social insurance funds.[38] Bank liquidity was dented temporarily but insufficiently to prevent record bank lending to non-banks. There was an air of desperation about Bundesbank actions, made worse by the decision by the Federal Reserve to cut its own discount rate in June 1960. In unusually dramatic language, the Bundesbank's later annual report for 1960 described this as 'a tragic coincidence'.[39] There was further correspondence with the federal government in September 1960, requesting that liquidity be removed from the economy via tax increases and higher social insurance levies and, on the expenditure side, by increased payments of development aid grants. Although the issue of revaluation was raised within the CBC by Otmar Emminger in particular and although Erhard had long been an advocate of flexible exchange rates, discussion/opposition to revaluation remained the preserve of interest groups and the newspapers. When the Bundesbank suddenly ended the brief squeeze by lowering the discount and Lombard rates on 11 November 1960, Germany's powerlessness to resist the contradictory pressures of the unequal development of linked economies in a system of fixed exchange rates were revealed for all to see. The undignified scramble which ended four months later in a 5 per cent revaluation started in earnest.

Otmar Emminger, Directorate member since 1953, had called for a DM-revaluation as early as 1956 but was isolated within the CBC and at odds, in particular, with Blessing and Troeger in the new Bundesbank line-up. Discussions about exchange rate parities had hitherto been deflected by calls for deficit countries like France or Britain to devalue rather than for surplus countries like Germany to

---

[37] Holtfrerich, 'Monetary Policy', op.cit. p.371

[38] Ibid. The banks were persuaded to keep voluntarily 1 billion DM worth of mobilization paper in their portfolios for at least two years.

[39] Quoted in Holtfrerich, 'Monetary Policy', op.cit. p. 371

revalue, particularly give Germany's trading deficit with the USA.[40] Now, with the United States suffering a cumulative deficit of $12 billion in 1958/59, such considerations were out of the question, given that the USA were the anchor of the Bretton Woods System. Emminger had consequently revived his campaign within the CBC in December 1959 and in a formal paper in January 1960 in which he proposed that the dollar rate of the DM be lowered from 4.20 to 3.90, a revaluation of the DM of 7.7 per cent, but again the overwhelming majority of the CBC rejected his view.

Erhard, increasingly convinced of the need to adjust the DM exchange rate upward attempted to convince the federal cabinet in the summer of 1960 but was voted down; he regarded the Bundesbank's recent squeeze as both appropriate domestically and also helpful in arguing for revaluation, given that the flow of hot money into Germany had not abated despite the Bank's targetted counter-measures. He was therefore dismayed when the Bundesbank reversed its short-lived restrictive moves (just 14 months), lowering central bank rates in November 1960, and shifted the focus of its policies to the maintenance of the DM's external stability, i.e. defending the low parity of 4.20: $1.00. Erhard and Etzel toyed with the idea of deploying the federal government's suspensive veto but confined themselves to public criticism of the Bank's decisions. The Bundesbank, in its November monthly report, had urged the government to increase its aid to developing countries to 4 billion DM per year, ensuring that such aid was not linked to purchases of German goods, as this would simply compound the structural trade surplus. International pressure on Germany was mounting; *The Economist*, in inimical fashion, noted that 'in the corridors, cocktail rooms and bedroom suites all the talk is of fears for the dollar' while Per Jacobsen, head of the IMF, with others was 'pointing accusing fingers at Germany'.[41] On 22 November 1960 a US delegation, headed by Dillon and Anderson, sought immediate measures from the German government to ease the USA's deficit via

---

[40] There are clear signs that the BdL sought to minimize the publicity given to dissenting voices within the central bank; for example, Heinrich Irmler, vice-president of the Land Central Bank of Lower Saxony and later Directorate member of the Bundesbank, raised the issue of devaluation in a public speech in November 1956, a speech which was published in the BdL's *Auszüge aus Presseartikeln* (21 December 1956) but without the extensive passage about revaluation.

[41] *The Economist*, 1 October 1960, p.61

the accelerated repayment of German debt and advance payment for existing arms orders, but had to wait until February 1961 for such an offer to emerge; the offer was not just below US expectations but was also linked in part to demands for concessions from the Kennedy administration on German assets confiscated during the war, considered an affront by the Americans.[42]

The Federation of German industry mounted an extraordinary campaign in November 1960 which included proposals for a voluntary pledge by industry to hold prices stable, binding commitments by industrial companies to buy development aid bonds, the freezing of investment capital in a holding account with the Bundesbank and a voluntary agreement between government and the construction industry to reduce public building projects. Adenauer, strongly influenced by his banking advisors Abs and Pferdemenges but also by veiled threats from Fritz Berg (BDI) to withdraw financial support from the CDU, allegedly promised that there would be no revaluation. It is now obvious that Adenauer came under considerable pressure from the Kennedy government in January and February 1961 which tipped the scales in favour of revaluation, making the fulfilment of this promise impossible. Meanwhile the Bundesbank was continuing to relax its monetary controls and at a special meeting of the CBC on 25 February voted to reduce minimum reserve ratios against Etzel's and Erhard's express wish. At the same meeting, Vice-President Troeger gave vent to his resentment over government criticism of the Bank, accusing the Adenauer administration of not supporting the Bank's liquidity policies.[43] Blessing repeated his threat to resign, according to Emminger, because of the unfair blame being placed on the Bank; Emminger, now with the open support of both Irmler and Wolf on the CBC, put the case for revaluation again and warned that in its absence, the Bundesbank 'will lose even more (sic JL) of its prestige'.[44] Blessing was summoned to a meeting in Bonn with Adenauer, Etzel and Erhard two days later, at which the political impasse was discussed and where Adenauer 'changed his mind over the revaluation issue with surprising speed.'[45] It was arguably not an on-the-spot conversion, as an *Economist* article suggested at the time: 'The cynic, reflecting that the

[42] See *The Economist*, 4 February 1961

[43] Troeger, quoted in: Holtfrerich, 'Monetary Policy', op.cit. p.373

[44] Otmar Emminger, *D-Mark, Dollar, Währungskrisen. Erinnerungen eines ehemaligen Bundesbankpräsidenten*, Stuttgart 1986, 122f

[45] Marsh, *The Bundesbank*, op.cit. p.183

case for all these measures was as strong, if not stronger, in 1957, may attribute their present realisation directly to the political fact that American pressure is now getting through at top level to Dr Adenauer, who probably never noticed earlier British representations in the same sense through OEEC.'[46] However, the chancellor only agreed to a revaluation of 4¾ per cent (from DM4.20 to DM4.00: $1.00), significantly less than the 7.7 per cent demanded by both Emminger and Erhard. The cabinet approved the decision on 3 March 1961 and Erhard attended a meeting of the Bundesbank CBC the same day to gain the Bank's agreement, even though formally the federal government had exclusive constitutional powers (GG§73.4) in relation to the exchange rate. The Bank had little option than to accept, however, and voted by a majority of 16 to 3 in favour of the motion. On Sunday, 5 March 1961, in a show of theatrical solidarity, Blessing, Etzel and Erhard announced the revaluation at a hastily arranged press conference in Bonn; it was a move obviously designed to preempt renewed speculation on the money markets the following day. Blessing was clearly the most uneasy, stressing that 'for a central bank, the exchange rate parity is sacrosanct, something which can only be changed when all other methods have proved unsuccessful'.[47] His honesty echoed the tenor of the November 1960 monthly report which had admitted that its policy hitherto had failed. Erhard was more upbeat in the radio broadcast of 6 March:

'It is undeniable that the revaluation means that exports will be made more difficult and more expensive to a certain extent, which will differ from branch to branch, but which will not lead to a sustained reduction of our sales abroad. On the other hand, making imports easier and cheaper will doubtless have a certain influence on German price levels but for this very reason help to maintain better economic stability.'[48]

Erhard was right. The revaluation reduced the visible trade surplus and in 1962 the current account slipped briefly into a deficit of DM − 686 million, but the balance of payments stabilised in 1963 and 1964 at a healthy but less menacing level of 1.9 and 1.6 billion DM respectively. With the possible exception of the coal industry, which was facing a severe structural crisis of overcapacity in any case, the dire

---

[46] *The Economist*, 11 March 1961, p.983

[47] Quoted in Marsh, *The Bundesbank*, op.cit. p.184

[48] Ludwig Erhard, 'Zur Aufwertung der Mark', in: *Deutsche Wirtschaftspolitik*, op.cit. 563f

warnings of the BDI of revaluation rendering German industry uncompetitive proved unfounded.[49] Indeed, the achievement of the highest levels of investment in post-war German history between 1961 and 1966 (average: 25.8 per cent) suggested a strengthened confidence on the part of industry with regard to their medium-term prospects. The temporary trade advantages enjoyed by Britain, France and other major industrial countries were quickly neutralised by higher levels of inflation than in Germany, but with strong growth in the United States, pressure on the DM was removed and did not re-emerge until renewed BOP problems in the US at the end of the decade. What neither Erhard nor Blessing conceded was that the structural problem of trade and payments surpluses was pre-programmed by the mercantilism of the early 1950s which sought systematically to maximise exports and to dampen domestic demand and that the state's difficulty in responding to this problem was not simply a function of a system of linked currencies of countries with differential growth and trade patterns but of Germany's institutional arrangements which condemned the country to five years of uncoordinated and often conflictual paralysis. Admittedly, west Germany's problems were the problems of success. The optimal conditions of the 1950s in which strong growth was achieved along with full employment, low inflation and export surpluses were unlikely to be repeated; accordingly, the absence of inflation made a policy of benign neglect, fudge or even paralysis irrelevant in the eyes of the majority of the population. The institutional rivalry between BdL/Bundesbank and central government was at most mediated not by recriminations over actual economic misfortune but by hypothetical debates about the potential for the abuse of monetary affairs by one or other agency. The Social Democrats – in unhappy opposition to the 'CDU-state' until 1966 – sought to make political capital out of Adenauer's ambivalence towards central bank autonomy in the election campaign of 1957 which coincided with the passage of the Bundesbank Law in July of that year and the introduction of new pensions arrangements. They exploited what *The Economist* described as the Germans' 'pathological fear of any rises in prices'[50] to imply that Adenauer and Erhard could play fast and loose with the currency if the Bank were rendered dependent again. While some Social Democrats, like Herbert Ehrenberg, had few illusions about central bankers, their

---

[49] The BDI nevertheless went through with its threat to deny the CDU 100 000 DM in an important election year.

[50] *The Economist* 27 October 1956, p.335

(at the time fruitless) electoral opportunism nevertheless contributed to the generation of the legend of 'good money and bad politics' which has been so mischeviously used since.[51] The reality of the 1950s was not of one state agency sovereign, authoritative and infallible, the other clientelistic, fallible and electorally compromised. The historiography of the Bundesbank in this period consistently identifies the predominance of 'dilemma'.[52] Rather, neither institution yet had the 'sovereignty' or 'authority' to influence decisively the monetary conditions enjoyed by German banks and German enterprises; if anything, the fiscal authorities had marginally more clout. Revaluation, when it came, was an option resisted by both until the last minute and then forced on both by the 'hot money'-market and by the US-government as bloc-leader.

At the famous meeting of the Bundesbank CBC on 25 February 1961, the Bank's vice-president, Heinrich Troeger made a strong plea for integrated and thus implicitly co-ordinated economic policy:

'The government, which wanted full employment, has achieved full employment and is maintaining full employment, must pursue an active and conscious stabilization policy. It pursued this actively – the economic miracle; it must also pursue it negatively, if this is required by the economic situation. The fact that it is not doing so, that is our real dilemma (and not the appreciation question) ... Monetary policy is part and parcel of economic policy'.[53]

The institutional lesson learned by the Bundesbank and its President, Blessing, after the revaluation scramble, was arguably in the opposite direction. 'The revaluation episode stiffened Blessing's conviction that the best way to deal with the government was through a policy of uncompromising monetary rigour' (Marsh).[54] There was still a considerable time-lapse before this 'rigour' manifested itself. After revaluation, interest rates and minimum reserve ratios were lowered and rediscount quotas removed. Monetary policy instruments went into virtual hibernation until 1964 when minimum reserve ratios were raised

---

[51] See J. Leaman, 'Central Banking and the Crisis of Social Democracy', op.cit. 26ff
[52] Marsh, *The Bundesbank*, op.cit. 180ff; Schlesinger, 'Geldpolitik', op.cit. p.605; Oberhauser, 'Geld- und Kreditpolitik', op.cit. p.614; Holtfrerich, 'Monetary Policy', op.cit. p.362ff (Section C is entitled 'Monetary policy on the horns of a dilemma: 1956–1961'.)
[53] Troeger, quoted in: Holtfrerich, 'Monetary Policy', op.cit. p. 373
[54] David Marsh, *The Bundesbank*, op.cit. 184f

slightly to counteract strong rises in bank liquidity[55], but both discount and Lombard rates remained unchanged until January 1965, when they were raised by ½ per cent to 3½ per cent and 4½ per cent respectively. The policy of benign neglect up until this time cannot be explained in orthodox monetarist terms, since price inflation jumped to uncharacteristically high levels between 1962 and 1966, averaging over 3 per cent and effectively producing negative interest rates (when central bank or market interest rates are below the rate of inflation), the well-known paradise for debtors. Bundesbank inactivity was determined by a new primacy of external targetting. 'The Bundesbank failed to counteract price increases with restrictive measures above all because of foreign economic considerations'.[56] By reducing bank refinancing costs to zero in real terms, by reducing bond yields and by tolerating slightly more internal inflation, the Bank sought to neutralise any residual attractiveness of German securities for foreign investors who might have been spurred on by the less than adequate rate of revaluation in 1961 to bet on an early second adjustment of the DM. With Blessing, an ex-industrialist, at the helm, Germany's exporters were again being protected. At the same time, Germany's consumption ratio was lower than its major industrial counterparts, offering some scope for increased domestic demand via a less severe attitude to wage rises. In contrast to the 1950s, where wage costs featured heavily in both central bank rhetoric and its sporadic credit squeezes, the high nominal wage settlements and the higher nominal rises in unit wage costs of the early 1960s excited little comment and even less action from the central bank.

Nevertheless, the Bundesbank's actions in 1965 and 1966 would seem to confirm Marsh's view of a firm resolve to demarcate itself from the fiscal state and to avoid taking the blame for too close an association with federal government policy. Erhard had succeeded Adenauer as chancellor in 1963 (against Adenauer's wishes and advice) and, despite the best intentions, was unable to paper over the cracks

---

[55] The liquidity figures are annualised and taken from Holtfrerich ('Monetary Policy', op.cit. p.312, Table 2); they are at odds with the liquid reserve figures provided by Oberhauser ('Geld- und Kreditpolitik', op.cit. p.635, which are quarterly but misleadingly show a sharp declining trend from 1958 through to 1966; Holtfrerich's figures show healthy bank liquidity after 1958, with reserves higher than lending to non-banks from 1962 through to 1970.

[56] Thus Oberhauser, 'Geld- und Kreditpolitik', op.cit. p.620

within the governing coalition (with the Free Democrats) and within the Christian Democratic group. The building of the Berlin Wall in August 1961 had helped to expose the structural vulnerability of an economy used to the steady supply of skilled labour from the East as well as the policy neglect of the Adenauer years, notably in social and educational affairs. While Erhard's advisors and quite a few influential Christian Democrats increasingly saw the advantages of interventionism, Erhard's ordo-liberalism rendered him intellectually isolated and certainly unable to face the challenge of the 'normal' cyclical conditions which had begun to emerge since 1960. Real shortages in the labour market began to emerge, notably for skilled workers, shortages which could not be compensated by the importation of labour from southern Europe. Nominal wages grew faster than nominal GDP and, despite strong investment in new machinery, unit wage costs grew at an uncharacteristically fast rate (1961–66: +4.2 per cent p.a.; 1952–1960: +1.5 per cent p.a.). With investment growth higher than GDP growth, capacity utilisation and capital productivity in Germany were falling in the first half of the 1960s, rendering enterprises more vulnerable to fluctuations in demand. Low borrowing costs reduced business concern about increased labour costs in the short term and businesses were lulled into thinking that the rates of growth and rates of return of the 1950s would be maintained ad infinitum. They were encouraged in this view by conservative politicians like Theodor Blank (CDU) who, at the party conference in March 1965, proclaimed that cyclical crises had been rendered obsolete by the 'social market economy' and full employment was a 'permanent condition'.[57] However, as Mandel pointed out at the time, Germany's productive potential was rushing ahead of potential demand. While demand for manufactured goods did not decline between 1965 and 1966, it did not rise sufficiently to halt the decline in utilisation, so that as early as the Spring of 1965 equipment purchases and building investments by manufacturing companies were being cut back. Construction order books were further hit by reductions in infrastructural investments by the regions and by local government. In 1966 the Bundesbank's own figures showed iron and steel production down on 1965 and capital goods production, including engineering, also down.[58] These early signs of the economy

---

[57] Theodor Blank, quoted in Welteke, *Theorie und Praxis der Sozialen Marktwirtschaft*, Frankfurt 1975, p.125

[58] See Bundesbank Monthly Report, January 1968; the Bundesbank's Annual Report for 1969 has a graph showing the flattening of industrial

cooling down were ignored by the Bundesbank. Instead it focussed on the sudden emergence and persistence of public sector borrowing which reached 1.9 per cent of GDP in 1965, with the bulk located at local government and regional level.

Most commentators chide the Erhard government for increasing social spending and making minor cuts in taxation in 1965, because they smacked of electoral gifts (1965 saw federal elections) and because they were 'pro-cyclical'.[59] The accusation is in part unfair, because demographic trends made increased expenditure on the social infrastructure a matter of urgency and because order books in the investment goods sector indicated (correctly) that the downswing had already begun. The Bundesbank, on the other hand, is applauded for anti-cyclical rectitude in raising discount and Lombard rates in August 1965 and May 1966 and counteracting Erhard's 'electoral gifts'.[60] Inflation did accelerate at the end of 1965, driven by consumer demand, but against the background of the tolerated 'adjustment inflation' of 1962 onwards which was helping to prevent external pressure on the DM. There is a stronger argument pointing to Bundesbank opportunism. The high levels of bank liquidity in the years of policy-hibernation (1961–64) would have made monetary countermeasures futile as they had been in the run-up to revaluation. Furthermore, consumer price inflation was distorted by the suspension of rent controls in 1960 and the doubling of rents by 1970; between 1959 and 1967, average annual rent rises of 6.2 per cent contrasted with still modest annual price increases for food (2 per cent), clothing (2 per cent), and energy (1.6 per cent) in the same period. With rent making up an eighth of household expenditure, the adjustment to market levels was bound to affect the general index and workers' demands for adequate pay increases. Again, for the Bundesbank to have taken strict countermeasures against consumer price inflation in this context would have been futile and unpopular. However, the sudden current account

---

orders in the second quarter of 1965 with an unbroken decline through to the second quarter of 1967

[59] Tax cuts were made 'in the wrong cyclical situation' (Oberhauser, 'Geld- und Kreditpolitik', op.cit. p.623; the government 'put its foot on the accelerator in pro-cyclical fashion', (Holtfrerich, 'Monetary Policy', op.cit. p.379; viz also Marsh, *The Bundesbank*, op.cit. 186f

[60] Holtfrerich, 'Monetary Policy', op.cit. p.379

deficit of at least 5 billion DM[61], together with three years of relatively heavy borrowing by the public sector (1964: 4 billion DM; 1965: 5.2 billion DM; 1965: 8.8 billion DM) made conditions on German capital markets sufficiently tight in 1965 and 1966 for the Bundesbank to exert some influence on monetary affairs. Even though much of the deficit spending was justified and Erhard was not the main 'culprit' , it is reasonable to conclude that Blessing and the Bundesbank CBC were actively demarcating themselves from the rest of the state, laying the blame for inflation squarely on the shoulders of profligate spending authorities and claiming the political high ground of anti-cyclical rigour. There is a strong flavour of humbug in Blessing's public upbraiding of the spending authorities in early 1966: 'The less it is supported by fiscal policy, the tougher monetary policy has to be ... Prices cannot continuously rise without producing dangerous economic, social and even political consequences'.[62] After all, the Bundesbank had itself allowed prices to rise continuously from 1961 to 1964 without batting an eyelid. Blessing's *Realpolitik* caused increased tension within Erhard's coalition, in which the Free Democrats were keen to impose the expenditure cuts demanded by the central bank. In October 1966, with the economy sliding into recession and the Bundesbank maintaining its monetary squeeze, Erhard resigned as chancellor. According to Marsh, 'Blessing bore an important part of the responsibility' for ousting Erhard, and it was a role which Blessing in part conceded when interviewed by Leo Brawand in 1971, stating that he had wanted 'to put things in order with an element of brute force'.[63] Even though the Bundesbank was criticized by some politicians for its untimely squeeze, the Bank had succeeded in disassociating itself from Erhard's perceived failure and deflecting blame for inflation onto the elected government. It was an important victory in a series of skirmishes between the Bundesbank and the federal government. The reality of the Bundesbank's corresponsibility in producing the brief recession in 1966/67 by maintaining its deflationary squeeze was

---

[61]These are year-end figures, taken from: Deutsche Bundesbank (ed.), *Vierzig Jahre Deutsche Mark. Monetäre Statistiken 1948–1987*, Frankfurt 1988; Oberhauser (op.cit. p.623) cites a higher current account deficit for the year of 6.2 billion DM

[62] Speech in Mainz, 24 February 1966, quoted in Marsh, *The Bundesbank*, p.187

[63] Leo Brawand, *Wohin steuert die deutsche Wirtschaft?*, Munich 1971, p.56

overshadowed by stronger public perceptions of a tired CDU-state, increasingly puzzled by unaccustomed economic problems and losing its 'miraculous' touch. The visible and accountable government lost out to the far less visible and unaccountable central bank.

The recession was a turning point for Germany's political economy in a number of senses. It marked the end of an almost unprecedented 18-year boom and with it the end of the post-war period qua reconstruction and rehabilitation. It marked the end of CDU supremacy and the baptism of the Social Democratic Party in federal government, which it would dominate for the next sixteen years. It marked the beginning accordingly of a brief experiment with Keynesian demand management, based on a consensus between Christian Democracy and Social Democracy in the framework of a grand coalition. Finally, in this context, it marked the beginning of a transition for the west German central bank from relative insignificance to politico-economic dominance at home and abroad.

The ideological core of the Grand Coalition's Stability and Growth Act of February 1967 was Keynesian; above all it set great store by co-ordination, co-operation and forward planning, such that the state, acting in concert, could implement policy 'appropriate to the economic cycle' (§§ 5–8, 14, 16 Stability Law). The central government was given powers to regulate all state revenue and expenditure to match the requirements of the business cycle; a Conjunctural Council was established, involving both area authorities and the Bundesbank to discuss the medium-term outlook for the economy and corresponding policy measures, while state representatives and the 'social partners' were organised in the (inappropriately named) Concerted Action forum, designed to achieve voluntary agreements on wages and profits.[64]

The Bundesbank's involvement in these new institutional arrangements was at best ambivalent. Despite immediate calls by the new Chancellor, Kiesinger (CDU), to halt its deflationary squeeze, the Bundesbank waited until 5 January 1967 to make a modest ½ per cent cut in the discount rate to 4½ per cent and ¾ per cent cut in the Lombard rate to 5½ per cent, by which time some 800 000 jobs had been shed, 300 000 migrant workers were being sent home and unemployment levels were moving to their highest level (February 1967: 673 000) since 1958. Further cuts in central bank rates came only gradually: , undoubtedly prolonging the downturn (however minor) and

---

[64] For further details of the Stability and Growth Act, see: J. Leaman, *Political Economy*, op.cit. 176ff

getting co-ordinated anti-cyclical behaviour off to a bad start. Quite rightly, the new Economics Minister, Karl Schiller, complained about Bundesbank recalcitrance in April 1967.

The Stability Law enshrined the 'magic square' of stable growth, prices, full employment and sound external balances as formal objectives of state economic policy. This was entirely in keeping with the Bundesbank Law in terms of both the Bank's primary task of safeguarding the currency and its duty to support government economic policy when this primary task was being fulfilled. However, the supply-side prejudices embedded in monetarism and underpinning the principle of an autonomous central bank were essentially at odds with demand-side values of the Grand Coalition's new Keynesianism or 'global steering' as it was confusingly called.

Table 4.1   Changes to Discount and Lombard Rates
and Inflation, 1961–1969

Change applicable from		Discount Rate % p.a.	Lombard Rate % p.a.	Annual Rate of Inflation %
1961	20 January	3.5	4.5	2.3
	5 May	3	4	
1962				3.0
1963				3.0
1964				2.3
1965	22 January	3.5	4.5	3.4
	13 August	4	5	
1966	27 May	5	6.25	3.5
1967	6 January	4.5	5.5	1.4
	17 February	4	5	
	14 April	3.5	4.5	
	12 May	3	4	
	11 August	3	3.5	
1968				1.5
1969	21 March	3	4	2.8
	18 April	4	5	
	20 June	5	6	
	11 September	6	7.5	
	5 December	6	9	

*Source:*Bundesbank, *Monthly Report* (various)

The Bundesbank could not afford to be inextricably linked to this new orthodoxy, because this could be seen to compromise its impartiality and involved the possibility of being associated with its failure. The Bank's annual report for 1967, while reflecting the new rhetoric of cooperation, nevertheless underscores 'the independent role of credit policy'.[65]

The 1967 report is indeed couched in terms of the general contribution of 'global steering' to monetary policy rather than vice versa: 'If the Federal and Länder Governments make energetic use of the means for conducting anti-cyclical policy which the Stability and Growth Law has given them, then, if the economy is again overstrained, not only will this create good preconditions for incomes to move in conformity with the needs of stability, but at the same time it will be possible for credit policy to be conducted on less restrictive lines than in the past.'[66]

In the immediate context of recession, however, the Bundesbank found it difficult to resist pressure to offer both an easing of rates and a degree of institutional cooperation. With domestic demand, investments, capacity utilisation and employment plummeting, it remains amazing that the Bank took as many as five steps in 1967 to reach an appropriate level of refinancing rates and another five steps to lower minimum reserve ratios. It was impossible to avoid negative growth in 1967 of 0.2 per cent, a situation made no better by the fact that the additional federal expenditure agreed for that year only restored the cuts made in 1966 and that regional and local authorities were continuing to cut their expenditure pro-cyclically. It was the Second Investment Programme of July 1967, for which the Bundesbank grudgingly agreed to additional deficit financing, that helped to kickstart recovery, a recovery evident in the last quarter of 1967, such that 1968 saw the restoration of the 'magic square', including real growth of 7.3 per cent; investments rose by 10.5 per cent, having slumped by 16.6 per cent in 1967, inflation remained modest at 1.6 per cent and the current account surplus rose to 13 billion DM. Compliance with 'global steering' nevertheless involved an amendment to the Bundesbank Act in November 1967, raising the credit limits for public authorities, which the Bank did not resist. The 1968 recovery was out of phase with global economic developments, coinciding with poor

---

[65] Deutsche Bundesbank, *Annual Report for 1967*, 1968, p.30
[66] Annual Report for 1967, p.28

economic performance in Britain, France and the USA and corresponding currency crises. Thus despite poor capital market returns in Germany, short-term capital balances rose by over 5 billion DM as a result of hot money escaping from the Dollar, the Franc and Sterling (already devalued in November 1967) and seeking refuge in a currency destined to appreciate in the short or medium term. The virtue of domestic monetary relaxation in Germany coincided with the necessity of avoiding excessive capital inflows. This was reflected explicitly in the opening lines of the Bank's 1968 report: 'The Deutsche Bundesbank's credit policy in 1968 was guided mainly by balance-of-payments considerations. The Bank thus tolerated the increase in liquidity resulting for credit institutions as well as for trade and industry from the market tendencies and to that extent continued its policy, already pursued in 1967, of keeping money and capital cheap by comparison with foreign countries'.[67] After the November 1968 conference of the Club of Ten in Bonn to discuss the currency crisis, the Federal Government introduced a system of licensing non-residents' deposits in German securities (22 November), while the central bank introduced 100 per cent minimum reserve ratios for all such deposits above their 15 November 1968 levels.

On the other hand, the Bank contributed to currency speculation by open criticism of the Bretton Woods system.[68] The inflow of hot money continued in the first half of 1969, affecting France and the US in particular. Britain's balance of payments was moving into surplus in 1969 and sterling was spared the major crisis which befell the Dollar and the Franc; both had chronic BOP deficits in 1969, that of the US exceeding \$7 billion. The French Franc's exchange rate parity was accordingly devalued unilaterally by 11.1 per cent on 11 August 1969, a move which merely compounded speculation against the Dollar and in favour of the Mark. In April and May, the Bundesbank's reserves grew by DM 16.7 billion and in the three week run-up to Germany's federal elections on 28 September a further 6.3 billion flowed in. As in

---

[67] Deutsche Bundesbank, *Annual Report for 1968*, 1969, p.1

[68] Thus in the 1968 Annual Report (p.30), where the Bank aligns itself with the view that the system is 'obsolete and stands in need of a basic overhaul'. Further: 'A system of basically fixed exchange rates can work satisfactorily only if the major countries of the world economy observe a minimum of harmony as to the aims and priorities of economic policy'. In the absence of such harmonisation 'excessive stress' may result for the international monetary system.

1960/61 transfers of this kind presented an impossible challenge to credit policy, however well it was supported by flanking fiscal measures. The restrictive measures adopted by the Bank in the course of 1969 were odd in the sense that it consciously acknowledged its powerlessness: 'The Bundesbank ...adopted a restrictive monetary policy, and tried step by step to increase its stringency – well knowing that, so long as the foreign trade and payments flank was open, there was not much chance of success'.[69] Four successive increases of the Bank's two main interest rates shadowed similar increases in France, the USA and the Netherlands, ostensibly designed to dampen domestic demand but functioning only to increase tensions within the Bretton Woods system. The Bundesbank's preference for a DM revaluation had already been communicated to the federal government prior to the Bonn meeting in November 1968; indeed, the Bank is reported to have worked out the operational details with the Banque de France beforehand.[70] Both chancellor Kiesinger and economics minister Schiller were opposed to revaluation at this stage and chose to impose dirigiste methods, favouring imports and deterring exports to reduce upward pressure on the Mark. The Bundesbank's measures will have only helped to undermine the government's resistance and can clearly be interpreted as deliberately aimed in that direction. Schiller came round pragmatically to the revaluation camp in the Spring of 1969, but Kiesinger's opposition meant that revaluation was delayed until after the formation of the new social-liberal coalition in October 1969. The federal government agreed to the removal of the Bundesbank's obligation to intervene on currency markets to defend existing parities from 30 September, a move sanctioned by the IMF. It meant the effective floating of the Mark for just under a month until, on 24 October 1969, the federal government announced a unilateral 9.3 per cent revaluation of the DM.

Even though the formal decision was that of the new social-liberal coalition, the 1969 revaluation had the Bundesbank's handwriting all over it. Raising German interest rates at a time when several of the IMF-group were suffering regular haemorrhages of their reserves, was tantamount to pouring petrol on the flames. Otmar Emminger, a long-time exponent of revaluation (and exchange rate flexibility) was being disingenous, if not dishonest, when he stated that: 'Through the repeated raising of minimum reserves, reduction of rediscount quotas

---

[69] Annual Report for 1969, Frankfurt am Main 1970, p.11
[70] Thus Marsh, *The Bundesbank*, op.cit. p.188

and a restrictive open market policy it (the Bundesbank JL) tried to render harmless the liquidity which had flowed in in the Spring of 1969'.[71] The liquidity had 'flowed in' firstly because the Bundesbank and its leading members were conducting an open debate about the virtue of German revaluation,[72] which international speculators will not have failed to note, and secondly because increasing the attractiveness of German securities made for a double bonus for those speculators, whatever short-term restrictions were placed on their holdings: revaluation gains and higher bond or deposit yields. If I, as a green undergraduate in 1969, managed to get the revaluation message with some piffling savings from working in Germany that year, hard-nosed financiers certainly will have. Holtfrerich is thus perfectly fair when he asserts that the Bundesbank was trying to force the issue by deliberately provocative behaviour:

'By its restrictive policy – this time fully aware of its inappropriateness – the Central Bank Council intended to exacerbate the external economic crisis, in order to force the Federal Government to revalue the currency'.[73]

The politico-economic problems of 1968/69 were multi-layered, there is no doubt: the Vietnam war, student unrest, the Czech crisis, the Grand Coalition, extra-parliamentary opposition and increasing growth disparities between IMF-countries all contributed to the cocktail of influences on policy-makers and corporate actors. But, with the increasing international strength of the German economy, the Bundesbank can be seen to identify a new and more assertive role for itself as a national and international actor. Where 'global steering' required a high degree of coordination in economic governance between monetary and fiscal authorities, Bundesbank action in 1969 was unquestionably a demonstration of breaking ranks, of denying support to government policy – on the pretext of 'safeguarding the currency' – where in the short-term the currency was subject to more violent external disturbances. Balance of payments stability could have been better ensured by 'clinging to low rates of interest' as Emminger

---

[71] Emminger, 'Deutsche Geld- und Währungspolitik im Spannungsfeld zwischen innerem und äußerem Gleichgewicht' 1948–1975', in: Deutsche Bundesbank (ed.), *Währung und Wirtschaft in Deutschland*, op.cit. p.519

[72] Emminger concedes that this month-long debate 'in the open market place' was an 'historically unique case' (ibid.)

[73] Holtfrerich, 'Monetary Policy', op.cit. p. 394

describes Bundesbank policy in 1968.[74] However, by convincing the ambitious Social Democrats within the federal cabinet that revaluation was the only feasible course of action, the Bank ensured a paralysing split in the Grand Coalition and a corresponding increase in its autonomous power. The interim float in October 1969 and the subsequent revaluation were only one stage in a more significant struggle which ended in flexible exchange rates and a qualitative shift in the Bank's room for manoeuvre.

Two factors made the transition to flexible exchange rates and a new enhanced monetary autonomy easier: an over-heating domestic economy and the rolling crisis of the Dollar and the US economy.

Firstly, the apparent success of Karl Schiller's Keynesian experiment in overcoming the 1967 recession and restoring the elusive 'magic square' was beginning to unravel in 1969. Trade union moderation in 1967 in the interest of boosting profits and employment had led to grass roots unease as profits grew far more strongly than forecast and many union members were still bound by 18-month pay deals. Attempts to rectify the anomaly within the tripartite forum of 'Concerted Action' proved fruitless, a situation made worse by the Social Democrat economics minister backtracking on his conception of 'social symmetry'; the pledge to restore pre-1967 distribution ratios, after union agreement to a temporary reallocation of national income in favour of profits, was altered to the objective of increased real incomes for all.[75] The result was an untimely series of wildcat strikes in September 1969 on the eve of the federal election and wage settlements which succeeded in bursting through the restraints of the voluntary incomes policy; order books were full and businesses could afford higher nominal increases. More specific problems of Schiller's demand management were becoming evident in the acceleration of state demand, not at the low point in the cycle but in 1969 when growth was most vigorous. With other unavoidable elements of state expenditure – on the educational and social infrastructure and on the Munich Olympics (!) – German Keynesianism produced a colossal pro-cyclical surge with rates of inflation reaching 3.7 per cent in 1970, 5.2 per cent in 1971 and 7 per cent in 1973. Even before the stagflationary crisis 1974–75, the contradictions of Keynesianism were becoming apparent which certainly weakened any residual commitment of the central bank to supporting state fiscal policy. By the same token it provided the bank

---

[74] Emminger, 'Deutsche Geld- und Währungspolitik', op.cit. p.517
[75] Further details in: Leaman, *Political Economy*, op.cit. pp.179–81

with powerful ammunition to support its own demands for enhanced monetary powers.[76]

Secondly, the exchange rate adjustments during 1969 were insufficient to alter the (long-standing) structural weakness of the US balance of payments; Emminger was arguably right in suggesting the revaluation was over a year overdue.[77] While Germany's liquidity surplus was eased by net outflows of capital in the final months of 1969, US rate reductions in 1970 – aimed at stimulating economic growth – produced a renewed migration of vagabond capital from the US into German and other European securities; by 1971 the 'influx increasingly swamped the German monetary system'.[78] The US current account deficit worsened in 1971 to $–10.6 billion, the overall balance of payments – including short-term capital transactions – fell to $–30.5 billion. Long before the globalisation of financial markets in the 1980s, there was already talk of international money markets representing a 'surrogate bank of issue'. The then vice-president of the Bundesbank, Otmar Emminger, asserts a virtual powerlessness of the Bank to influence affairs: 'In this period it was no longer the German currency authorities but predominantly the liquidity policy changes of American credit policy and the speculative to and fro of vagabond masses of Dollars which determined the supply of money to the German economy'.[79] The crisis of the US economy was undoubtedly also a crisis of the trading and payments system of which it was the anchor. When it is no longer the anchor currency which supports the currencies of junior bloc partners, but vice versa, the dangers of the 'predatory hegemon' (Susan Strange) become apparent. A mutual, if unequal interdependence obliges the junior partners to sustain the purchasing power of the bloc leader through contractually (not economically) based interventions, allowing the latter's population to live above its means for an extended period. The extent of these interventions between 1970 and 1973 was undeniably disruptive to the pursuit of stability in European economies.

The dysfunction of German Keynesianism and the weakness of the US economy nevertheless do not absolve the Bundesbank from all responsibility, as Emminger (above) would like us to believe. It had

---

[76] Further to the problems of German demand management see: Leaman, ibid. pp.181–93

[77] Emminger, 'Deutsche Geld- und Währungspolitik', op.cit. p.520

[78] Deutsche Bundesbank, *Annual Report for 1971*, p.30

[79] Emminger, ibid. p.523

views about the resolution of its monetary policy dilemmas and it pursued measures which, however haphazardly, sought to achieve that resolution. In essence this involved weakening or breaking the Dollar link and the strengthening of monetary controls either in the framework of European monetary cooperation or on its own.

This helps to explain why, after the October 1968 realignment, the Bank chose to push the Lombard rate to 9 per cent in December 1969 and then to 9½ per cent in March 1970, with a parallel rise in the discount rate in March from 6 per cent to 7½ per cent, and why it chose not to allow the disequilibrium of US and German balances of payments time to resolve themselves, if only marginally. Rate rises in Germany, combined with rate reductions in the US noted above, could only have the opposite effect of reversing the stabilising effects of capital outflows from Germany in the last quarter of 1969. Bank policy thus contributed in part to the worsening of the dollar crisis, i.e. to undermining the Bretton Woods system. This coincided with discussions at EEC level about enhancing monetary cooperation. The Hague Conference of December 1969, designed to 'deepen' European integration, commissioned among other things a report on the modalities of monetary union by a special committee chaired by Werner, the Luxembourg Minister-President. An interim report was presented to the Council of Ministers in May 1970, with the final document released in October the same year. Although the report's recommendations were ultimately overturned by renewed currency crises in 1971, they are significant inasmuch as they foreshadowed a new primacy of monetary policy, acknowledged the need for a critical mass in international monetary affairs (including a European central bank) and, by implication, sought to neutralise the negative effects of association with the USA. To this extent, the Bundesbank was content to be associated with the project, even though it did not hide its scepticism.[80] The Werner Report also recommended the establishment of narrower bands within which linked EC currencies could fluctuate with each other in relation to the Dollar. This objectively meant a tightening of the IMF margins but was generally perceived as containing 'the beginnings of a detachment from the dollar'.[81] The plan to narrow fluctuation bands was agreed by the Committee of Central

---

[80] Viz. Deutsche Bundesbank, *Annual Report for 1970*, pp.42–43; also Dorothee Heisenberg, *The Mark of the Bundesbank. Germany's Role in European Monetary Cooperation*, Boulder/ London 1999, p.29

[81] Heisenberg, *Mark of the Bundesbank*, ibid. p.30

Bank governors, with implementation earmarked for June 1971, but was abandoned in the wake of renewed turbulence in early 1971; hot money flooded into Germany in even larger waves, resulting in the closure by the Bundesbank of foreign exchange markets from 5 May to 9 May, when they reopened on 10 May, the Bundesbank announced a temporary halt to its interventions in support of the dollar, thus effectively floating the DM once more, as in September 1969. The promise of monetary cooperation à la Werner Report evaporated. However, there were no significant changes in the direction of global capital flows out of the dollar. In August 1971 the US government therefore suspended the dollar's gold convertibility which signified the effective floating of most of the other IMF currencies until the formally agreed realignment of the Smithsonian Agreement in Washington in December 1971: this saw the 7.9 per cent devaluation of the Dollar, the IMF's anchor currency, and the revaluation of other member currencies, including a 4.6 per cent rise in the DM parity. Furthermore, the fluctuation margins for currencies within the system were widened to ±2¼ per cent from ±1 per cent. While EU-countries sought closer cooperation in the 'Snake' established in April 1972, the inadequacy of the December 1971 adjustment became apparent in June 1972 with a further crisis of sterling, which ended in its being floated unilaterally. The final nail in the Bretton Woods coffin was delivered by massive sales of the Dollar in January and February 1973, where IMF member states were obliged to make repeated and expensive interventions in the currency markets. The Bundesbank alone bought some 24 billion DM worth of foreign currencies in this period, including $2.7 billion (DM 7.5 billion) on just one day, 1 March; on 2 March the Bundesbank German currency markets were closed. In the interim period, EEC member states voted to implement a block floating of their currencies. This followed on 17 March; interventions in support of the dollar were ended. With this the remains of Bretton Woods were laid to rest.The politics of Bundesbank decisions in this period are highly significant, in that the Bank's urging of a joint floating of EEC currencies in March 1973 came at the end of a momentous struggle with the federal government, in which a majority of CBC members doggedly opposed floating and urged swingeing capital controls instead. The new president of the Bundesbank, Karl Klasen, like his predecessor Blessing stressed the importance of maintaining the competitiveness of German exporters and upholding international monetary commitments. It was a view shared initially by a majority of CBC members and by a majority of the Brandt Cabinet but in opposition to Karl Schiller (who by 1971 held both the Economics and the Finance portfolios) who favoured a collective float of European currencies. Schiller's fierce rejection of capital controls and preference for market mechanisms produced a direct confrontation firstly with the Bundesbank in May 1971 and secondly with both the Bank and the federal cabinet a year later after the floating of sterling in June 1972. The cabinet, constantly irked by Schiller's imperious style, unanimously sided with Klasen and rejected a group float. Schiller resigned both his cabinet posts and was replaced as Economics Minister by Helmut Schmidt. Government and Bank continued to improvise a rather hapless set of dirigiste measures, including the licencing of foreign purchases of German securities and the imposition of a cash deposit obligation for all loans taken out abroad by German individuals or companies.

There was far less unanimity within the Bundesbank than within the cabinet. The majority in the CBC in favour of capital controls in May 1971 was only 11 to 7, with Klasen heading the dirigiste group and his vice-president Emminger the collective float group.[82]   The ineffectiveness of dirigiste controls, together with the increasing confusion in foreign exchange relations produced a gradual conversion of the CBC to joint floating. The process was aided by the absence through sickness of Karl Klasen in the crucial period in early 1973. It is sufficient to note that within less than a year of Schiller's resignation, his proposal for a collective floating of EEC currencies was finally implemented by the federal government, urged on by the Bundesbank, the Council of Economic Experts and the Academic Sub-Committee in the Economics Ministry. Helmut Schmidt remained unconvinced of the case for floating, but circumstances and a vigorous campaign by Emminger pushed cabinet opinion towards the inevitable.[83] In both instances, however – in the initial rejection of floating and the subsequent advocacy of floating – the Bundesbank's view prevailed, suggesting not just inconsistency but a high degree of opportunism in establishing its domestic political supremacy.

The route to the Bank's 'new-found freedom' (thus Marsh),[84] had certainly not been a direct one, based on doctrinal purity. From the

---

[82]   Thus Heisenberg, *Mark of the Bundesbank*, op.cit. p.31

[83]   It should be noted that Brandt also acknowledged the virtue of removing the dollar peg and acting independently of the US and had supported the principle of floating proposed by Schiller, even if he did not support him personally in the resignation issue.

[84]   Marsh, *The Bundesbank*, op.cit p.192

mid-1950s it had become increasingly aware of the 'cleft stick'[85] in which it found itself, where an exposed 'external economic flank' and the straitjacket of intervention obligations made domestic monetary measures largely 'self-defeating'.[86] In this context, but also in the practical context of furthering the recovery and expansion of German production and trade, policy responses were inevitably going to be spasmodic and non-doctrinaire. In addition the culture of expectations built up around the institution of an autonomous central bank – that it would regularly demonstrate its imperviousness to government influence – produced a number of symbolic skirmishes which signified no more than the need for self-demarcation. Towards the end of this period, however, the erratic deployment of monetary policy levers reflected both an (understandable) dissatisfaction with the US-led system of fixed exchange rates and an attempt to make it less rather than more workable. The Bank's annual reports from 1968 onwards demonstrate this growing disillusionment, even though the language is diplomatic. The 1972 report, published in the Spring of 1973, expresses the certainty 'that a future exchange rate system will contain a greater measure of flexibility than hitherto for the adjustment of external disequilibria'.[87]

In retrospect, there seems to be little doubt that the Bank's exercising of autonomy in this period was driven by the need not just to maintain but to extend that autonomy, above all to remove the dysfunctional influence of an exchange rate system that made its job impossible. Emminger's judgement from 1976 that the end of Bretton Woods meant 'the recovery of control over the money supply' and the beginning of 'a completely new era for German monetary policy'[88] is echoed by several Bank and other commentators.[89] More significantly

---

[85] Schlesinger, 'Geldpolitik' op.cit. p.555

[86] Emminger uses the English metaphor to characterise the Bank's fundamental dilemma in the final stages of Bretton Woods, 'Deutsche Geld- und Währungspolitik', op.cit. p.533

[87] *Annual Report for 1972*, p.38

[88] Emminger, 'Deutsche Geld- und Währungspolitik', op.cit. p.533

[89] Norbert Kloten, who joined the CBC as president of the Baden-Württemberg LCB in 1976: 'At last the Bundesbank regained control of monetary affairs', 'Erfolg und Mißerfolg der Stabilisierungspolitik', in: Deutsche Bundesbank (ed.) *Währung und Wirtschaft in Deutschland*, op.cit. p.658; Jürgen von Hagen talks extravagantly about the 'emancipation of monetary policy', 'A New Approach to Monetary

for this study, it represented a qualitative shift in the power of the Bundesbank in relation to all other domestic political actors. Keynesianism, with its implied need for coordination, became unworkable as a result of its own contradictions, the onset of stagflation and the central bank's increased manoeuvrability. The era of full-blown German monetarism had arrived.

Policy 1971–8', in: Deutsche Bundesbank (ed.), *Fifty Years of the Deutsche Mark*, op.cit. 411ff

5   Towards Dominance: Central Bank Politics 1973–1982

The proponents of flexible exchange rates advanced two core hypotheses which can, but need not necessarily be linked. Firstly, Milton Friedman argued that the replacement of the Bretton Woods system by a 'system' of floating currencies would reduce exchange rate volatility, by allowing financial markets autonomatically to interpret the macro-economic signals of national GDP growth, inflation, trade and payments balances with adjustments which would tend towards equilibrium.[1] Secondly, Robert Mundell and others maintained that national monetary policy could be considerably more effective under a system of flexible exchange rates, since it would liberate policy makers from the dilemma of defending both external and internal stability, when either international growth cycles or structural trade asymmetries made this impossible under a system of fixed exchange rates.[2] While subsequent empirical evidence indicates that the first hypothesis was seriously flawed and that the twenty-six years since the end of Bretton Woods has been characterised by severe and disruptive exchange rate volatility,[3] the second hypothesis has at least some measure of plausibility about it, even if this applies more to the Bundesbank than to other agencies of monetary policy. Certainly, the Bundesbank's operational room for manoeuvre was greatly increased by the suspension of the dollar peg, such that Jürgen von Hagen can talk of the

---

[1] Milton Friedman, 'The Case for Flexible Exchange Rates', in: M.Friedman, *Essays in Positive Economics*, Chicago 1953, pp.157–203
[2] Robert Mundell, 'A Theory of Optimum Currency Areas', in: *American Economic Review*, Vol. 51 (1961), pp. 657–65
[3] In particular, see: Barry Eichengreen, Andrew K. Rose and Charles Wyplosz, 'Exchange Market Mayhem: the antecedents and aftermath of speculative attacks', in: *Economic Policy*, No.21, 1995, pp.251–312

'emancipation of monetary policy' in 1973.[4] This was reflected in a new confidence within the CBC, boosted by its victories over the federal government and the partial discrediting of Keynesianism, a confidence which was initially expressed in the transition to monetary targeting in 1974. While policy hitherto had been driven by improvisation and (sporadic) attempts to manage bank liquidity, announcing a single percentage target for the expansion of narrow money (the 'central bank money stock') was deemed less of a hostage to fortune than in the reconstruction period when high rates of GDP growth were accompanied by high and unpredictable rates of growth for both narrow and broad money. As well as being more feasible, the CBC perceived a political value in a specific target, making it 'easier to withstand political pressure' and 'signalling to the public ....the intention of not allowing monetary growth to get out of control'.[5]

At the same time, while 1973 may have marked a temporary resolution to the crisis of exchange rate speculation and management, it also signalled the transition to an extended period of global disequilibrium in which the underlying asymmetries of the Bretton Woods crisis actually increased – contrary to expectations – with corresponding shifts in the balance of power within the global economy. Thus, within the industrialised 'North' the economies with higher levels of productivity and trade growth, higher investment ratios and a relative intensity of research and development (Germany and Japan) tended towards structural surpluses, while less successful economies with lower investment ratios and lower productivity growth (Britain) tended towards structural deficits.   Similar asymmetries emerged in relations between developed and the majority of developing countries. Apart from oil, the relationship between high grade exports from the industrialised North and the primary and semi-finished goods of the developing South has consistently favoured the North since the Second World War; the falling terms of trade of developing countries mean that larger volumes of coffee, cocoa, copper or other primary goods have to be traded to finance the purchase of the same volume of imported finished goods.   The leverage of both German private economic actors and German political agencies, like the Bundesbank, was thus increased vis-à-vis both other OECD countries and less developed countries. This new hierarchy of global power relations was

---

[4] Jürgen von Hagen, 'A New Approach to Monetary Policy' (1971–8), op.cit. 411ff
[5] von Hagen, ibid. p.425

emerging before the onset of the first oil crisis in 1974. Given that the reputation of the Bundesbank (and of German economic governance in general was enhanced by experiences of the 1970s ('Modell Deutschland'), 'An object-lesson in economic management'), it is important to stress this fact both to qualify the blanket assertion that floating benefits (all) monetary policy and to develop a broader case for questioning the notion that the institutional form of monetary policy in Germany can be seen as a paradigm that can be transplanted into utterly different politico-economic contexts.

The title of this chapter – 'towards dominance' – should nevertheless not be understood in terms of progress towards a strengthened primacy of (monetary) politics in relation to 'the' market but rather in terms of a less obvious erosion of state powers compared a) to other (fiscal) agencies of the German state b) to both the fiscal and monetary agencies of other developed countries and c) to both private and state agencies in less developed countries. The Bundesbank's 'hegemony' is thus relative: to the powerlessness of other central banks, to other state agencies and to some other private economic agents. It also reflects the shift to the new dominance of monetarist thinking which, in the apparent absence of other presciptive policy solutions, represented a *faute de mieux* to policy makers at the time. Furthermore, monetarism as an 'order political' rather than 'process political' doctrine,[6] is closely related to neo-liberal thinking and thus implies a desire to strengthen the power of market forces and to minimise state interference. What this and the following chapter are at pains to demonstrate is that the monetarist revolution did not simply help to destroy the so-called Keynesian consensus but contributed to the weakening of all state power, including that of central banks, by aiding the birth of 'casino capitalism' and its fundamental form of 'monetary accumulation' (see below).[7] For a time, central banks like the Bundesbank may, under optimal circumstances, be able to influence domestic and international flows of capital and corporate decision-

---

[6] The German category of *Ordnungspolitik* expresses policy orientation towards maintaining a healthy framework for market activity, in contrast to *Prozesspolitik* which is more akin to Keynesian fine-tuning of the business cycle via regular fiscal and other interventions.

[7] Elmar Altvater uses the category monetary accumulation to describe the self-adequate sphere of financial investments which since the end of the 1970s has operated separately from the 'real productive' economy; see E. Altvater, *Die Zukunft des Marktes*, op.cit. 143ff

making marginally, but the exchange rate crises of recent years have demonstrated that no central bank, not even the Bundesbank or the Federal Reserve, has the resources to outmanoeuvre the unfettered forces of global financial markets as they exist today.

To return to the 1970s, the accession of the Bundesbank to the key position in the economic governance of the Federal Republic coincided with the onset of stagflation. This combination of stagnation/recession with inflation had been considered a theoretical impossibility by all major schools of neo-classical economics, which had always postulated a 'trade-off' between the movement of prices and employment: the Phillips-Curve had – using long-series data from the British economy – seemingly demonstrated that high unemployment always coincided with low inflation and vice versa. Keynesian demand management was based on the trade-off premise. Helmut Schmidt, successor to Schiller as economics minister in 1972 accordingly expressed the preference for 5 per cent inflation rather than 5 per cent unemployment.[8] When he took over from Willy Brandt as chancellor in 1974, the option of one or the other had evaporated: German domestic price increases, already high as a result of cyclical overheating, were driven even higher by the raising of crude oil prices from a mere $1 a barrel to over $10 by the the the Organisation of Petroleum Exporting Countries (OPEC); industrial employment fell by 3.6 per cent, private investment by 13.2 per cent in real terms, GNP-growth slumped from 4.9 per cent in 1973 to just 0.4 per cent in 1974. 1975, the year of severe recession (GNP: –1.9 per cent) saw a clear demonstration of the demise of the Phillips Curve with 6 per cent inflation and 4.7 per cent unemployment; 1976 – the year of recovery – still showed inflation of 4.5 per cent and unemployment of 4.6 per cent, together with a further rise in bankruptcies over 1975 (9362 compared to 9195), and this despite real GNP growth of 5.1 per cent. The Keynesian option of counter-cyclical fiscal management was rendered problematic by the coincidence of features of both boom and slump in a configuration considered impossible in textbooks hitherto; by the pro-cyclical surge of the state ratio (share of state expenditure in GDP), which rose from 41.6 per cent in the recessionary year of 1967 to 45.6 per cent in 1973 when the rate of growth hit 4.9 per cent; within overall state expenditure, the key Keynesian variable of state investment had also developed pro-cyclically (notably within the period of open Keynesian experimentation), but began a period of consistent decline from 1970 (16.4 per cent) through 1974 (13.1 per cent) to 1977

---

[8] *Süddeutsche Zeitung*, 28 July 1972

(10.2 per cent), while expenditure on state personnel rose from 27.9 per cent of total expenditure in 1967 to 33.4 per cent in 1974;[9] the renewed reluctance of regional and local authorities to cooperate in coordinated fiscal programmes (like the two investment programmes of 1967) since these had ended up burdening them with significant subsequent costs, despite generous initial grants from the federal government;[10] the structural impediment of an independent central bank with increased scope for autonomous action.

The deep recession of 1975 obliged all levels of government to increase their expenditure to absorb some of the direct cost of unemployment, which rose to 1.07 million; in turn public borrowing was increased because of the indirect effect of recession on tax revenues. The full effect of the decline in employment (22.9 million in 1973 to 22.0 million in 1975) was cushioned by the official stop to labour immigration in 1973 and the subsequent repatriation of 706 000 foreign workers between 1974 and 1977. Nevertheless, the surge in state borrowing had significant implications for capital markets and for the operation of monetary policy. With free liquid reserves dropping very significantly from over 30 billion DM in 1969 to 14.8 billion DM in 1971 and to 3 billion and 4.5 billion in 1973 and 1974, and with the country's capital balance moving into a considerable deficit in 1974 (– 25 billion DM) and 1975 (–13 billion DM) the scope for monetary policy to bear down on domestic inflation was suddenly considerable. After a pro-cyclical relaxation of both discount and Lombard rates through 1971 and 1972, the Bundesbank proceeded to raise both rates rapidly in 1973, despite the initial signs of cyclical weakness, and maintained relatively high rates through to May 1975 (see Table 5.1 below).

The indicators of investment activity, unemployment trends, capacity utilisation and bankruptcies all suggested problems during 1974 at the latest. The Bundesbank's own figures for industrial production showed a peak in September 1973 and rapid deceleration from April 1974. The construction sector displayed year-on-year

---

[9]   Figures from Kurt Biedenkopf & Meinhard Miegel, *Die programmierte Krise*, Bonn 1979 and own calculations
[10] Further details in: J.Leaman, *Political Economy of West Germany*, op.cit. p.190; the borrowing requirement of German local authorities rose to 7.6 per cent in 1971 and 8.1 per cent in 1972, considerably higher than central government

negative growth rates from March 1973 and absolute monthly falls
from June 1973.

Table 5.1   Monetary Policy and Stagflation, 1973–75

Date	DR %	LR %	IR %	UE %	CU %	B	I
1973							
(12 Jan)	5	7	0.3	1.3	86.7	5 515	6.9
(4 May)	6	8					
(1 June)	7	9					
1974							
(25 Oct)	6.5	8.5	–13.2	2.6	81.7	7 772	7.0
(20 Dec)	6	8					
1975							
(7 Feb)	5.5	7.5	–4.5	4.7	77.7	9 195	6.0
(7 March)	5	6.5					
(25 April)	5	6					
(23 May)	4.5	5.5					
(15 Aug)	4	5					
(12 Sept)	3.5	4.5					

DR: Discount Rate; LR: Lombard Rate; IR: change in per cent; UE:
Unemployment rate; CU: Capacity Utilisation (WSI definition); B:
bankruptcies; I: rate of inflation (CPI)

Sources: Bundesbank, Monthly reports, own calculations

The decline in consumer goods production was sharp from 175.6 (1962
= 100) in September 1973 to 150.3 in January 1974 and 136.6 in July
1974. The development of industrial orders, also monitored by the
Bundesbank, showed monthly falls for all industry from June 1973;
aggregate industrial orders were prevented from falling too far by
buoyant foreign demand through 1973 and 1974 but the global trade
crisis brought on by increased energy costs produced a slump in
international orders of –12.2 per cent in 1975, neutralising a slight
recovery in domestic demand. The Bundesbank was clearly not blind
to these developments, but asserted strongly that they were a necessary
'price' for monetary stabilisation. The Bank used the price metaphor in
its annual report for 1974, i.e. before the full impact of its deflationary

policies had fed through.[11] The irony of the high macro-economic price for a lower macro-economic price-level clearly escaped the authors of this and later reports. The justification, or rather 'the only justification' for the credit squeeze is significantly doctrinaire: 'there was no real alternative to the stabilisation policy'.[12] Both 1974 and 1975 Annual Reports are at pains to stress that Bank policy had been coordinated with the federal government. The assertion is disingenuous in three senses. Firstly, the federal government was being made painfully aware of the inflationary mess caused in part by ill-conducted fiscal policies between 1968 and 1972 and of the new political leverage of the central bank; institutionally, there was no alternative but to subordinate itself to the Bank's monetary priorities. Secondly, the fact of an anti-inflationary squeeze has to be distinguished from its intensity, its timing or its duration; in this latter respect, there were very clear worries within the Social Democratic Party that policy on the part of an unelected and unanswerable central bank would exact an electoral as well as an economic price.[13] Thirdly, the Bundesbank – while acknowledging the imported nature of oil-price inflation – proceeded to treat price rises in Germany as a domestic phenomenon, by exerting pressure on factors of domestic production and demand like investment, wages and employment. The postulated absence of an alternative conflicts with the reality of alternative policies in other OECD countries, where institutional arrangements allowed a different policy-mix; in Britain and France, for example, the political and social dangers of high unemployment convinced both governments to prioritise the fight against recession and unemployment; Britain and France were able at least to assert Helmut Schmidt's preference for inflation over unemployment, an option denied the Schmidt government itself. Admittedly, the British and French policy mix failed in the medium term, but this failure can in part be ascribed to the international effects of high interest rates on capital flows and the balance of payments (i.e. to the application of monetarism in countries like Germany) and more broadly to the failure of the whole industrialised world to devise a

---

[11] Stabilistion could not be achieved 'without exacting a price from the economy as a whole and without individual sacrifices', *Annual Report* 1974, p.1

[12] *Annual Report* 1974, ibid.

[13] See in particular the lengthy article in *Der Spiegel* (17 February 1975), 'Stürzt knappes Geld die SPD'

coordinated and consistent response to what was an extraordinary exogenous shock to the global business cycle.

Within the post-Bretton-Woods hierarchy of political agencies worldwide, the central bank of Europe's dominant industrial economy with its long-standing structural trade surpluses was in an optimal position to pursue national economic and domestic political priorities without the encumbrance of a coordinated supra-national strategy. Understandably, perhaps the domestic economic and political cost of Bretton Woods commitments (and the flaws of domestic policy coordination under Schiller) had taught Bundesbank strategists the advantages of autonomy (qua self-legislation). The Bank's statutory duties were also more clear-cut than those of other central banks, including the Federal Reserve, whose remit explicitly includes furthering growth and employment. According to German national law, the Bundesbank arguably had no option in the impossible choice between inflation or unemployment but to attack inflation with the limited indirect weapons at its disposal, and the federal government had no other option than to accept the consequences of the separation of monetary and fiscal powers.

It is undeniable that German price inflation was more readily brought under control in 1976 (4.3 per cent) 1977 (3.7 per cent) and 1978 (2.7 per cent) than in most other OECD countries,[14] but it is naïve firstly to ascribe this record predominantly to the influence of German monetary policy and secondly to assume that this 'success' was not accompanied by significant macro-economic and macro-political costs.

A major contributory factor in delivering low inflation in Germany, not just in the period under discussion but throughout the post-war period, was the particular nature of the country's political economy:

Institutionally, the time horizons of German companies are longer than those in other economic cultures. The interpenetration of industrial and finance capital through the unique system of universal banks provides medium-term security for the larger manufacturing and service enterprises which are the main exporters, the main employers and the main corporate taxpayers. The long-term and substantial stakes of

---

[14] Germany's inflation record in the 1970s was the best of all industrialised countries, with an average of 4.89 per cent p.a., almost matched by Switzerland (4.98 per cent), but considerably better than major European partners: Netherlands (7.06), Belgium (7.13), France (8.90), Denmark (9.29), Italy (12.33), UK (12.63); the USA (7.10) and Japan (9.09) are also significantly adrift.

German universal banks in companies like Daimler-Benz, Bayer, BASF, Hoechst, Krupp-Thyssen, Hochtief etc. provides a reciprocal quality of security which does not exist in the standard creditor-debtor relationship of a British, French or American retail bank. The latter seek an asset security from corporate borrowers, but provide no more security themselves than the credit contract terms. Deutsche Bank, in operating as both major shareholder and house bank to Daimler-Benz and many other major companies, sits on both sides of the creditor-debtor divide; it lends itself money in effect and has indubitably a corresponding interest in ensuring the medium- and long-term commercial effectiveness of its credit operations, just as it would in self-financed investments in its core banking activities. Corporate credit in Germany is thus to a very large extent distinct from corporate credit in countries where universal banks are illegal; it is *more strongly immunised against the short term manipulation of central bank discount rates or indeed to short-term market rates*. While it would be naïve to suggest that German companies do not seek to take advantage of the price advantages of booms to protect themselves from future cyclical downturns, the pressure to profiteer is reduced by the reduced short-term pressure to ammortize debt and by longer-term prospects of healthy returns on capital. Furthermore universal banking helps to neutralise the debtor's interest in devaluing debt via inflation because, with the reciprocal holdings of non-banks in banks, the big corporate debtor would undermine its own financial assets as shareholder.

The long-termism of Germany's private economy is strengthened by a corporate culture which is historically 'risk-averse' and which seeks protection from the vicissitudes of the market in a way which is uncommon in, say, Anglo-Saxon economies. Such protection is offered by highly disciplined and effective trade associations which impose strict rules of corporate behaviour on their members in terms of contract compliance (prompt payment, above all) and facilitate a variety of cooperative activities in research, development, consortial export projects and – historically – in straightforward cartel activities.[15] Trade associations have also traditionally provided the basis for centralised pay-bargaining with branch-based trade unions which ensure a higher degree of cost-predictability than in the decentralised, enterprise-based

---

[15] J. Leaman, 'Industrial and commercial cultures in Britain and Germany: Rivalry or Reconcilability?' in K.Larres and E.Meehan (eds), *Uneasy Allies: British German Relations and European Integration since 1945*, Oxford 2000, 212f

systems of industrial relations elsewhere. Long-termism is also built into the consistently highly-refined system of training and craft skills which ensures predictability of the supply of skills for all agents within the labour market to operate with and accordingly helps to avoid wage inflation as a result of sudden and unforeseen skill shortages.

Finally, the generalised fear of inflation has not been simply embedded in political institutions but in the collective memory of the German population, as has been observed at several stages in this study. The inappropriateness of price- and wage-inflation as a strategic option for enterprises, workforces or policymakers is thus more strongly fixed in German economic culture and manifested itself in the actions of trade unionists and companies in the wake of both the 1974 and the 1979 oil crises.

These are the specific reasons why the culture of expectations regarding price levels and the timescale of economic processes operated differently in the mid-1970s (and continues to operate now). Even if the transmission mechanisms in other market economies operate according to monetarist assumptions of responsiveness to the indirect leverage of short-term interest rates, there is a strong case for arguing that these mechanisms apply far less in Germany. However, there is also a clear case for doubting the general argument of efficacious monetarist policy, as it applied in the 1970s.

MONETARY TARGETING

The transition to monetary targeting in 1974 was a strange affair. It was presented as an act of decisive, scientific and authoritative policy which deserved the complete confidence of other political agencies and the general public. The background to the transition, as von Hagen has described it, was anything but authoritative: 'There was initially some reservation about publishing the target. A number of members (of the CBC: JL) were of the opinion that the flexibility of monetary policy ought not to be restricted by artificial barriers. Others expressed doubts whether the money stock could be controlled precisely enough. It was also questioned whether the relationship between nominal output and the money stock could be quantified with sufficient accuracy'.[16] The doubts were entirely justified. In the first four years of the operation of single figure targeting (1975–78), the targets were never met. Despite

---

[16] Jürgen von Hagen, 'A New Approach to Monetary Policy', op. cit. p. 425

significant fluctuations in economic fundamentals, the CBC stuck to the same target for the expansion of the central bank money stock of 8 per cent for four successive years; in each year there was an overshoot, in 1975 of 2 per cent, in 1976 and 1977 of 1 per cent and in 1978 of 3 per cent. CBC discussions suggest that the choice of 8 per cent was essentially symbolic. The sudden reference to a monetary target would, according to a majority view within the CBC, 'in the case of recession ... make it easier to withstand political pressure for more rapid monetary growth. Last but not least, a monetary target was in accordance with the wishes of those calling for a steadier, more rules-based policy. The decisive point was that setting a monetary target was opportune for a number of reasons and thus received majority support'.[17] 8 per cent happened to coincide with official forecasts of 2 per cent growth and 6 per cent inflation, such that it would not be too much of a hostage to fortune nor suggest too deflationary a stance; secondly it coincided with the potential-oriented view that sought to match the growth of productive potential with an unavoidable level of price inflation. Given that forecasts for these were 3 per cent and 5 per cent respectively, the 8 per cent target was again a safe bet. The fact that inflation in 1975 ended at 5.9 per cent and there was a severe recession did not shake the Bundesbank's resolve, nor decisively public confidence in the institution.

What this reveals about the social psychology of targeting is a matter for a great deal of speculation. It is clear that the success of the target indicator was less important to the main economic agents and to informed observers than the success of the general task of 'safeguarding the currency'. The strengths of Germany's trading economy and its economic culture made an inflationary spiral much less likely than in other (deficit) countries. Monetary activism was thus a politically astute option. Setting an exclusively monetary target had the added advantage that it underscored Germany's single agency approach to currency stability, indeed it was a more effective signal of the end of Keynesian mixed targets (the 'magic square') than an inflation target. This was one the Stability Act's four targets and could be more readily reconciled with the general state function of economic governance, even with a clear separation of responsibilities. The money stock target signalled the transition to monetarism and a new hierarchy of responsibilities in a very obvious way. There was also a feeling within government circles, during the period of interest relaxation (1976–1978) that money stock

---

[17] von Hagen, ibid.

targeting 'served to steady monetary policy and take it out of day-to-day politics',[18] i.e. by providing an orientation point for economic actors it signalled the possibility of the threat of intervention as a preemptive means of discipline rather than a response to already existing indiscipline.

Nevertheless, there were doubts within the CBC about the implications of monetary targeting for both its theoretical stance and public perceptions of its role. In 1977 an internal discussion paper questioned the danger of linking money stock growth to national output in any given year, because this conflicted with the (monetarist) view of clear time-lags between money stock changes and real economic outcomes. At the end of the year 'one member of the Directorate voiced strong opposition to the policy of monetary targeting. Looking retrospectively at 1977, an improved interest-rate policy, involving earlier cuts in rates, would, he argued, have improved the state of the real economy, eased the external position and perhaps even enabled the Bundesbank to control the monetary expansion more effectively by blocking the inflow of foreign currency'; there was a real danger that the Bank would 'allow itself to become the slave of a mere number'.[19] Such doubts were not aired in public and clearly failed to alter the Bank's long-term commitment to monetary targeting, even if it moved to the more flexible 'corridor' system in 1979, with a 3–4 per cent band within which the money stock would be allowed to fluctuate.

DOMESTIC TRANSMISSION PROCESSES

The mythology of the Bundesbank's 'object lesson in economic management' is based on the assumption of the effectiveness of its policy instruments. This applies above all to the responsiveness of the users of credit finance to the central bank's manipulation of its main levers, in the 1970s discount and Lombard rates and minimum reserve ratios: the central bank can control the money stock (and thereby inflation) by increasing/reducing pressure on commercial banks in their granting of credit to third parties. The primary problem about this hypothesis is that the levers remain very indirect instruments, 'blunt weapons', according to Reinhard Kohler, a contemporary observer.[20]

---

[18] von Hagen, ibid. p.429
[19] von Hagen, ibid. p.430
[20] Reinhard Kohler, 'Die Bremspolitik der Bundesbank hat noch nie richtig funktioniert', *Frankfurter Rundschau*, 27 June 1979; Kohler

As the fifties and sixties revealed, the central bank's leverage was considerably reduced by the existence of high bank liquidity and a correspondingly low demand for central bank money, as well as by high levels of corporate self-financing. Even in situations of lower bank liquidity and higher ratios of corporate borrowing ('gearing'), apart from the very exceptional use of rediscount quotas, the Bundesbank is not able actually to stem the flow of cash into the national economy; it is in fact obliged to exchange bank securities for cash whenever banks request it. Increased interest charges clearly do affect short-term costs but, according to Kohler, companies set cost calculations in the context of the expected short-, medium- or long-term return on investment, depending on the nature of the enterprise.[21] Banks in turn provide credit to companies, state bodies and private individuals in relation to the security of the lending risk which varies significantly and, in the case of German banking, is strongly coloured by bank equity holdings in non-banks, as noted above. Kohler's conclusion is that the Bundesbank's 'blunt weapons' cannot and do not illicit a unitary response from the suppliers or users of credit and 'have never functioned properly'.

Profit expectations vary widely from branch to branch, from year to year, but most significantly in relation to the timescale of the investment and the size of the firm. The time horizon of a small textile manufacturer, thinking of purchasing additional machinery to fulfil a short-term order to one of a variety of customers, is radically different from that of a power company, needing to construct new capacity to fulfil expected demand in five-to-ten years time. The latter has to ignore short-term variations in credit costs in order to maximise the medium-term commercial advantage of being able to satisfy customer demand. (This is even more critical when, as is the case in Germany still, private power companies enjoy regional monopolies and are obliged to satisfy current and future demand of all users in that region). The former, particularly if operating within very tight margins, is self-evidently more sensitive to immediate rises in interest costs and does have the choice between consolidation and expansion. Even at the theoretical level, therefore, sharp credit squeezes by the central bank cannot have uniform effects and must thus be inefficient. It is also important to point out that, even when monopolistic enterprises borrow at higher rates of interest, the transmission effect is not to reduce price levels, since these

---

was assistant to the later Bundesbank director Claus Köhler from 1972 to 1974.

[21] Ibid.

can – in the case of the electricity company – be passed on to the consumer, but at best to encourage rationalisation of investments and reductions in the workforce.

The inefficiency/unfairness of the blanket short-term squeeze is reinforced by the fact that larger companies frequently have access to cheaper foreign credit, using their foreign assets as security, a facility clearly not available to medium-sized to small enterprises with their exclusive national location. For example, larger west German companies more than trebled their foreign borrowing in 1973 to 17.5 billion DM, when central bank rates leapt to 7 per cent and 9 per cent.[22] Unsurprisingly, in the same year 92 per cent of the bankruptcies were among companies employing fewer than 200 people.

The inherent danger of using the blunt weapons of interest rate manipulation or of altering minimum reserve ratios is that it accelerates the process of concentration by making life difficult for the enterprises who are not immune to or cannot escape from the policy effects. Already in 1960, the top fifty industrial companies turned over 33.5 per cent of all industrial turnover; by 1967 this ratio had risen to 42.5 per cent and has continued to rise since then.[23] Given the access of all these companies to credit outside the direct orbit of the German central bank, there is certainly room to doubt that a macro-economic policy aimed at influencing all credit decisions can hope to succeed if at least half of the objects of that policy are immune to its direct effects.

Given that the Bundesbank was aware during earlier crises of the existence and effect of foreign borrowing, the question arises as to the intended transmission effect of a contractive policy, if not to deter corporate credit. Herbert Schui concluded at the time that the primary object of this policy was wage settlements.[24] Schui quotes Norbert Kloten, chair of the Council of Economic Experts and from 1976

---

[22] See Herbert Schui, 'Opfer für die "Stabilität" - die krisenverschärfende Politik der Bundesbank', in: Huffschmid, J. & Schui, H. (eds), *Gesellschaft im Konkurs*, Cologne, 1977, p.368. In 1980, during the major credit squeeze of 1979–1982, the proportion of foreign borrowing to overall short-term loans by German industry stood at 40 per cent; thus *Frankfurter Rundschau*, 16 October 1980

[23] By 1997 the turnover of Germany's top fifty companies (industrial and commercial) corresponded to 48.2 per cent of GNP. Further details, J.Leaman, *Political Economy*, op.cit 65f; same author, *'Mergers and the unsocial market economy'*, in *Debatte* 5/2 (1997), pp.235-248

[24] Herbert Schui, 'Opfer für die "Stabilität", op.cit.370ff

President of the Baden-Württemberg LCB, commenting on wage settlements in 1974, that they had 'far exceeded anything that the macro-economic situation justified'. The disciplining effect of the crisis is articulated clearly in comments by the Academic Sub-Committee to the Economics Ministry from the year before: 'Negotiators in wage agreements can only be persuaded to take account of the stability of the value of money, if excessive increases of the nominal wage level can lead to reductions in employment without this causing immediate compensatory measures on the part of economic policy.'' This view of wage-driven unemployment (which in part sets aside the effect of the explosion of energy costs on corporations and households) is strongly evident in Bundesbank pronouncements in the wake of the oil-crisis: the 1976 Annual Report concludes that the 'major set of causes of the present labour market problem is the movement of wages in the first half of the decade' and that the solution lies in an 'income trend compatible with stability' and an 'improvement in basic conditions for investment'.[25] In this and subsequent reports the Bundesbank talks explicitly about the need for a 'correction of distribution ratios', and in the 1978 report expresses its satisfaction in the 'shift in the distribution of income in favour of entrepreneurial income' as a result of the 'sense of responsibility' exhibited by employers and trade unions.[26]

It is clear that, while the central bank was not able to influence the cost inflation involved in oil price rises nor the borrowing behaviour of the country's largest enterprises, wage costs could be influenced both by the rhetoric of moral suasion and via the leverage of employers' organisations which also represented the smaller and medium-sized enterprises which were more acutely exposed to higher credit costs. The success of employers in the engineering sector in negotiating a 5 per cent wage deal in the spring of 1978 with the biggest union, IG Metall, is acknowledged as contributing to the 'favourable' outcome of higher nominal increases in entrepreneurial income for that year (+11 per cent), compared to overall national income (+7.5 per cent) and wages and salaries (+6 per cent).[27] It represented the success, not of a refined coordinated policy strategy, but of a rather brutal, dishonest and inequitable approach that sought to manage the crisis on the back of wage and salary earners, using unemployment as a central lever. Shifting the distribution ratios in favour of capital pursued a well-

---

[25] Deutsche Bundesbank, *Annual Report* 1976, p.36 and p.38
[26] *Annual Reports*, 1976, p.39; 1977, p.40; 1978, p.9
[27] *Annual Report*, 1978, p.9

rehearsed logic of liberating resources for investment to boost production and employment, while depressing wage costs and thus mass consumer demand in order to generate growth through exports; the strategy was typical of post-war reconstruction and explicit in the Keynesian reforms of 1967, where the Council of Economic Experts (SVR) stressed the virtues of 'a wage policy which has a neutral effect on cost levels',[28] in the 1976 report the strategy was expressed in terms of 'minimum wage unemployment', caused not by technological nor exogenous factors but by trade unions which priced their members out of jobs.[29] While there were minority views within the SVR which rejected the crude analysis of 'minimum wage unemployment' (notably Claus Köhler, Werner Glastetter and later Dieter Mertens), the federal cabinet, led by the junior partner, the liberal Free Democrats, accepted the crisis strategy of boosting exports at the expense of mass incomes and social expenditure. This clearly had deeply felt implications for the political strategy of the senior coalition partner, the Social Democrats under Helmut Schmidt. While the latter sought to bask in the reflected glory of the country's relative success in conquering stagflation, the persistence of high unemployment and of costly government borrowing produced a fatalism within the party which is best reflected in the supposedly upbeat *Long-Term Programme*, published by the party in 1975. This 'orientation framework for the years 1975–1985 qualified its ambitious economic and social policy aims by underscoring the 'narrow limitations of our potential political actions'.[30]

The domestic transmission process of monetary policy in the first stagflationary crisis of 1973–75 was inevitable in the sense that the Bundesbank was statutorily obliged to address currency stability as its primary task and that the doctrinally prescribed credit squeeze would have a negative impact on domestic factors of production, most notably labour. Beyond this, however, the problematic domestic dimension of applying the monetary brakes involved persisting with the squeeze long after the recessionary signals had become clear; here, even in supply-side terms, unemployment would have risen to sufficiently critical

---

[28] Jahresgutachten, 1967 paras 248ff

[29] Jahresgutachten, 1976, para 278

[30] SPD (ed.), *Zweiter Entwurf eines ökonomisch-politischen Orientierungsrahmens für die Jahre 1975–1985*, Bonn 1975, § 2.1.2; for further analysis of the dilemmas of German Social Democracy, see: Leaman, *Political Economy*, op.cit 212ff; also Leaman, 'Central Banking and the Crisis of Social Democracy', op.cit., 28ff

levels to have influenced pay settlements without the burden of twelve
months worth of high interest rates.

Were monetary policy to have operated on a basis that was
'compatible' with the growth cycle the discount rate curve in the graph
above would have shadowed the growth curve of real GDP
approximately and been the mirror image of the unemployment curve.
As the graph shows, however, the squeeze intensified during 1973, as
unemployment rises and growth declines dramatically; the discount rate
only begins to come down in 1974 when the unemployment curve
climbs steeply upwards and real GDP contracts to –1.9 in 1975.

Chart 5.1   Stagflation and Monetary Policy in Germany,
                     1972–1978

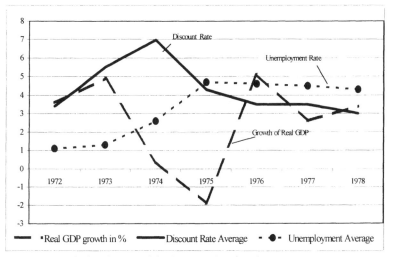

Source: Bundesbank, Monthly Reports (various).

Typically, the relaxation of monetary policy takes more incremental
changes over a longer period of time; while the application of the
squeeze in 1972 and 1973 took six steps over eight months, with three
half-point and three full-point changes, easing to pre-squeeze interest
rate levels (DR: 3 per cent; LR: 4 per cent) took eleven steps over a full
38½ months. This asymmetry of application patterns has no logical
explanation in terms of monetary theory – time-lags are assumed to
operate in reverse – so that one must conclude that the reasons were
contextual or structural: the global economic context will be discussed
below but, with the double shock of currency floating and oil price
rises, was clearly more volatile; the domestic political context involved

a social-liberal central government with at least residual welfarist and deficit-spending ambitions which, in terms of the new monetary orthodoxy still needed to be disciplined by raising the cost of such deficits. The Bundesbank's hagiographer dignifies the Bank's campaign in terms of its struggle with the 'expenditure beast', 'corrosive fiscal socialism';[31] while there were no such flights of rhetoric from Bank officials, Schlesinger's retrospective study of Keynesianism and state debt leaves little doubt that the Bank was involved in an ideological struggle with the deficit-spending mentality. The structural dimension to the asymmetry of squeezing and easing could be explained in terms of the psychology of authority examined in Chapter Two: the decisive stroke to demonstrate determination and power, the slower loosening to indicate that it represents a concession on the part of the powerful. In short, it resembles the psychology of the bully.

INTERNATIONAL TRANSMISSION MECHANISMS

When stagflation struck in 1974, the Bundesbank was operating in a radically new international context of flexible exchange rates and weakened fiscal regimes, a context which not only increased the relative strength of central banks and monetary policy but which above all favoured independent central banks, like the Bank of Switzerland and the Bundesbank, who could operate free from government instruction. This abstract structural power of the autonomous Bundesbank was buttressed in a crucial manner by the long-termism of Germany's economic culture and above all by the structural trading surpluses achieved by its key exporting industries: engineering, motor manufacturing, electro-technology and chemicals. The advance of the Deutsche Mark to become the second strongest reserve currency made the Bank's leverage among the global family of central banks, but in particular among the smaller family of European central banks linked through the 'snake' decisive and dominant. Within a system of freer capital movements, the interest rate behaviour of a leading central bank presiding over structural surpluses would of necessity influence the interest rate behaviour of subordinate, weaker central banks in countries with structural deficits, and in a fundamentally asymmetrical way. This is most easily demonstrated by the graphs below detailing the movements of selective central bank discount rates between 1973 and 1998. All the OECD countries selected were subject to similar effects

---

[31] Balkhausen, *Gutes Geld und schlechte Politik*, op.cit. 107f and 43ff

of imported inflation after 1973 and to different domestic factors like the growth patterns of GDP, productivity, unit wage costs which can also be deployed to explain the divergence of central bank discount rates in this and subsequent periods. Nevertheless, the core relevance of reserve currency status and external balances cannot be ignored: in 1975 (when statistical records of the composition of global currency reserves began), the dollar represented 78 per cent of all reserves, followed by the DM with 8.8 per cent and way in front of sterling (2.8 per cent), the Swiss Franc (2.2 per cent), the Yen (1.8 per cent) and the French Franc (1.8 per cent); by 1980, in the wake of the depreciation of the dollar and the appreciation of both DM and Yen, the dollar had slipped to 68 per cent, the DM had almost doubled to 15.3 per cent while the Yen had moved to 4.4 per cent of total reserves.

Chart 5.2　　　Discount Rates Compared, 1973–1998

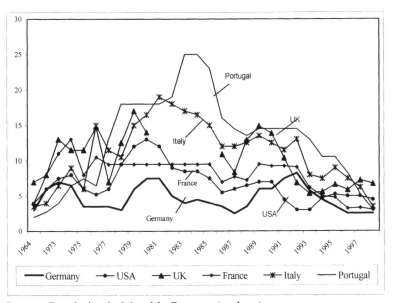

Source: Bundesbank, Monthly Reports (various).

With a permanently positive balance of visible trade and a current account balance record which was better than that of any other OECD country, with the possible exception of Japan, Germany's main problem throughout the 1970s was having a currency which appreciated too steeply against other major currencies. This reduced the pressure to use high interest rates to protect the exchange rate from declining. Conversely, major OECD countries like France, Italy and the UK exhibited persistent balance of payments problems throughout the period of stagflation, putting downward pressure on their currencies and obliging them to deploy higher interest rates to maintain capital inflows and prevent excessive devaluation.

Nevertheless, between 1972 and 1980 the DM rose in value by 46 per cent against as basket of 23 other currencies, the French Franc fell by almost 3 per cent, the pound by 22 per cent and the Italian Lira by 47 per cent. These asymmetries are observable in the spread of interest rates which widened in the 1970s after lower and narrower averages in the 1960s; in 1964 the spread in the sample above was a mere five percentage points with a Portuguese discount rate of 2 per cent and the UK base rate of 7 per cent; in 1976 the spread was 11.5 percentage points and in 1978 fifteen. While Germany's current account balance remained positive the OECD aggregate was negative in 1974, 1976 and 1977.

This in turn increased the pressure within the OECD to repress domestic demand and to boost exports to return to balance. The deflationary effect of higher interest rates is evident in domestic demand growth in the whole of the OECD between 1976 and 1979 which averaged 4.15 per cent p.a., compared to German domestic demand growth of 4.38 per cent in the same period. OECD export growth averaged 7.6 per cent in these critical years, that of Germany only 5.45 per cent. The most dramatic changes in international macro-economic indicators were:

a) the rise in structural unemployment within the OECD in general, from a rate of 3.1 per cent in 1970 to levels persistently above 5 per cent between 1975 and 1979, with steeper rises within the EU from 2.6 per cent in 1970 to 5.7 per cent in 1979;

b) the deterioration of government finances from a position of relative balance between 1970–73 to persistent budget deficits throughout the next decade and a half; within the average annual PSBR for the OECD of 2.5 per cent between 1974 and 1979, there were significant variations, with Scandinavian countries in surplus, the UK averaging 4.1 per cent and Italy 9.95 per cent; again there is a strong correlation between high interest rates and high PSBR rates, as well as higher ratios of interest to total government expenditure.

c) the emergence of persistent consumer price inflation within industrialised countries which rose from an average of 5.1 per cent to 14.1 per cent in 1974 and settled at over 8 per cent for the rest of the decade, again with marked variations between the German low average of 4.6 per cent (1974–1979) and Italy's 16.8 per cent and Britain's 15.6 per cent; the transmission effects of both devaluation and higher interest rates can again be assumed here.

German success in neutralising the effect of imported inflation and the reallocation of national income to absorb the immediate shock is clearly linked to the appreciation of the DM against the dollar, the currency in which oil prices were denominated, and secondly in the rapid reversal of the country's balance of trade deficit with OPEC countries (Table 5.2 below).

The disadvantage of currency appreciation was limited by Germany having the lowest rate of inflation among OECD countries. The 'real value' of the DM, measured by the Bundesbank according to the domestic devaluation of eighteen other currencies as well as exchange rate changes, changed little during the decade. The stronger DM-exchange rate nevertheless favoured the country's preponderant importation of raw materials and semi-finished goods.

Table 5.2　　　German Trade with OPEC countries, 1972-78

	1972	1975	1978
German Exports to OPEC Countries as % of total exports	3.2	7.6	8.6
German Imports from OPEC Countries as % of total imports	6.5	11.0	8.0

Source: Bundesbank *Annual Report*, 1978

The recycling of petro-dollars back from OPEC countries towards the industrialised countries of the OECD took both the direct form of orders for manufactured goods and the use of western banks as depositories for cash reserves and as mediators of other security transactions (equity and bond purchases, for example). It is clear from both Table 5.2 and Chart 5.3, relating to external balances, that Germany was relatively more successful in maintaining a steady surplus, while the OECD as a whole only managed a significant surplus in 1979, just before the second oil-price shock.

The core hypothesis being elaborated here is that the volatility of exchange relations in the mid- to late 1970s was reinforced by the asymmetry of national economies and the asymmetry of institutional power within the family of European and OECD central banks. Thus, while the Bundesbank's interest rate levels look tame compared to those of other European countries, they exercised a powerful and exaggerated drag effect on economies with weaker currencies, compounding the unemployment but also the inflationary effect of higher credit costs for both foreign enterprises and foreign governments. The incremental reduction of German discount rates in eleven stages over 38½ months between 1974 and 1979 will have contributed to these effects.

Chart 5.3   Current Balances, OECD, Germany, USA, 1963–1998
                   in $ millions

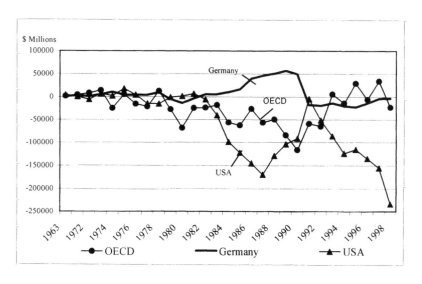

Source: OECD, *Economic Outlook* (various).

A further significant transmission effect of Bundesbank dominance over policy-making will have been the (resignative or otherwise) acceptance of the orthodoxy of monetarism. With the exception of France, which resisted the abandonment of planification and welfarist Keynesianism until the early 1980s, most European countries shifted towards both monetary management and more restrictive budgetary measures. The British balance of payments crisis of 1976, in which Dennis Healey was obliged to seek a short-term loan from the IMF, is a strong demonstration of the capitulation of a welfarist party to an institution already converted to neo-liberal thinking and which was able to impose the kind of conditions on British fiscal behaviour that became famous in the Third World debt crisis of the 1980s.

A significant vehicle for the transmission of the Bundesbank's monetarist preferences and the negative effects noted above was the so-called 'Snake' which linked the currencies of Germany, the Netherlands, Belgium, Luxembourg, Denmark, Sweden, Norway and – sporadically – France in a joint float.[32] The 'Snake' committed members to observe fluctuation bands of ±2.25 per cent in the group's exchange rate movements in relation to the dollar but, with no sanctions against non-intervention and no rules governing who should intervene when bands were breached, the burden of compliance fell on countries with weaker currencies. This was an important reason for Britain and Italy not joining the March 1973 joint float and for France (which was 'keenly aware of the asymmetries of the Snake')[33] deciding to withdraw in January 1974 and again later, after a further eight month stint from July 1975, in March 1976. The Snake carried little cost for the Bundesbank but, as such, it was an early indicator of the leverage which was later to be brought to bear within the EMS.

The OPEC-revolution was a brief attempt to redress the unequal balance in global terms of trade between the former colonial powers and associated oil companies and the small group of oil-rich developing countries. It effected a significant redistribution of global wealth in favour of this small group. It also created a large new pool of liquidity which was recycled into the major banks of the 'North' and which was used, in the short term, to cushion the effect of rising oil prices for the majority of non-oil producing developing countries. With the encouragement of both the private banks in OECD countries and international lenders like the IMF, the World Bank and individual states, developing countries took out large and predominantly long-term loans at real rates of interest which allowed a real return on investment.

The total long-term debt of non-oil developing countries accordingly rose from $96.8 billion in 1973 to $375.4 billion in 1980 and $505.2 billion in 1982.[34] Up until 1980, as the table below

---

[32] Britain and Italy, which had been brief members of the earlier 'Snake in the Tunnel' before the end of Bretton Woods, had floated their currencies unilaterally. Further details, see: Heisenberg, *The Mark of the Bundesbank*, op.cit. 35ff, 39ff.

[33] Heisenberg, ibid. p.41

[34] Figures from Karel Jansen, *Introduction to Monetarism, Economic Crisis and the Third World*, The Hague 1983, p.13

indicates, the rate of real economic growth exceeded the real interest rate by a considerable margin, allowing a benign interpretation of credit conditions and future prospects. It allowed developing countries to ignore the higher debt servicing ratio (interest plus amortisation as a percentage of total exports) as well as increases in their current account deficits,[35] firstly because borrowing was essential to development and secondly because debt servicing could be accommodated comfortably within increased national wealth.

Table 5.3   Growth Rates for Non-Oil Developing
               Countries (excluding China) and Real Interest Rates
               1973-83

19..	73	74	75	76	77	78	79	80	81	82	83
GDP	6.1	5.4	3.3	6.0	5.2	5.4	4.6	4.3	2.5	0.8	1.2
RIR	1.2	-3.5	-0.9	1.6	1.0	1.1	-0.2	0.6	4.3	6.3	6.2
CG	4.9	8.9	4.2	4.4	4.2	4.3	4.8	3.7	-1.8	-5.5	-5.0

GDP: Annual growth rate of real GDP of non-oil developing countries in per cent; RIR: real interest rate; CG: critical gap between GDP and RIR

Source: Susan George, *A Fate Worse Than Debt*, London 1989, p.197

As the table also indicates, however, in 1981 the relationship between growth and real interest rates was reversed. The calculation on the viability of international borrowing became considerably more risky, a theme which will be developed later. The important message at this stage of the analysis is that developing countries – with their very different strategic priorities – became committed to a process of debt-financed growth with assumptions about future conditions over which

---

[35] The ratio of debt repayments (interest plus capital) to total exports, paid by non-oil developing countries rose from an average of 14 per cent in 1973 to 16.3 per cent in 1980 (IMF, *World Economic Outlook*, Washington DC, 1982) and the average current account deficit (as a percentage of GDP) for the same group of countries rose from 2 per cent to 4.8 per cent in the same period (IMF, *World Economic Outlook*, Washington DC, 1981); this compared to the healthier current balances of industrialised countries which varied between a surplus of 0.1 per cent in 1975 and deficits of 0.7 per cent in 1974 and 0.8 per cent in 1980 (OECD: *Economic Outlook*, December 1981)

they had little or no control. Interest rates were just one of the factors defining the trap into which developing countries were about to fall; the practice of using new debts to pay off old ones also contained the seed of disaster, because the new credits granted in the 1980s were at higher and frequently variable levels of real interest and were increasingly short-term; additionally, the price-trend of non-oil primary products began to drop in around 1977, worsening the terms of trade between the bulk of developing countries and their trading partners in both the industrialised world and in OPEC countries. Between 1981 and 1988 all food prices fell, with the exception of pepper (!), likewise all vegetable oils, all agricultural raw materials, apart from pelts and tropical timber, and all minerals, apart from aluminium.[36]

The debt-trap, while compounded by bad planning, inefficiency and corruption in the countries affected, was laid by a combination of external factors, including above all the new orthodoxy of monetarism. While monetarism was certainly inappropriate to development in advanced capitalist countries, it was brutally inappropriate for less developed countries. The function of the mercantilist state in the development of a basic economic, educational and social infrastructure, was still highly relevant; no different, in fact, from the developmental function of mercantilist European states in the nineteenth century. The crucial difference was that the dominant institutions of the developed world (central banks, commercial banks, IMF, World Bank, national governments) decreed that the state was a dysfunctional economic agent that should confine itself to framework policies and proceeded to construct a global system of liberalized exchange rates, capital and other factor markets which made it impossible for states in the developing world to perform an enabling, mercantilist function. The astonishing thing about orthodox accounts of the evolution of Bundesbank monetarism is that they confine their attention at most to the transmission effects within the industrialised world. The idea that monetarism affected other parts of global capitalism is entirely absent from their discussions. The cumulative index of the articles in the 516 Bundesbank's monthly reports published to date contains one single contribution on German trade with developing countries, but nothing on the rolling crisis of Third World debt. The huge and generally very well written retrospective volume, *Fifty Years of the Deutsche Mark*, edited by the Bundesbank thematises the balance of payments crises of

---

[36] UNCTAD figures, quoted in: Michael Barratt Brown, *Fair Trade*, London 1993, p.62

industrialised countries but not those more consistently critical crises of non-industrialised countries. There is also an odd change in the Bundesbank's monthly statistical records, in that up until 1986 it included updated figures on the central bank discount rates of ten non-European developing countries, as well as those of 22 other industrialised countries. After that it confined itself to the rates of just sixteen industrialised countries. The records went on long enough to register the rise in the Brazilian discount rate from 18 per cent in 1974 to 49 per cent in 1985; what is missing are the subsequent rises to 401 per cent in 1987, 2494 per cent in 1991 and 5756 per cent in 1993. Admittedly, the figures are exceptional even by developing country standards, but the shunning of developing world statistics is symptomatic of the doctrinaire blindness of an institution which asserts the primary domestic focus of its monetary policy instruments. It parallels the 'total ignorance' of economists in the developed world about debates in Latin America about monetarism in the 1950s and 1960s, noted by Dudley Seers: 'they seem to know little or nothing about the results of attempts there to apply monetarist policies'.[37]

However, the governments and central banks of the developed world cannot deny co-authorship for the new global order: the abandonment of fixed exchange rates, the removal of exchange controls and reduction of state regulatory controls of market 'actors' were all deliberate political decisions, urged and applauded by the leaders of financial and industrial institutions, by their academic advisors and by successive leaders of the Bundesbank. They created the new global space within which the major corporations of the North could thrive and above all within which new forms of monetary accumulation took root (see Chapter 6). They created the pre-conditions for the scandal of the redistribution of wealth from the poorest to the richest in the 1980s:

'By 1983 the flow of funds into developing countries from export earnings and from new (more probably renewed) borrowing was for the first time exceeded by the outflow of interest and other payments. In other words, the Third World was financing the First World to the extent of some $25 billion a year in the mid-1980s, rising to $40 billion

---

[37] Dudley Seers, 'Structuralism vs Monetarism in Latin America: A Reappraisal of a Great Debate, with Lessons for Europe in the 1980s', in: Jansen, K. (ed.), *Monetarism, Economic Crisis and the Third World*, London 1983, p.110

in 1989, compared with about $40 billion net flowing into the Third World in the 1970s'.[38]

There is an indisputable link between monetarism, the debt crisis and the environmental disasters of deforestation and cash-cropping in developing countries, a theme that will be developed further in the next chapter. It is sufficient here to point out that the initial implementation of monetarism by the Bundesbank and fellow central banks in the North was at best disingenuous. It assumed a transmission process which was somehow territorially discreet and which was appropriate to all market actors within that given territory. The reality was and remains one of widely varying market conditions, where monopolistic and oligopolistic behaviour does not (does not have to) respond to monetary policy signals in the same way as firms and workers operating in more open markets; the asymmetry of market power in Germany is matched by a set of asymmetries within the global economy and within the global hierarchy of central banks which mediate monetary policy signals differently, according to the position of state or market actors in given power hierarchies. There is no equal pain or equal gain for all those affected; the law of unequal development should make that perfectly plain to all those who do have market power or policy leverage. Self-interest, however, is notorious for repressing such knowledge.

STAGFLATION ROUND TWO AND THE EUROPEAN MONETARY SYSTEM

The figures cited below for Germany and other OECD economies indicate that by 1979 the effects of the first oil shock had been absorbed, firstly in terms of the return to modest growth and secondly in terms of reduced levels of price inflation; unemployment, while declining, was still considerably higher than in 1973. The trebling of OPEC oil prices in the course of 1979 delivered a severe blow to the fragile stability of those OECD economies, affected – for the first time – the pricing structures of soviet-bloc economies and reinforced the critical balance of payments problems of developing countries. Increased energy costs had almost immediate effects on net industrial production which fell by 0.4 per cent in 1980 and on capacity utilisation; agricultural production shrank for the second year running but the clearing of manufacturing stocks and strong growth in the service sector helped prevent an immediate slide into recession.

---

[38] Barratt-Brown, *Fair Trade*, op.cit. p.113

However, the acceleration of consumer price inflation (1979: +4.1 per cent; 1980: +5.2 per cent) and even sharper rises in factory gate prices (+4.8 per cent & +7.5 per cent respectively) confirmed the danger of further stagflation. Table 5.4 shows the full course of the subsequent stagflationary crisis. As in the first stagflationary crisis, the west German state was faced with the dilemma of addressing either the problem of recession and mass unemployment or domestic price inflation. But, as in the earlier crisis, the dilemma was resolved in terms of the Bundesbank's statutory obligations and its diagnosis of the crisis; the fiscal state had a higher debt ratio in 1979 (30.3 per cent), compared to 1973 (18.2 per cent) which reduced further its room for manoeuvre relative to the central bank. Discount and Lombard rates, which had only just reached their 1972 levels in January 1979, were raised again, largely in single point moves to reach 6 per cent and 7 per cent respectively by 1 November the same year; further rises followed in February and May 1980 (to 7 ½ per cent and 9 ½ per cent) and in February 1981 ordinary Lombard credits to commercial banks were halted completely until May 1982.

Table 5.4   Stagflation in West Germany, 1979–82

	1979	1980	1981	1982
GNP (real growth in %)	4.0	1.0	0.1	-1.1
Net industrial production	5.4	-0.4	-1.9	
Investment (growth in %)	0.3	0.5	-9.0	-3.4
State investment (growth in %)	-0.5	7.7	-3.0	-3.9
Consumer price inflation (in %)	4.1	5.5	6.3	5.2
Unemployment Rate (in %)	3.8	3.8	5.5	7.5
Productivity (growth in %)	7.1	4.6	4.4	8.8
Capacity utilisation in %	86.7	81.7	77.7	81.7
Bankruptcies	5515	7772	9195	9362
Notifiable Mergers	243	294	445	453
Discount Rate % Average	4.4	7.2	7.5	7.25

Sources: Bundesbank Monthly Reports, Statistisches Jahrbuch der Bundesrepublik Deutschland, Creditreform, Bundeskartellamt

Instead, a 'special Lombard rate' was introduced, offering variable volumes of short-term credit at 12 per cent, three percentage points above the old Lombard rate. Furthermore, outstanding Lombard credits worth 6.5 billion DM were called in. The discount rate remained at 7½ per cent until 27 August 1982; the easing of central bank rates to approximately pre-recessionary levels (3 per cent & 4½ per cent) took 12 moves over 85½ months to 1987.[39] There is a common but by no means unanimous view that the Bundesbank's exclusive focus on price stability intensified the 1981–82 recession, a view which is supported by most of the indicators in Table 5.4. Helmut Schmidt and the governing Social Democratic Party became increasingly critical of the pro-cyclical policies of the central bank.[40] Significantly, Schmidt's judgement that the Bank's policy was 'extremely dangerous' was not shared by his liberal coalition partners, in particular economics minister, Lambsdorff, who asserted that the Bank 'has no other choice' and who was otherwise critical of deficit spending as a strategy against unemployment.[41] Schmidt did, however, receive support from a number of academic sources, including the Keynesian Deutsches Institut für *Wirtschaftsforschung* in Berlin, Rüdiger Pohl (Hagen) and Hanns-Joachim Rüstow (Kiel), as well from leading bankers who contributed to a highly contentious domestic and international debate about the timing and effects of Bank policy.[42] Implicit in the critique of monetary

---

[39] It should be noted that the Bundesbank did not deploy its minimum reserve ratios as deflationary levers in the 1979–83 stagflationary crisis, since there was an increasing view that these were another and less direct way to influence interest rate levels.

[40] See, for example, the leading article in *Der Spiegel* (No.17 1981), 'Bundesbank: Der Zwist mit dem Kanzler' 19ff; also the earlier interview with SPD budget specialist, Wolfgang Roth, 'Zeit für einen Kurwechsel', *Der Spiegel*, 35/1980, p.33; 'Bundesbank kann SPD-Fraktion nicht überzeugen', *Frankfurter Rundschau*, 18 March 1981, p.5

[41] Der Spiegel, 17/1981, p.21; predictably the Bundesbank used identical phrasing to support their policy in the March 1981 Monthly report.

[42] DIW weekly report, quoted in: *Frankfurter Rundschau*, 12 February 1981; Rüdiger Pohl, 'Hohe Zinsen schädigen Konjunktur zunehmend', Frankfurter Rundschau, 25 March 1981; H-J Rüstow, 'Bundesbank in der Zinspolitik auf einem verhängnisvollen Kurs', *Frankfurter Rundschau*, 9 April 1980; Deutsche Bank chairman, Christians, was convinced that higher interest rates would not cure stagflation (thus Kennedy, *The Bundesbank*, op.cit.45f); in May 1980 Dieter Hoffmann, head of the Bank für Gemeinwirtschaft, expressed the fear of a repeat of the 'bitter experiences of 1975', with the Bundesbank driving

policy was the acknowledgement that the state's fiscal latitude was constrained yet further a) by the direct burden of increased borrowing costs and b) the indirect effects on budgets of lower revenue and higher expenditure. Budgetary pressure after 1973 had forced all levels of government to reduce the proportion of expenditure allocated to state investment from 15 per cent (1974) to 11 per cent (1979), while state budgets increased spending on interest repayments from 4 per cent of total expenditure to 5.3 per cent in the same period. By 1983, interest payments on government borrowing rose to 9 per cent of all expenditure, exceeding for the first time the state's investment ratio of 8.8 per cent.[43]

The strongest argument in defence of the Bank's position was Germany's particular exposure to foreign exchange pressure where, in contrast to the 1975 crisis, the dollar was appreciating at the expense of most other currencies. The dollar rate was driven strongly by both record discount rate levels in the US (1980: 13 per cent year end; 1981: 12 per cent) and by massive borrowing by the US federal government to finance Reagan's extravagant military programme (the 'Star Wars' project), which produced US federal bond rates in excess of 19 per cent in 1981 and thus, with US inflation running at 10.8 per cent, a real interest rate of over 8 per cent; unsurprisingly, the demand for US securities from European banks and corporations increased; in the absence of exchange controls, billions of DM and other European currencies moved over the Atlantic, seeking both higher bond yields as well as speculative gains from dollar appreciation. The Bundesbank, along with other European central banks, chose to raise their own short-term interest rates not just to control imported inflation but also to prevent large capital outflows and contributed thus to a profoundly damaging (real) interest rate competition.[44]

Germany into a new recession (interview in: *Frankfurter Rundschau*, 6 May 1980).

[43] The claim that ostensible Bundesbank concessions to Schmidt on higher federal borrowing in 1979 constituted a victory of Keynesians over monetarists in the CBC (Kennedy, *The Bundesbank*, op.cit. p.63) is extraordinary, given the monetarist straitjacket already imposed on the fiscal authorities, the maintenance of monetary targeting (via corridors) in 1979 and the beginning of a new squeeze.

[44] Rather disingenuously, US critics accused the Bundesbank of starting 'an interest rate war' in 1979; thus Ernst Baltensperger, 'Monetary Policy under Conditions of Increasing Integration (1979–1996), in:

There was certainly some confusion at the time about whether the Bundesbank was targetting the internal or the external stability of the currency.[45] Keynesian and other critics, while conceding short-term disadvantages for Germany's current account balance, argued that these would soon be rectified and that the greater dangers to international and national economic stability were the stagnation of GDP and trade growth and the persistence of structural unemployment.[46] While the federal government had been prepared even to concede that a monetary brake was appropriate in 1979, when growth was still strong and inflation rising,[47] they along with other critics of monetary policy became alarmed at both the continuation and the intensification of the squeeze when all indicators were pointing towards recession and, by implication, to market driven adjustments to wage and price levels. Rüdiger Pohl set the cost effects of devaluation, emphasised by the Bundesbank, against the cost effects of monetary policy:

'(I)t makes no sense to calculate the cost effects of a devaluation but to negate the cost effects of an alternative policy of high interest rates. The cost effect of a variation in the level of interest of one percentage point is approximately four billion DM. If one were to lower interest rates in Germany by two percentage points, for example, and were this to be accompanied by a ten percent devaluation, the cost calculation for the economy would not be bad at all. Certainly the net burden effect of devaluation would be around three billion DM, but the relief of interest costs would at the same time amount to eight billion.''

The turbulence on foreign exchange markets in the early 1980s in fact produced a devaluation of the DM of 37.8 per cent against the currencies of 18 other industrialised countries between 1980 and 1985 and a corresponding appreciation of the dollar of 38 per cent. Whether the degree of change was worsened by interest rate competition is a matter for speculation. What is irrefutable, however, is that German export growth averaged 5.33 per cent in the same period compared to

---

Deutsche Bundesbank (ed.), *Fifty years of the Deutsche Mark*, op.cit. p.449.

[45] Thus Baltensperger, 'Monetary Policy', op.cit. p. 443

[46] See Rüdiger Pohl, 'Bundesbank im Schlepptau des Auslands? Eine geldpolitische Analyse', in: *BfG-Wirtschaftsblätter*, 29/7, pp.1–5; also DIW, 'Muss der deutsche Zins im Schlepptau Amerikas bleiben?', *Wochenbericht* 13, 1984

[47] See, for example Wolfgang Roth, 'Zeit für einen Kurwechsel', *Der Spiegel*, 35/1980, p.33

just 0.67 per cent for the USA, while the US current account balance slid from a surplus of $1.37 billion to a deficit of $-122.38 billion, with Germany's brief deficit of $-10.75 billion improving to a healthy surplus of $49.17 billion. This development arguably lends weight to the position adopted by Rüdiger Pohl, the DIW and others that interest rate competition was fruitless from the start and that the greater danger to a nation's productive capacity and competitiveness lay in an appreciation of the currency based not on US trading strengths but on artificially high real US bond yields. From this, it could also be argued that shadowing US central bank and, above all, market rates gave the wrong signals to currency markets, to wit: that US rates represented fundamental economic strength rather than – as was clearly the case – severe structural trading weaknesses.

Germany's external economic position was complicated politically by the operation of the newly established European Monetary System. The EMS was the child not of central bank cooperation but of EEC heads of state, in   particular of Helmut Schmidt and the French president, Valéry Giscard d'Estaing.   Indeed the Bundesbank was initially sceptical of the value of tighter banding arrangements for the European 'snake', having benefitted from the latter's minimal commitments to intervene: 'Judging from past experience, an attempt to defend exchange rates that have ceased to be credible leads to an increase in interventions and thus to a rapid reduction in the monetary autonomy of the countries with more stable currencies'.[48] However, both Schmidt and Giscard, as former finance ministers, were united by a common scepticism about freely flexible exchange rates and by a particular irritation over US indifference to the volatility of the dollar rate. Anticipating the hostility of the Bundesbank, discussions about the fundamental framework of the EMS were held in some secrecy. Schmidt, exploiting the sovereignty of the federal government in external currency affairs, was also clearly seeking to bind the German and other central banks to a new set of politically defined rules. Heisenberg suggests that Schmidt was 'foolish' in antagonizing the Bundesbank with public remarks which certainly exceeded his political ability to deliver. In her recent study of the Bundesbank's role in European monetary cooperation, she quotes an interview with Schmidt in Business Week, where he talks about 'additional instruments of monetary assistance', redefining monetary policy with longer time

---

[48] Bundesbank Monthly Report, March 1979 (the month of the EMS launch)

horizons, of 'sacrificing some of our reserves' and 'expand(ing) our monetary supply somewhat more rapidly than we have done until now'.[49] There was a strong monetary Keynesian whiff about these remarks which, together with the prospect of a new supranational regime, would inevitably provoke resistance from the Bundesbank, headed as it was at the time by the long-standing advocate of flexible exchange rates, Otmar Emminger.

The resistance which emerged was vigorous and effective and, while it did not prevent the project from proceeding, it shaped EMS arrangements in such a way as to allow significant leverage for the Bundesbank within the new system. In a number of positional papers and in correspondence with the federal government, objections were made in particular to a system which prevented regular changes to currency parities and which was based on a pool currency (the ECU); the Bank's preference for a system based on bilateral parities which could be adjusted frequently when the ceiling/floor margins covering just two currencies were breached, would minimise the need for the central bank of either the stronger or the weaker currency to intervene. The other major objection was to the establishment of a European Monetary Fund which, like the IMF before it, would provide bridging support to weaker currencies via special drawing rights to overcome temporary balance of payments difficulties. By formulating its objections in terms of the challenge to the statutes of the Rome Treaties, the German constitution and the Bundesbank Law, a united CBC achieved the capitulation of both French and German governments to its preferences. The introduction of the ECU as an 'indicator of divergence' was no more than a token gesture to the French whose brave attempts to create a stronger symmetry of influence within the EMS foundered on the real power asymmetries within European economic governance. As Emminger's successor, Karl-Otto Pöhl, later remarked: the Bundesbank 'turned the original concept on its head by making the strongest currency the yardstick for the system'.[50] The technical details of the EMS were completed in a very short period of time (by EEC standards) between April and November 1978. The system itself came into force on 13 March 1979. Its birth thus coincided with the second oil price shock and was followed almost

---

[49] *Business Week*, 28 June 1978; see also D. Heisenberg, *The Mark of the Bundesbank*, op.cit. 54ff

[50] Pöhl, Speech in Frankfurt's Paulskirche, 27 August 1991, quoted in Marsh, *The Bundesbank*, op.cit. p.233

immediately (30 March) by the Bundesbank's sudden raising of its short-term interest rates by a full percentage point. Some commentators note with surprise the stability of the system in its first two years of operation, which experienced only two realignments (in September and November 1979); while Heisenberg endorses the view of the Bank for International Settlements that the system's stability was down to the weakness of the DM,[51] there is little doubt that the asymmetrical shadowing of Bundesbank interest rates by participant states (see Chart 5.2 above) helped to produce a (deflationary) stability within the new system. Kennedy, in contrast, speaks of an 'initial phase of relative instability' by taking a more realistic four-year view up to March 1983, a period which includes the global recession of 1981 and 1982, the lag-effects of a prolonged credit squeeze and a full seven alignments of EMS bilateral rates.[52] Four of the realignments to 21 March 1983 involved a revaluation of the DM within the system, three the devaluation of the French franc, four the devaluation of the Italian lira; the first four years of the EMS thus permitted a 28 per cent appreciation of the mark against the franc and a 31 per cent rise against the lira. While the EMS clearly settled down in the second half of the 1980s, its beginnings can barely be described as stable.

Von Hagen claims interestingly that the EMS was the 'saviour of monetary targeting' within the Bundesbank, i.e. that it strengthened monetarist orthodoxy at a time when some members of the CBC were suggesting the abandonment of targeting, as this 'had long exposed (the Bank) to ridicule'.[53] The eventual decision to retain money stock targets would seem to have been taken for symbolic reasons rather than because of overwhelming convictions about their technical value: it was the wrong time, considering the upturn in domestic inflation, and there was a clear desire to demonstrate the Bank's monetarist credentials to other, fiscally more lax participant countries like Italy.[54] Ironically, therefore, it could be argued that the introduction of the EMS encouraged the Bundesbank in its deflationary endeavours, even

---

[51] Heisenberg, *The Mark of the Bundesbank*, op.cit. p.77; this is also the view of Baltensperger, 'Monetary Policy', op.cit. p.443

[52] Kennedy, *The Bundesbank*, op.cit. p.82

[53] Von Hagen, 'A New Approach', op.cit. p.431f

[54] Von Hagen, ibid. p.433; there is an interesting parallel between the Bundesbank's symbolic gesturing at the birth of the EMS and its later tightening of the 1992 credit squeeze immediately after the signing of the Maastricht Treaty; see Chapter Seven below.

that some of its counter-inflationary zeal was driven by the desire to demonstrate both its power and its autonomy after its newly-won influence on the exchange rate had been reduced (if only slightly) by the inter-governmental agreement on intensifying exchange rate cooperation.[55]

THE BUNDESBANK'S ROLE IN THE REMOVAL OF HELMUT SCHMIDT FROM OFFICE

The corresponsibility of the Bundesbank in the premature end of the social-liberal coalition in October 1982 is a commonplace in surveys of the Bank's history, even in those of its ardent supporters.[56] Some accounts talk in dramatic terms of a 'three year battle of attrition between the Bundesbank and Bonn',[57] a conflict which 'amounted to a virtual declaration of a state of emergency'[58] which ended in the ousting of Schmidt as chancellor in the only successful 'constructive vote of no confidence' in the history of the Federal Republic. The parliamentary vote was swung by the simple and virtually unanimous abandonment of Schmidt and the SPD by the Free Democrats. Schmidt's political base had also been weakened by the unpopularity of his (expensive) defence policies among the SPD's grass roots, trade unions and the increasingly vocal and successful Green movement. Nevertheless, the main force undermining Schmidt domestically was the central bank and the strident new anti-fiscalism which it shared with leading members of the FDP, with the Christian Democrats, the Council of Economic Experts and Germany's neo-liberal research institutes. It thus set both the institutional and the ideological conflicts at the heart of German economic governance in the Schmidt era in sharp focus. Who governs? Who decides the guiding principles of economic policy?

---

[55] While the Bundesbank was able to advise the federal government on exchange rate issues after the launch of the system, decisions on changes were the exclusive preserve of heads of government. Interest rate changes and open market interventions by the System's dominant central bank nevertheless remained powerful instruments levering governments into essentially unavoidable decisions, as Europe discovered to its cost in 1992 and 1993.

[56] Marsh (*The Bundesbank*, op.cit. 172ff) and Kennedy (*The Bundesbank*, op.cit. 40); Balkhausen, op.cit. pp.138–48.

[57] Marsh, *The Bundesbank*, op.cit. p.174.

[58] E. Kennedy, *The Bundesbank*, op.cit. p.40.

The battle lines were fairly clearly defined. The interest rate juggernaut was relentless and immovable, defining both the conditions of state expenditure (qua costs of unemployment) and of deficit financing (borrowing costs). Even though the Schmidt cabinet had achieved a comfortable majority in the 1980 federal elections, the loyalty of the FDP under the ideological leadership of Economics Minister Lambsdorff to cabinet economic policy was flaky; furthermore an opposition majority in the upper house (Bundesrat) weakened Schmidt's ability to outmanoeuvre the Bundesbank.

The shared preference of both Schmidt and Giscard d'Estaing was to target unemployment and stagnation with increased state expenditure, in particular to boost innovate investment in alternatives to oil-based energy. As the Bundesbank intensified its squeeze in February 1981 – with the 'closing of the Lombard window' (Kennedy)[59] – it also intensified its public criticism of federal budgetary and energy policy as well as of trade union wage negotiators; Bundesbank vice-president Schlesinger even advocated a wage freeze, in other words – in a year of 5.9 per cent inflation – a real wage cut of over 5.5 per cent. Direct appeals by Schmidt and Finance Minister Matthöfer were ignored. A joint Franco-German plan in 1981 to arrange a large Saudi-Arabian loan was essentially thwarted by the Bundesbank's refusal to administer the corresponding issue of federal bonds.[60]

While the 'Special Lombard' affair was dramatic, there was no doubt that the Bank acted within its statutory rights; the refusal to cooperate on the Saudi loan scheme was arguably more serious constitutionally, in that its duty to support government policy (§12 Bundesbank Law), for example through the issue public securities for the federal government (§20) was being interpreted in an excessively narrow manner.

There is no doubt that the federal government was facing serious fiscal problems in 1981: the budgetary provisions of the 1980 budget law estimates were 5 billion DM short on unemployment, 1 billion DM on defence (notably on the costs of the Tornado), and 700 million short on interest payments.[61] With revenue over 1 billion DM lower than forecast and a looming EC budget crisis for 1982–84, the need to plug gaps was increasing every month. Public sector borrowing to bridge the deficit would have to take place via the normal channels of the

---

[59] Kennedy, ibid.44f

[60] For a detailed account of the Saudi loan affair, see Kennedy, ibid.48ff

[61] Figures from *Der Spiegel*, 11 May 1981

German capital market. The proposed deal with the Saudis had four key advantages in the eyes of the chancellor's negotiators: a) it would not put additional pressure on German capital market rates via 'crowding out' effects; b) it would be at a favourable rate of interest; c) it would provide funding for targetted programmes assisting small and medium-sized enterprises via interest-subsidies; d) it would solidify bilateral relations with Saudi Arabia and thereby oil the wheels of Germany's export trade, where the promise of large deals on armaments, construction and engineering projects was already being generated.[62] Schmidt's plan to channel the loan through the Credit Agency for Reconstruction (*Kreditanstalt für Wiederaufbau*) was clearly an attempt to outmanoeuvre the Bundesbank and prettify the federal budget deficit, since the KfW was nominally an agency independent of the federal government and its liabilities were not included in the PSBR.

Notwithstanding the wording of §20 of the Bundesbank Law that foreign loans should be arranged 'with the agreement of the German Bundesbank' (*'im Benehmen mit ..*), refusal to cooperate – as per §12 BBLaw – could in this instance be seen as colliding with the principles of democratic government and accountability, in particular as outlined in Articles 65, 67 and 68 of the Basic Law which cover the powers of the Federal Chancellor and his removal.[63] In §65 *Grundgesetz*, the 'Federal Chancellor shall determine, and be responsible for, the general policy guidelines. Within the limits set by these guidelines, each Federal Minister shall conduct the affairs of his department autonomously and on his own responsibility'. In the case of budget deficits, it is the Federal Minister of Finance, not the central bank, that provides consent 'in the case of an unforeseen and compelling necessity' (§112GG). The constitutional limitation on deficit-financing (§111GG) allows the federal government to 'borrow the funds necessary for the conduct of current operations up to a maximum of one quarter of the total amount of the previous budget'. The 1981 federal deficit, while large, fell easily within that limit at 17.4 per cent of the 1980 budget and the overall PSBR for 1981, although at record levels at 4.9 per cent, was certainly not critical by international standards. Within the context of the 'unforeseen and compelling necessity' of the second oil shock, stagnation and rising unemployment, Bundesbank

---

[62] See *Der Spiegel*, 6 April 1981, 27 April 1981, 4 May 1981
[63] Herbert Ehrenberg (*Abstieg vom Währungsolymp*, Frankfurt 1991, 73f) sees this collision as a fundamental contradiction of the Bundesbank Law and of the Bank's interpretation of its role.

behaviour over Schmidt's foreign borrowing plans were arguably tantamount to a monetary 'coup d'état', i.e. an anti-constitutional abuse of its autonomy. Ellen Kennedy's summary of the government-bank conflict in 1981–82 is utterly convincing, to wit: 'The Bank is willing to transgress the line dividing the government's rightful sphere of "general economic policy-making" from its own area of monetary responsibility when its chances of winning against a relatively weak opponent seem good'.[64]

While the FDP was unwilling to show open dissent in the 1981 budget debate, its scepticism over deficit-spending was already on record and when the predicted recession hit the beleaguered Schmidt administration in 1982, the preparedness to abandon ship was palpable. The ideological affinity of the FDP with the neo-liberal and monetarist orthodoxy of the Bundesbank was a key factor in the dynamics of Schmidt's downfall. 'Without a parliamentary ally of that stature, it is unlikely that the Bank would challenge an elected government so directly.'

---

[64] Kennedy, *The Bundesbank*, op.cit. p.54

6   The Emperor's New Clothes: Monetarism, Monetary Accumulation and the Blindness of Power 1982–1990

The fourteen years of social-liberal rule under Brandt and then Schmidt from 1969 to 1982 witnessed dramatic global events: the end of the Bretton Woods years, two oil price shocks, two waves of global recession, the emergence of structural unemployment throughout the industrialised world and the beginnings of the debt crisis throughout the developing world. If one were to choose when to be chancellor and when not, the Brandt-Schmidt era would certainly not be top of the list, given the constellation of circumstances and the economic and political forces ranged against them. The regime which succeeded Schmidt's after the 'palace coup' of October 1982 arrived under the banner of the 'great change' (*Wende*) and was headed by the leader of the Christian Democratic Union, Helmut Kohl, who became Federal Chancellor in November. The rhetoric of change was typical of the pseudo-revolutionary propaganda manifested by conservative political forces in the twentieth century; it masked a reactionary purpose: to restore the social disparities of income distribution characteristic of the 1950s in favour of capital, dampening the growth of domestic consumer demand as a precondition for encouraging export-led growth. The rhetoric of the *Wende* stressed the need to maintain German competitiveness in changed circumstances of increasingly harsh international market conditions. The flag of deregulationism and supply-sidism, already hoisted in Britain under Margaret Thatcher and in the United States under Ronald Reagan was run up the German political flagpole with the support of leading research institutes in Germany and abroad, most notably the OECD in Paris. The OECD saw in Germany a prime case of over-regulation, of 'sclerotic' market conditions preventing the dynamism necessary for reversing the trend of mass unemployment[1]. The 'sclerosis of the German economy'[2] was matched conveniently by the notion of 'Euro-sclerosis', of bureaucratically protected markets and social arrangements which were said to cost companies time, money and jobs; the blame could be spread widely and the message was appealing, as successive election victories for the Kohl administration demonstrated.   German regulatory culture was indeed dense and cumbersome: planning law and procedures made the implementation of private and commercial construction projects lengthier and more expensive than in most other European countries; guild-based trade associations maintained high levels of professional skill but at some cost in flexibility and adaptability (the medical profession is a good example of strategic professional power which has long dictated cost structures in the German health system); shop opening hours were (and are still) deemed excessively restrictive; taxation law was and remains a paradise for accountants and a misery for regional tax offices with high marginal rates and myriad offset facilities for private and corporate taxpayers; the long-standing natural (private) monopolies in gas and electricity supply were subject to extensive political controls to prevent the abuse of power; last but not least, Germany's renowned consensual labour relations remain heavily juridified and administered by an extensive and separate branch of public law. Unlike Britain, the German state's direct control of economic assets had always been limited; for this very reason, conspicuous regulatory regimes like those now prevalent in post-privatisation Britain were standard features of Germany's political economy throughout the post-war period. The fact that they functioned relatively well did not alter their visibility and the ease with which many Germans could identify with the critique of an overweening state.

The constellation of political forces surrounding Kohl's neo-liberal agenda was arguably optimal. The ideological affinity of the new federal coalition of Christian Democrats (CDU and CSU) and Free Democrats (FDP) with the monetarism of the Bundesbank has already been established; supply-sidism and monetarism were essentially twin branches of the Chicago school of economics with its core preference for *Ordnungspolitik* (framework policy) and its core prejudice against

---

[1] OECD (ed.), *Economic Surveys: Germany* (various), also OECD (ed.) *Progress in Structural Reform*, Paris 1990
[2] Thus the title of a long article by Renate Merklein ('Die Sklerose der deutschen Wirtschaft'), in: *Der Spiegel*, No.1 1985

interventionism (process policy). Additionally, however, the government's majority in the lower house of parliament (Bundestag) was replicated by a conservative majority in the upper house, representing Germany's regions. Theoretically, at least, the potential for implementing a coordinated (neo-liberal) agenda within a short period was greater than for some considerable time, greater even than in the 1950s when policy sovereignty was constrained both by formal international obligations (Bretton Woods) and by the need for considerable international sensitivity (see above). The economic circumstances were also auspicious to the extent that by October 1982 the recession was coming to an end, the balance of payments difficulties associated with the second oil shock were also receding and export orders were increasingly healthy.

If one were to measure the success of the Kohl government by the degree to which Germany's external balances recovered their traditional surpluses from 1982 onwards, by the fact that in 1987 the country became briefly the strongest exporting nation in the world, even in front of the far larger US economy, or that corporate profitability and the profits ratio (ratio of profit income to national income) rose considerably at the expense of mass incomes, the *Wende* might indeed be dubbed a revolutionary shift towards sound liberal economics. The relative success of German corporations on the global stage nevertheless conceals a number of key structural deficiencies in the national and international political economy, several of which can be ascribed to the influence of the new monetarist orthodoxy and the Bundesbank as its leading European institution. The neo-liberal prescriptions espoused by the Kohl government (and most other OECD governments) and warmly supported by the Bundesbank, assumed above all a virtuous circle of cost relief for private companies, leading to higher profits, then to higher investments, then to higher capacity, higher levels of employment, higher levels of growth and so on. The first link in the chain – cost relief via fiscal adjustments and lower wage bills leading to higher profits – was demonstrably successful.[3] Dieter Eissel has shown how corporate profits grew from 287 billion DM in 1980 to 604.2 billion DM in 1990, while the share of profit taxes in overall taxation fell from some 37 per cent to 24 per cent in the same

---

[3] For details, see J. Leaman, 'The Rhetoric and Logic of the *Wende*', in: *German Politics* Vol 2, No 1, 1993, pp.124–135; Dieter Eissel, 'Distribution Policy in the Kohl Era. The Impact of Neo-Liberalism on Wealth and Poverty in Germany', in: *Debatte*, Vol.7, No.1, May 1999

period.[4] After this first link in the chain, however, neo-liberal growth strategy was a resounding flop in Germany; the investment ratio continued to decline, the GDP growth trend weakened further, unemployment remained doggedly high and employment growth was virtually non-existent, a feature shared with most other European countries.[5]

Clearly, the failure of neo-liberalism in practice, evidenced in Table 6.1 below, has much to do with the naïvety of its theory: the hypostatisation of 'the' market, of 'competition' and its benign results, of supply as the key factor in market efficiency and dynamics (Say's Law), the quasi-religious faith in the reality of infinite economic growth, of infinitely expanding human consumption and investment, the cavalier or even hostile attitude to the public regulation of economic and social affairs. The dismal failure of neo-liberalism to address the core issue of unemployment and to reverse its rise was thus all too predictable.

The zealotry with which it was applied, however, in particular the new centrality of monetarism in neo-liberal *Ordnungspolitik*, created seismic shifts in the structures of global accumulation, reinforcing the destructive features of capitalism already present. The new dominance of *monetary accumulation* represents the most significant of these shifts. It was presided over by the major agencies of monetary policy with a blitheness which will leave future economic historians scratching their heads in disbelief.[6]

Monetary accumulation has always been a feature of capitalism. It is a core principle of 'rent-seeking' capital, where the accumulated money assets of individuals or organisations are provided to other economic agents (banks, insurance companies, joint stock companies, the state) to generate new wealth via production and distribution for a fixed or variable price (interest, dividend) and possible additional benefits (increased equity or bond values). Historically, however, monetary

---

[4] Eissel, ibid. p. 46f

[5] Leaman, 'Rhetoric and Logic of the *Wende*', op.cit. p.132

[6] Mari Marcel Thekaekara passes a similar judgement on contemporary economics: 'Fifty years from now, when people read about the economic theories of this century, I suspect they will do so with the same degree of disbelief and horror that we experience when we read the rationale of the generations who advocated slavery or colonialism …', 'Global Free Trade: the View from the Ground', *New Political Economy*, Vol.1, No.1 (1996), 102ff

accumulation was an integral part of general accumulation through production and trade; the unearned income of the rentier class, of private and corporate shareholders and of smaller savers was derived, by and large, from a portion of the borrower's traded profits; the growth of unearned income thus bore a clear relation to the growth of traded goods and services.

Table 6.1   Profit Ratio, Investment Ratio,
Growth and Employment in Europe, 1980–88

	PR %	GNP p.a %	I p.a. %	IR 1988	IR 80–88 (+/–)	E p.a %
Belgium	+6.9	1.6	0.3	18.6	–3.7	–0.2
Denmark	+1.1	2.0	1.8	22.3	+0.7	0.8
Germany (W)	+5.0	1.8	0.6	20.9	–3.0	–0.1
Spain	+4.7	2.6	2.3	–	–	0.4
France	+4.7	1.9	1.1	21.0	–3.2	–0.1
Ireland	+5.2	2.5	–2.6	18.4	–11.6	–1.4
Italy	+1.1	2.2	1.2	20.4	–4.1	0.7
Luxembourg	+4.3	3.1	1.1	22.4	–3.9	1.3
Holland	+6.7	1.4	2.0	21.3	–0.9	0.0
Portugal	+4.3	2.2	2.0	22.7	–5.0	–0.9
Britain	+5.8	2.8	4.5	18.1	–0.3	0.1

*PR=Profit ratio (share of national income taken by incomes from profits and wealth, change in percentage points); GNP=average annual growth of real GNP 1980–88; I=average rate of growth of real investments; IR = investment ratio, share of gross fixed capital formation in GNP: E = average annual employment growth in per cent

Sources: Eurostat National Accounts, Luxembourg 1991; own calculations (calculations on ECU basis).

The 1980s, under the auspices of the world's major central banks, produced a 'decoupling of monetary from real accumulation' (Altvater)[7], in other words a situation where money assets could generate further money assets without the interplay of real production,

[7] Elmar Altvater, *Die Zukunft des Marktes*, Münster 1992, p.143ff

real distribution and real consumption. The roots of this new alchemy can be found in both long-term structural economic trends in major industrial countries as well as in the political management of those countries. The two key trends are GDP growth and the investment ratio. The average annual rate of growth of gross domestic product in Germany (as in most other OECD countries) has been diminishing consistently since the 1950s and is mirrored in particular by the decline in the growth rate of domestic demand. The effect of slower domestic demand growth was only partly neutralised by the remarkable growth of trade in the post-war period.

Table 6.2   Growth of trade and GDP, 1913–84

	1913–50	1950–73	1973–84
World Trade (average annual growth in %)	0.49	9.42	3.61
GDP of six industrial countries (average annual growth in %)	1.85	5.31	2.10

Source: Maddison, A. 'Growth and Slowdown in Advanced Capitalist Economies', *Journal of Economic Literature* XXV, 1987, p.670

Trade growth in the second half of the twentieth century has been consistently stronger than that of GDP in the six major industrial countries featured in Table 6.2 above. The figures for 1950 to 1973 indicate the favourable effects of post-war reconstruction and dynamic global trade guaranteed by the United States within the Bretton Woods system, in contrast to both the war-torn and protectionist global economy between 1913 and 1950 and the recession-plagued decade between 1973 and 1984. The decline in GDP growth rates is mirrored in the reduced willingness of companies to reinvest corporate or social surpluses in new capacity; the proportion of GDP reinvested annually in Germany (investment ratio) fell from 27.8 per cent in 1970 to 23.5 per cent in 1980, to 21.4 per cent in 1990; since 1992, within unified Germany, it has been consistently below 20 per cent.[8] The emergence of structural unemployment can be ascribed to both the decline in the investments ratio and to the preference – within investment strategies –

---

[8] The decline in the investment ratio is common to the vast majority of OECD countries. See OECD Basic Statistics in: OECD (ed.) *Economic Surveys* (various)

for rationalisation investments rather than investments aimed at extending or simply maintaining capacity. The resulting higher levels of labour productivity helped corporate earnings and corporate reserves to rise. Even so, and despite a parallel rise in the mass of private savings, significantly less of this increased reserve of liquid assets was being invested in domestic instruments of real wealth creation. Under normal circumstances the excess supply of liquidity would tend to put downward pressure on the price charged for borrowing money (real rate of interest); this was in part the case in the second half of the 1970s when banks and corporations in developed countries provided low-interest credit to domestic borrowers and to developing countries. However, with the onset of the second oil price shock in 1979 and the application of monetarism and Reagonomics to global economic affairs, the price of credit rose to hitherto unprecedented levels, indeed to a position where *the real rate of interest remained persistently above the real rate of economic growth.*[9] In a system of credit-based (real) accumulation this is fundamentally subversive.

Table 6.3   GDP Growth and Real Interest Rates, 1970–1990

	Germany GDP*	G7 GDP*	EU GDP*	OECD GDP*	Real Interest Rates (US)**
1970–80	2.7	3.3	3.0	3.6	–0.27
1981–90	2.26	2.95	2.4	3.0	3.97

* Average of annual real growth of GDP; ** 3-Month US Treasury bills, average

Source: OECD, *Economic Outlook*, own calculations

Monetarism helped to generate a new and seductive entrepreneurial logic. Why should enterprises invest in machinery, plant and buildings when the growth of the national economy (of private, corporate and

---

[9] This point is underscored by Stephan Schulmeister in his critique of Bundesbank policy, 'Euro-Projekt. Selbsterhaltungsdrang der Bundesbank und das Finale Deutschland gegen Italien', *WSI-Mitteilungen* 5/1997, by Stefan Collignon in an article advocating EMU, 'Der EURO als Ausweg aus der Krise', *WSI-Mitteilungen* 5/1997, and by Michael Barratt, *Fair Trade*, op.cit. 112ff, to name but a few.

state demand) is less than the real return on financial assets, i.e. when a company can earn more lending its reserves than selling its products? OECD data show clearly a leap in real long-term interest rates within the G7 group and the wider OECD between 1979 and 1981 and their persistence for most of the 1980s in excess of 5 per cent.[10] Real growth in the 1980s was consistently lower than it had been in the 1970s (when lower real interest rates applied). The contradiction between higher real yields on financial investments than on additional real productive capacity manifested itself in a number of ways, in particular in the way in which corporations managed their assets. Increasingly, companies employed their cash reserves not for reinvestment in their own commercial operations but for the purchase of financial securities, in the first instance in government stock which – in the US in the early 1980s – frequently offered yields in excess of 10 per cent. The facetious remarks about Daimler-Benz and Siemens being banks with industrial subsidiaries were becoming all too accurate descriptions of how these companies thrived. Table 6.4 shows the change in the structure of corporate assets in Germany between the 1970s and the 1980s.

Table 6.4   Asset Ratios for German Industries, 1970–97

	1970	1980	1985	1990	1995	1997
All Enterprises	66.6	0.75	0.84	0.99	1.03	1.11
Manufacturing All	64.2	0.77	0.96	1.01	1.22	
Chemicals	76.7	0.87	1.21	1.41	2	
Engineering	86.9	0.93	1.07	0.95	1.117	
Motor Vehicles	47	0.85	1.04	1.02	1.57	
Electro-technical	95.6	1.3	1.59	1.53	1.76	
Retailing	42.3	0.41	0.41	0.46	0.54	

Source: Bundesbank, 'Ertragslage und Finanzierungsverhältnisse westdeutscher Unternehmer. Article Series in Monthly Report, October/November (various).

Whereas in 1970 German enterprises had a comfortable but not excessive cushion of financial assets equivalent to two thirds of their tangible assets, the transition to monetarism and Reagonomics saw the rapid increase of financial assets, such that by 1984 the core manufacturing branches of chemical, engineering, motor vehicle and

---

[10] OECD, *Economic Outlook*, No.47, Paris June 1990, Chart A, p.6

electro-technical industries had acquired portfolios of cash, short- and long-term claims and other securities which exceeded the book value of their real assets (see Table 6.4); the electro-technical industry had nearly three-quarters more financial than tangible assets as early as 1983. These branches had effectively become net creditors, a position reached by all manufacturing branches by 1987 and by all enterprises by 1991.[11]

The Federation of German Trade Unions (DGB) charts the trend in terms of the ratio of new corporate financial assets in a given year (net profits plus investment subsidies plus depreciation) to net private (real) investments; here corporate funds exceed corporate investments in 1983 already by 14 per cent; by 1990 the ratio had risen to 1.30 and by 1997 1.61.[12]

The sudden emergence of a wide gap between low real GDP growth and high real interest rates in 1981 and the persistence of the gap until 1988 (Chart 6.1) is a watershed in the political economy of west Germany and typical of other OECD economies. Schulmeister draws a direct causal link between the 'regime-change' to monetarism, corporate and private savings surpluses and structural state deficits in terms of 'primary economic balances':

'The transition – caused essentially by central banks – to a system in which the rate of interest remains permanently above the rate of growth, generated the following 'systemic' problem: Since the sum of all primary balances (of income and expenditure) is equal to zero, the state was quite unable to achieve primary surpluses, given the constant primary surpluses of the enterprise and household sectors. It therefore "suffered" virtually permanent primary deficits: the investment weakness of enterprises depressed tax revenues and led to increases in payments to the unemployed and in other social transfer. The rupture of the accumulation system driven by private credit from private savings for private real investments (the classical economic 'contract' of capitalist economies) left the state to maintain an increasing proportion of both social consumption and social investment, for which it was forced to borrow and at rates driven by the inflated expectations of monetary accumulation.

---

[11] The aggregate is clearly distorted downwards by the low financial asset ratio of the retail sector.

[12] DGB, *Zur Entwicklung von Löhnen, Gewinne, Kapitalrendite und Lohnstückkosten in Deutschland. Informationen zur Wirtschafts und Strukturpolitik*, 2/1998, p.27

Chart 6.1   GDP Growth and Real Long-Term Interest Rates in
                     Germany, 1970–1997

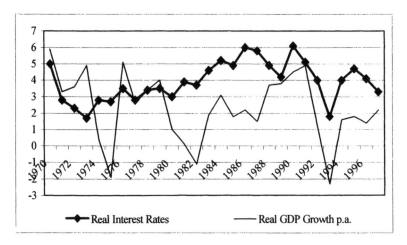

Source: Bundesbank Monthly Reports (various), *Statistisches Jahrbuch
der Bundesrepublik* (various), own calculations
* Public Sector Fixed Interest Securities (annual mean) adjusted for
inflation

Monetarism, far from solving the fiscal crisis of the state, compounds it.
The emergence of vast corporate and household surpluses in the early
1980s gives the lie to the monetarist myth of state borrowing
'crowding out' private demand for credit. 'The reduction of their
(corporate JL) demand for credit was so great that their primary balance
"turned" into a permanent surplus.'[13]   The non-use of credit for real
accumulation by companies left a vacuum which the state was obliged
to fill, or risk social and economic disintegration. The persistence of
high real interest rates beyond the onset of economic recovery in 1983
represents the consolidation of the new system of accumulation and the
subordination of national fiscal policy to its artificial dynamic. The
growth of corporate reserves via financial speculation both increases
expectations of the potential yields from such speculation and reduces
the willingness to pursue real investment for real accumulation. There
emerges therefore an increasing mass of vagabond capital with no 'real'
home to go to. Even when bond yields begin to fall (after the

---

[13] Schulmeister, ibid.

abandonment of hard-dollar policies in the United States in 1986), the reservoir of vagabond capital cannot be redirected back to real accumulation, because global real demand is quite insufficient to promise either increased turnovers or increased rates of profit for this self-inflated pool of money. It is attracted rather to other forms of monetary accumulation: via equity markets, via predatory or speculative takeovers, currency markets and derivative trading (of which more below).

One of the contributory factors in the depletion of potential real demand in the world economy was the parallel and colossal crisis of 'Third World' debt. The emergence of the debt crisis in developing countries is well researched and relatively well understood: the coincidence of high bank liquidity in developed economies, low real rates of interest in the global economy and non-oil developing countries threatened by the impact of huge energy bills in the 1970s produced a situation where these countries could sustain development programmes through low-cost borrowing (see Table 6.3), the repayments for which could be financed out of the proceeds of economic development. Borrowing within both the developing and the developed world grew significantly in the 1970s, creating what Altvater has called the new 'debt economy', encouraged by real interest rates averaging 1.3 per cent between 1973 and 1980;[14] the volume of private international credit grew by 900 per cent in the 1970s and a further 400 per cent in the 1980s.[15] The second oil crisis after 1979 produced a similar recycling of petro-dollars through banks in the 'North' but borrowing conditions became suddenly and punitively stringent, influenced by the rigorous application of monetarist credit policy as well as by the absorption of large tranches of global capital through US government borrowing. The *repayment of old debt by new but more expensive debt* became a fatal path of least resistance for developing countries keen to maintain their modernisation programmes in the face of further energy cost increases; they were actively encouraged to do so by transnational banks in aggressive campaigns selling debt.[16] Debt repayment conditions also changed. The relative security of long-term, low, fixed-

---

[14] Altvater, *Die Zukunft des Marktes*, op.cit. p.153 and p.155
[15] Source: *Globale Trends 1996*, Frankfurt (Fischer) 1995, p.191
[16] See S. C. Gwynne, 'Adventures in the loan trade', *Harper's Magazine,* September 1983, pp.22–6; also Richard Lombardi, ex-vice president of the First National Bank of Chicago, *Debt Trap*, New York 1985

interest loans was replaced in large measure by short-term, flexible rate loans at generally far higher rates. Increasingly, developing countries – also plagued by corruption, mismanagement and wasteful military expenditure – were unable to sustain debt repayments from development gains; in many instances 'development' evaporated. On the advice of both private banks and international banking institutions like the IMF and the World Bank, developing countries were encouraged to boost the production of (basic) commodities for export and to use the proceeds to meet their interest and repayment obligations and to resolve their balance of payments problems. The widespread adoption of such production and export programmes produced both dramatic crises of overproduction in most major commodities, massive environmental damage to areas subjected to slash-and-burn cash-cropping, and social devastation as traditional mixed farming was replaced by monocultures, populations forcibly removed or driven into destitution by the collapse of household incomes. While some dollar-based commodity prices had been falling in the 1970s and others (coffee, tea, rubber, tin, tungsten) rising, the oversupply of the 1980s produced more severe falls in commodity prices right across the board.[17] With the nominal price of manufactured goods rising by 32 per cent between 1981 and 1990 and those of primary products falling by 21 per cent in the same period, the terms of trade for developing countries deteriorated more severely and faster than at any time since the 19th century.[18] These were compounded by the devaluation of many 'Third World' currencies. Cash-cropping was both damaging in social, economic and environmental terms and ineffective in terms of boosting export yields and expunging debt. Individual countries (like Argentina, Peru and Mexico) came close to defaulting on debt (as the United States

---

[17] Between 1980 and 1988 maize prices fell by 10.4 per cent, sugar by 17.3 per cent, coffee by 1.9 per cent, cotton by 7.7 per cent, rubber by 5.5 per cent, tin by 15.1 per cent and tungsten by 20.8 per cent; figures from UNCTAD, *Monthly Commodity Price Bulletins* (various); the bleak situation of Third World producers of primary products was clearly compounded by the fact that the trading control of these products was predominantly in the hands of a few transnational corporations; e.g. 85–90 per cent of world coffee, 80 per cent of tea, 80–85 per cent of copper, 75–80 per cent of tin are traded by between three and six large corporations; see Barratt Brown, *Fair Trade*, op.cit. p.51
[18] Figures from: M Barratt Brown, *Fair Trade*, op.cit. p.37

actually did in the 1840s, and most Latin American countries in the 1930s). In general, however, and under enormous global pressure from both private and state financial institutions in the developed world[19], debts were 'rescheduled', perpetuating the absurdity of net transfers of wealth from the poor to the rich nations of the world:

'Between the mid-1950s and 1980 the annual flow of funds into the Third World had averaged about \$40 billion. After 1982 the flow of funds *out of* the Third World averaged about \$35 billion a year, amounting to nearly 10 per cent of the value of the Third World's total exports. For some of the Third World countries the flow of debt payments took as much as 50 per cent of the earnings from their annual exports. Out of the \$1,200 billion which the Third world owed in 1990, only \$400 billions constituted the original borrowing. The rest consisted of accrued interest and capital liabilities'.[20]

The gradual integration of developing economies into the global economy via trade was reversed significantly between 1977, when they accounted for 26 per cent of total world trade, and 1987 when this proportion had dropped to just 20 per cent. Significantly, trade between developed countries intensified – rising from 46 per cent of world trade to 54 per cent in 1987 – and manufacturing and other exports from the developed to the developing world fell to just 13 per cent of global trade flows. The greater demand potential of less developed countries was thus perversely damaged by the economic policies of developed countries, whose markets were showing clear signs of saturation, reducing still further the motives of industrial corporations in the North to spend their reserves on additional capacity. Assuming that the distribution ratios of 1977 had remained constant up to 1987, along with the volume of trade, the value of Third World exports would have been \$650 billions (rather than just \$500 billions) and its ability both to repay debt and to buy manufactured goods from the developed world would have been significantly increased. As it was, real purchasing power was leached out of developing countries, allowing even greater volumes of surplus liquidity to accumulate in the asset portfolios of banks and corporations in the North. The skewing of distribution ratios in favour of rich, developed countries and at the expense of poorer nations thus will have provided a further perverse boost to the development of pure monetary accumulation.

---

[19] See, in particular, Susan George, *A Fate Worse than Debt*, op.cit. 67ff

[20] Barratt Brown, *Fair Trade*, op.cit. p.43

The new *monetary architecture* established by central banks and private financial institutions in the 1980s generated innovative circuits for money and credit:

A new breed of 'money-centre banks' broke the traditional symmetry of depositors' savings funding bank lending: 'an MCB does not loan money on the basis of its own clients' deposits or its shareholders' equity. Rather, it buys money, either on the Eurodollar market or from other banks, and becomes less a banker in the classic sense than a financial broker.'[21]

Table 6.5   Large-Scale Mergers in Germany and Europe 1983–90
a)   Notifiable Mergers in (West) Germany

1982	1983	1984	1985	1986	1987	1988	1989	1990
506	575	709	802	887	1159	1414	1548	2007

b)   Mergers and Takeovers by 1000 largest EU Industrial Companies

1982/3	1983/4	1984/5	1985/6	1986/7	1987/8	1988/9	1989/90
117	155	208	227	303	383	492	622

Source: *Der Spiegel* 15/1992

Merger and acquisition activity accelerated markedly and was driven increasingly by the prospects of short-term gains by speculators who borrow large volumes of money against minimal security and thus at high cost to purchase majority holdings in joint stock companies with the intention not of developing the companies commercially but simply of disposing of all or parts of their assets; this form of speculation was commonly associated with high yielding 'junk bonds'.

Other examples of M & A activity were driven both by the promise of improved scale economies (the more efficient and productive use of capital stock and human resources) and market power and by the expectation of associated boosts to the share value of the merged operations, normally measured in terms of the number of redundancies delivered by the merger; this kind of activity is associated with the voguish term 'shareholder value'. As Chart 6.2 indicates, the modest rise in the 1970s of both the Dow Jones index and the DAX-30 blue chip index (where economic growth was stronger) was followed in 1984 by extraordinary rises in equity values. While the DAX grew

---

[21] Susan George, *A Fate Worse than Debt*, op.cit. p.35

nominally by just 26.8 per cent and the Dow Jones by 51.9 per cent between 1977 and 1983, the years 1984–90 produced rises of 69.6 per cent and 120.3 per cent respectively. Nominal GNP growth in the two periods, however, was almost identical at 39 per cent and 38.3 per cent respectively. There would seem to be a clear correlation between the acceleration of national and trans-national mergers and steep rises in equity values.

Banks, private corporations but also public institutions (like local authorities) and mutual funds have used assets or loans to speculate in exchange rate fluctuations, forward trading in commodities and – most notoriously – in so-called derivative 'products'.[22] The rhetoric of the financial 'products' in general is, in the context of monetary accumulation, a grotesque distortion of language, since their relationship to real economic features of production, distribution, service provision and consumption is at best tenuous and at worst non-existent.[23]

The asset ratios of Germany's large corporations continued to shift significantly in the direction of financial holdings, reducing their susceptibility to credit squeezes because they were increasingly less reliant on borrowing. A recent study by the Bundesbank of company finances in Germany and France demonstrates empirically that large companies in Germany as well as in France have become virtually free from credit-dependency, even though it asserts bizarrely that 'the influence of interest on borrowing increases with the increasing size of the enterprises'.[24]

The credit dependency of German enterprises with over 2000 employees – as a ratio of overall finances – was already below 4 per cent in 1987 and fell to just 1.3 per cent in 1995. The reality is that many (the largest) of Germany's corporations will have become net creditors, that they will be operating not as borrowers but as financial

---

[22] A clear (if benign) exposition of the operation of derivatives is provided by David N. King, *Financial Claims and Derivatives*, London (Thomson) 1999, Chapters 4–9

[23] It is nevertheless a rhetoric deployed by most of those involved in financial services and bank supervision; the Bundesbank, in a well-known commentary on financial derivatives (*Monthly Report*, November 1994) is not embarrassed to describe them as products (p.42 etc.)

[24] 'Zur Unternehmensfinanzierung in Deutschland und Frankreich: Eine vergleichende Analyse', Bundesbank *Monatsbericht* October 1999, p.45

institutions as well as commercial companies and that – beyond their relative immunity to short-term interest-rate fluctuations, noted above – they are essentially immune to most forms of restrictive credit policy per se. This reinforces the disadvantage of small and medium-sized enterprises that have higher debt 'gearing' (are more heavily reliant on bank lending) and whose shorter-term investment strategies are more sensitive to short-term changes to interest rates.

Chart 6.2   DAX and DOW Jones Share Price Indices, 1977–90

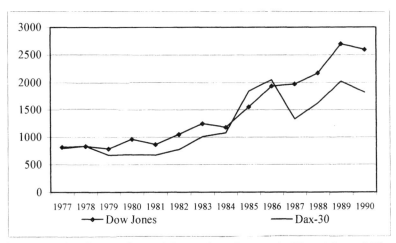

Source: Index figures for end December. *Investor's Chronicle* and *The Economist* (various issues)

In the context of monetary accumulation, an undifferentiated monetary policy (one which does not distinguish between the interest sensitivities of differing categories of borrower) contributes even more to the process of economic concentration than in periods of real accumulation. The increasing role played by monetary accumulation in the wealth-creation of large commercial companies in fact benefits from the manipulation of short-term interest rates, either directly when industrial or commercial corporations play the securities markets and bid up the varying forms of rent (interest) yielding investments or indirectly through speculation on *interest-based* derivatives, which represent the majority of such 'instruments'.[25]   Far from being deterred by high

---

[25] Interest futures, interest swaps and interest options constituted 81 per cent of derivative instruments worldwide in 1987, rising to 91 per cent

central bank and money market rates, the new corporate 'rentiers' have further options for deriving rent from their liquid reserves. Furthermore the dynamics of interest rate 'swaps' (a common derivative instrument) are frequently dependent on one contracting party being a greater credit risk than the other and therefore keen to 'hedge' his credit risk by speculating on the future movement of his and/or the other party's borrowing costs.[26]

The phenomenon of monetary accumulation, while it produces a relative immunity to the effects of short-term credit policy by dint of a lower net dependence on credit for real investment, nevertheless generates new and more dangerous credit circuits in which the artificially inflated asset values of financial securities are used as collateral for further speculative forays into equity, currency, commodity futures and derivative markets. Individuals, money centre banks, corporations and public authorities began to borrow large sums of money in the 1980s against the higher value of their financial portfolios in order to acquire additional and potentially higher-earning securities. The perils of derivative trading are amply illustrated by the spectacular losses of Metallgesellschaft, the Schneider group, Orange County (in the USA), the Party of Democratic Socialists in Saxony-Anhalt, Barings Bank and others, but these victims should not be regarded as typical for the processes of monetary accumulation, rather as the exceptions that prove the rule of a large-scale global shift of accumulated assets into trading modes which yield high.

Monetary accumulation, based as it is on the generation and inflation (in the literal sense of filling with air) of fictitious values, has given rise to a psychology of delusion and self-delusion which is akin to that of Hans Christian Anderson's naked emperor who is persuaded by a couple of savvy tricksters that the fine suit of (invisible) clothes they design and sell him is only visible to the clever observer and not to the dim-witted; the dim-witted emperor and his intimidated subjects are not prepared to concede their stupidity and resolutely deny the evidence of their senses. The major difference between Andersen's fairy-tale and the real world of monetary accumulation is that the process of social reproduction has become so dependent on the growth dynamic of

---

in 1993, while equity-based derivatives made up only 2.7 per cent in 1987 (2.6 per cent in 1993) and currency derivatives 16 per cent (6.4 per cent); see Bundesbank *Monatsbericht* November 1994, p.43

[26] These 'vanilla' or 'generic' interest rate swaps are described by King, *Financial Claims and Derivatives*, op.cit. 315ff

fictitious values – in the shape of bank assets, pension funds, corporate profit strategies – that no-one is prepared to question the intellectual or economic basis of fictional wealth creation; there is no boy in the crowd. We, within western societies, are increasingly trapped in the convenience of 'casino capitalism' and unwilling to doubt its efficacy or wisdom. Orthodox economic discourse on the disparity between equity market valuations and real economic growth is a truly extraordinary phenomenon. Alan Greenspan, chairman of the world's most powerful central bank, raised the innocent but intellectually alarming question concerning stock market speculation in December 1996: 'How do we know when irrational exuberance has unduly escalated asset values, which then become subject to unexpected and prolonged corrections.'[27]   Greenspan's tacit answer to the rhetorical question is: 'We don't' or – and this is the alarming implication of his innocence – the economics profession is ignorant either of the logic which drives equity values or the transmission mechanisms linking the real economy with the fictitious economy; but in the absence of any such knowledge, we will assume a Panglossian position of benign neglect. There is vague talk of 'corrections', 'adjustments', 'consolidation' in equity market prices, there were indeed real 'corrections', as in October 1987 (see Chart 6.1) or in the middle of 1998. However, whereas monetarism brings the full weight of its intellectual rigour to bear on the structural causes and triggers of inflation and on the transmission mechanisms, circuitry and time-lags of corrective monetary policy, with the assistance of elaborate econometric models, the phenomenon of financial asset inflation has hitherto excited little concern among most monetary economists[28]. The DAX-index of share prices rose by 30.3 per cent between December 1982 and December 1983 in a year of modest GDP growth of 1.8 per cent, and by 72 per cent in 1985, when real growth was a mere 2 per cent. There was barely a murmur from the inflation-slayers of the Bundesbank, in contrast to their regular imprecations against public

---

[27]   Alan Greenspan, chairman of the Federal Reserve Board, 5 December 1996, quoted by Martin Wolf, 'Greenspan's big experiment', *Financial Times* 3 November 1999, p.25
[28] Martin Wolf cites some very recent work of monetary economists who are starting to consider the influence of financial asset prices on consumption and suggest that these be included in the construction of new inflation targets; 'Greenspan's big experiment', *Financial Times* 3 November 1999, p.25 (see below Chapter 7)

sector borrowing, when these showed signs of modest growth. There is an interesting and marked disparity between the Bundesbank's account of equity market rises in 1985 and the sharp falls of October and November 1987. In its December 1985 monthly report, the Bank notes the 'strong upward tendency of share prices' in Germany and the doubling of transaction volumes in the year past with considerable satisfaction: 'The extraordinarily solid condition of the equity market is founded on the unchanged optimistic expectations of enterprises with regard to profits and profitability, for which the truly positive perspectives for the development of the German economy seem to provide a secure foundation'. This and the successful flotation of new stocks meant that the attractiveness of shares 'as an instrument of capital investment and financing' was increasing.[29] Two years later the fall in stock market prices of one third during 1987 is seen as 'a correction of the preceding speculative exaggerations' but more particularly is explained not by indigenous factors but 'above all (sic JL) by the fact that foreign investors have become the dominant group of buyers in recent years who have a decisive influence on market tendencies', frequently as a result of 'undifferentiated' views of the relationship between equity markets worldwide. The reassuring conclusion of the Bank is that 'the financial sector will in general produce hardly any negative effects worth mentioning on the real (sic JL) sphere of the economy'.[30] The real economy can therefore take credit for the share price boom (17 times the growth rate of nominal GDP) but remains untarnished and unaffected by the share price slump.

The external linkages of monetary accumulation are self-evident but cannot be admitted selectively. International share transactions had increased markedly in the 1980s, along with international currency, bond and derivative dealings. The disproportionate influence of market conditions in the US or of Japanese demand for financial securities in this decade cannot be denied, but nor can the co-responsibility of public and private institutions in all industrialised countries for the new 'architecture' of financial deregulation, which had above all dispensed with the fiscal means of deterring short-term speculative flows. The Bundesbank was no exception in its espousal of market freedom for international capital; monetarist doctrine assumes the collective rationality of market actors in their deployment of financial assets as a means of achieving optimal exchange rate levels. It is difficult to justify

---

[29] Bundesbank, *Monatsbericht*, December 1985 p.18
[30] Bundesbank, *Monatsbericht*, December 1987, 22ff

any implication of irrationality in the shape of 'speculative exaggerations'. Karl-Otto Pöhl focussed on the malign influence of US politics on international financial affairs, linking the decline in share prices to the decision by the US treasury under James Baker to allow the dollar to weaken more rapidly than agreed in the Louvre Accord of February 1987. He was subsequently reluctant to accede to Kohl's request for co-ordinated central bank action to reduce interest rates and prevent the slide from stock market crash to recession.[31] Monetary conditions in 1987 were showing renewed tensions between domestic priorities of money stock control and the need to ward off the inflow of hot money out of the dollar into DM securities. Despite the Bank's own central bank money stock exceeding the preset target corridor (3–6 per cent growth) by two percentage points, interest rates had to be kept low (and even eased later) to prevent external boosts to the money supply. This enduring contradiction of monetary policy in the context of flexible exchange rates and severe current account asymmetries helped persuade the Bank to change its target money stock for 1988 to M3, the growth of which had been closer to the 1987 corridor. This did not alter the fact that there was no coincidence of excessive money stock growth and inflation. The collapse of commodity prices, including for oil, in the mid 1980s ensured that there were no dangers of imported inflation, while persistently high unemployment of over 2 million maintained pressure on wage settlements. Rising terms of trade also helped to achieve record exports (in value terms) and a growing BOP surplus.

Returning to the issue of equity markets, the Bundesbank asserted confidently that the October crash would have a minimal effect on the 'real' economy, because neither investments nor consumption were guided by short-term fluctuations in stock market prices. Certainly, private households in Germany held smaller volumes of equities, compared to Anglo-Saxon households, and most ceded their voting rights as a matter of course to the big universal banks; furthermore, share flotations were less intensively used as sources of finance by

---

[31] See Trevor Evans, 'Dollar is likely to rise, fall or stay steady, experts agree', *Capital and Class*, no.34, Spring 1988, 13f; also David Marsh, *The Bundesbank*, op.cit. p.40; Baltensperger, in contrast to the other two commentators, describes the Bundesbank's easing of its short-term rates in November 1987 as a spontaneous response to the October crash, 'Monetary Policy under conditions of Increasing Integration', op.cit. p.471

German corporations with their high reserves. Nevertheless, there is a qualitative change in corporate behaviour with the emergence of strong and persistent stock market gains (c.f. Chart 6.2 and Table 6.4). Even the European Commission noted a rapid acceleration of M & A activity between 1987 and 1990.[32] In Germany, the quality of merger activity, while still dominated by horizontal mergers (of firms producing cognate products), shifted significantly in the direction of both vertical and diagonal (conglomerate) links.[33] While horizontal and vertical mergers combine (in theory) the advantages of scale economies and intra-firm trading with equity-based speculation, conglomerate holding operations reflect the dominance of pure rent-seeking from dividends and the appreciation of financial asset values (from share price rises) (figures Cartel Office). German businesses, generally slower to adopt the more risk-laden practices of their Anglo-Saxon counterparts, had thus made a significant step in the direction of highly speculative monetary accumulation.

THE DECEPTIVE STABILITY OF THE EMS

Parallel to the major qualitiative shifts in the secular economy in the direction of monetary accumulation and to the massive crisis of debt and poverty in the Third World, the political economy of Germany and other EU states manifested few signs of serious instability. This was reflected in the development of the European Monetary System which corresponded to the priorities set by the Bundesbank, rather than to any initial illusions about shared, intergovernmental responsibility around a core basket of currencies (ECU). The lesson learnt brutally by Schmidt in the Autumn of 1982 – of monetarism driving all economic policy – was also dealt out to the French government, the last of the EU governments to abandon fiscalism. The election of a socialist president, François Mitterrand, in May 1981, together with socialist gains in the national assembly elections the following month had raised false hopes of prioritising the fight against unemployment. An appropriate expansion of French state expenditure in the following summer months produced significant speculative attacks on the French Franc, resulting

---

[32] European Commission, 'Economic Evaluation of the Internal Market', *European Economy*, 4, 1996
[33] Ansgar Richter, 'Corporate Restructuring in Britain and Germany: an overview', in: G. Owen and A. Richter (eds), *Corporate Restructuring in Britain and Germany*, London 1997, p.7

in a realignment of the EMS' major currencies on October 5 1981 (see Table 6.6 below), including a 3 per cent devaluation of the Franc. The Bundesbank was highly critical of French government policy in its 1981 Annual Report, calling essentially for the convergence of EMS state economic policies along neo-liberal and monetarist lines.[34] Significantly, the French socialists received little support from Schmidt and fellow German social democrats, who – themselves under considerable pressure from both FDP and Bundesbank – endorsed the calls for French budgetary cuts. French concessions were reluctantly given in negotiations over two subsequent EMS realignments (in June 1982) and, after Schmidt's departure, in March 1983. There is a strong view that French fiscal policy was being 'dictated' by Germany and the Bundesbank in this critical stage of the EMS.[35] This is matched by Ellen Kennedy's assertion that '(f)rom 1981 to 1985 the Bundesbank could successfully pursue a line of "insular monetarism"',[36] which required no less than compliance from other, weaker members of the EMS group (as well as from its own government).

'Following the pivotal 1983 realignment, a period of stability resulted from a gradual convergence of economic policies of the EMS member states. With the exception of France, all of the ruling governments were conservative, and France had demonstrated that it too had adopted the norms of disinflation and fiscal austerity.'[37] It was a stability assisted by the strength of the Dollar and the indifference of the US to their twin deficits as well as by the growing interdependence of industrialised countries in their new export-led growth strategies; the share of the First World in all trade rose from 67 per cent in 1981 to 72 per cent in 1990, while the ratio of intra-First World trade rose from 67 per cent to 77 per cent in the same period.[38] There was also a degree of convergence between EU economies in terms of their current account balances, key determinants of market perceptions of currency values (Chart 6.3). Even when James Baker and Paul Volcker instituted long-overdue moves to reduce the over-valuation of the Dollar in 1985, the EMS succeeded in surviving the Dollar's decline with just minor

---

[34] Deutsche Bundesbank, *Annual Report*, 1981, p.79
[35] E.g. Heisenberg, *The Mark of the Bundesbank*, op.cit. 83ff; Favier, P. and Martin-Roland, M., *La Décennie Mitterand*, Paris (Seuil), 1990, p.476
[36] Kennedy, *The Bundesbank*, op.cit. p.63
[37] Heisenberg, *The Mark of the Bundesbank*, op.cit. p.86
[38] Source: Michael Barratt Brown, *Fair Trade*, op.cit. p.37

realignments in July 1985 and April and August 1986. While the background to the January 1987 realignment was surprisingly heated, with the French attempting to force a German revaluation by refusing to halt the Franc's slide towards the bottom of its parity margin and Chirac accusing the Germans of being 'a little selfish',[39] the event was relatively minor and certainly overshadowed by US attempts to encourage German growth stimuli and the later stock market mayhem in October 1987.

More remarkable was the absence of any further realignments for over five years (between 1987 and 1992), despite the 'exogenous' shocks of financial market volatility, the collapse of east European communism and German unification. Chart 6.3 shows the relative stability of current account balances, notably of France, Germany Italy and the Netherlands, even if Britain (a non-member of the EMS) experienced a serious balance of payments crisis in this period and paid for it with ongoing devaluations. The very marked convergence of the external positions of major EU and the US economies after 1991 would, in the absence of other factors, imply an even lower susceptibility to speculative attacks, but this was clearly not the case, as the following chapter will show.

Chart 6.3   Current Account Balances as per cent of GDP, 1981–1998

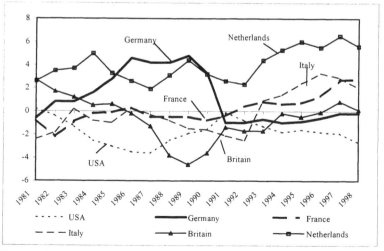

Source: OECD, *Economic Outlook*, June 1999

---

[39] Heisenberg, ibid. p. 90

Table 6.6　　　Realignment of the European Monetary System, 1979–1998

Date	EMS Realignments
1979 (24 September)	Revaluation of the DM by 2 per cent, devaluation of Danish Krone by 2.9 per cent
1979 (30 November)	Devaluation of Danish Krone by 4.8 per cent
1981 (23 March)	Devaluation of Italian Lira by 6 per cent
1981 (5 October)	Revaluation of the DM and the Dutch Guilder by 5.5 per cent, devaluation of French Franc and Italian Lira by 3 per cent
1982 (22 February)	Devaluation of the Belgian Franc by 8.5 per cent and of the Danish Krone by 3 per cent
1982 (14 June)	Revaluation of the DM and the Dutch Guilder by 4.25 per cent, devaluation of the Italian Lira by 2.75 per cent and of the French Franc by 5.75 per cent
1983 (21 March)	Revaluation of the DM by 5.5 per cent, the Dutch Guilder by 3.5 per cent, the Danish Krone by 2.5 per cent and the Belgian Franc by 1.5 per cent; Devaluation of the French Franc and the Italian Lira by 2.5 per cent and of the Irish Punt by 3.5 per cent
1985 (20 July)	Devaluation of the Italian Lira by 6 per cent; revaluation of all other EMS currencies by 2 per cent
1986 (7 April)	Revaluation of the DM and the Dutch Guilder by 3 per cent, the Danish Krone by 2.5 per cent and the Belgian Franc by 1 per cent; devaluation of the FF by 3 per cent
1986 (4 August)	Devaluation of the Irish Punt by 8 per cent
1987 (12 January)	Revaluation of the DM and the Dutch Guilder by 3 per cent and of the Belgian Franc by 2 per cent
1989 (19 June)	Entry of Spanish Peseta into EMS (within fluctuation bands of ± 6 per cent)
1990 (8 January)	Devaluation of Italian Lira by 3.7 per cent while it enters narrow bands (± 2.25 per cent)
1990 (5 October)	Entry of British Pound into EMS (within wider band of ± 6 per cent)
1992 (4 April)	Entry of Portugues Escudo into EMS (within wider band of ± 6 per cent)
1992 (13 September)	Devaluation of the Italian Lira by 3.5 per cent, devaluation of all other currencies by 3.5 per cent
1992 (16 September)	Departure of both British Pound and Italian Lira from EMS, devaluation of the Spanish Peseta by 5 per cent
1992 (22 November)	Devaluation of the Spanish Peseta and the Portuguese Escudo by 6 per cent
1993 (30 January)	Devaluation of the Irish Punt by 10 per cent

1993	Devaluation of the Spanish Peseta by 8 per cent and of the
(14 May)	Portuguese Escudo by 6.5 per cent
1993	Fluctuation bands of the ERM widened to ±15 per cent; DM-
(2 August)	Guilder bands stay at ± 2.25 per cent
1995	Austrian Schilling enters EMS
(7 January)	
1995	Devaluation of Spanish Peseta by 7 per cent and of Portuguese
(6 March)	Escudo by 3.5 per cent
1996	Finnish Markka enters EMS
(12 October)	
1996	Italian Lira reenters EMS
(24 November)	
1998	Greek Drachma enters; Irish Punt revalued by 3 per cent
(14 March)	

Source: Dorothee Heisenberg, *The Mark of the Bundesbank*;
Bundesbank, Monthly Report (various)

CONCLUSION

The important message of this chapter, in conclusion, is that the stabilisation of economic reproduction and of exchange relations within the First World concealed significant qualitative shifts in the nature of global accumulation, establishing monetary accumulation as a primary source of capital reproduction, and above all significant quantitative shifts in the distribution of global wealth, both within the developed countries (see Table 6.1) and from developing to developed countries. The share of the industrialised world in global currency reserves rose from 59.2 per cent to 65.7 per cent in the 1980s, that of developing countries fell to 34.3 per cent, that of the least developed countries (excluding OPEC and the Asian 'tiger' economies) fell from a meagre 16 per cent to just 13 per cent. An arguably more critical development was the dramatic shift in the flow of global direct investments away from developing countries towards the triad of industrialised countries of Europe, Japan and North America; while developing countries still attracted 35 per cent of direct investments between 1981 and 1985 (industrialised countries: 65 per cent), the increasing public poverty of the Third World in the second half of the 1980s, together with inflationary and BOP turmoil produced a virtual stagnation of investment volumes and a halving of the Third World's share to just 17 per cent. This is indicative of the effective autarkisation of the developed world's productive economies as well as the more specific autonomisation of the monetary sphere of accumulation, whereby the capital surpluses of the North no longer had to run the risk of uncertain returns from investments in less developed countries but could be placed in the surprisingly robust financial markets of the North itself. The stability of the North's new system of capital reproduction and of the new regulatory mechanisms like the EMS/ERM was purchased at a very high price, therefore: the brutal subordination of the developing world to the new hegemony of monetarism to add to the existing domination of Third World markets and products by trans-national corporations. Monetarism and debt crisis softened up the credit- and aid-dependent developing countries for the neo-liberal 'cures' of market liberalisation, deregulation, privatization, roll-back of the state as economic manager, wage reductions and location competition.

Table 6.7   Distribution of World Currency Reserves, 1980–90 in per cent

	1980		1990	
	Billion $	%	Billion $	%
Industrialised Countries	251.4	59.2	622.7	65.7
All Developing countries	173.2	40.7	324.4	34.3
of which Less Developed Countries*	(68.8)	(16.2)	(123.2)	(13.0)
Total	424.6	100	947.1	100

Source: Bank for International Settlements, *Annual Report* various

The generalisation of the new economic orthodoxy of the OECD to cover the dependent and subordinate developing economies took no account of the law of unequal development, of the dramatic asymmetries of power between private and public agencies in the developing world and their counterparts in the developed world, of the advantage these asymmetries bestow on the few and the costs they impose on the many.

The corresponsibility of agencies like the Bundesbank in imposing this new orthodoxy and in constructing the foundations of 'casino capitalism', and of monetary accumulation is clear and culpable. A report by the Deutsches Institut für Wirtschaftsforschung in 1985[40] argued cogently against the high interest rates of the Bundesbank in general and against the specific mirroring of US central bank rates. In retrospect, the preparedness of Europe's key central bank to tolerate/encourage high US rates, while adhering to a very strict quantity theory, and of European private and public capital to satisfy Washington's fiscal hunger by purchasing vast quantities of Federal paper, made the disaster of Third World debt and poverty inevitable. The blindness to the detrimental transmission effects of First World monetary policy on Third World economics was more culpable still. It was a blindness which – in the face of relative domestic stability – agencies like the Bundesbank could afford at the time. The long-term consequences of this blindness will, in my view, be very considerable for the very well-being of mankind.

---

[40] Deutsches Institut für Wirschaftsforschung, 'Geldpolitik nicht wachstunsgerecht: Hoher Realzins hemmt la restitionen', *Wochenbericht* 52, 1985, pp. 374–81

7 The Final Chapter? Germany, EMU and the Bundesbank

When future histories of European politics are written, it is likely that the final decade of the 20th century will be seen to have been dominated by three major developments: by German unification, by the realignment of central and East European states to the economic and political norms of the EU and thirdly by EMU. It will be important to see all three (interconnected) developments set in a broader global context of political and economic upheaval, of a new and profound uncertainty about fundamental human ideologies and associated policy priorities.

This chapter is concerned with the attitudes and behaviour of just one of the major actors in Europe's political economy, namely the German Bundesbank. The chapter will focus on very specific relationships and on the specific problem of the Bank's attitude towards EMU, but this focus must not be allowed to conceal the uncertainty and disequilibrium which have characterised the global political economy in the last quarter of this century. This prefatory qualification is important both because national and super-regional affairs are decisively influenced by global economic and political determinants and also because the major agencies of economic and political governance are driven in part *by the need to appear certain, authoritative, sovereign and 'in control'*. That is, they are driven by the need to conceal the reality of both uncertainty and impotence. This kind of self-presentation is seemingly demanded by the dynamics of global markets and of modern media-sensitive democracies. The dilemma of establishing or maintaining one's legitimacy as an agency becomes particularly problematic when a set of potentially contradictory imperatives (supra-national, national, political, constitutional, technical etc.) collide, as has clearly been the case with the EMU project.

In one very obvious sense, the Bundesbank itself has epitomised the collision of two of these imperatives. Firstly, as the independent agency of German monetary policy and a strong public advocate of central bank autonomy, the Bundesbank must be expected to approve of the abstract institutional arrangements agreed at Maastricht in December 1991, given in particular that these arrangements are modelled almost exclusively on the 1957 Bundesbank Law. Bundesbank representatives were indeed involved in the work of the Delors Committee in 1988, in the vetting of the Maastricht agreement, the formulation of the convergence criteria and the provisions of the later Stability Act.[1] On the other hand, the Bundesbank had many reasons to disapprove of the project: its operational preference had always been for flexible exchange rates and against pooling its sovereignty in linked currency regimes with their collective commitments to intervene to defend agreed parities.[2] Bretton Woods, the EC's 'Snake' and the later EMS clearly reduced the latitude of this autonomous institution, even though in each case it was able to exploit its leverage to use all three schemes (particularly the EMS) to pursue its core task of 'protecting the currency'.[3] Above all, there were always strong doubts within the Bank about the creation of currency blocks which were not accompanied by corresponding fiscal harmonisation; monetary union without political union would leave the potential for member states to jeopardise monetary stability either directly through divergent fiscal regimes or indirectly through divergent real economies.[4] More specifically, the Bundesbank's ambivalence

---

[1] See in particular the Bundesbank's 'Statement on the Establishment of an Economic and Monetary Union in Europe' (*Monatsberichte*, October 1990, pp.41–45), which sets out a set of preconditions (sections V–VIII), all of which were incorporated into the Maastricht Treaty; see also Ken Dyson & Kevin Featherstone ' EMU and Economic Governance in Germany', *German Politics*, 5/3 1996, pp.325–55

[2] C.f. Dietrich Dickertmann, 'Die Autonomie der Bundesbank unter dem Einfluß gelpolitischer Entwicklungen', *Wirtschaftspolitische Chronik*, 1975/1, pp.23–45; in its March 1979 Monthly Report, coinciding with the launch of the EMS, the Bundesbank poured cold water on its chances of success: 'Judging from past experience an attempt to defend exchange rates that have ceased to be credible leads to a rapid increase in interventions and thus to a reduction in the monetary of the countries with more stable currencies. Such risks must be kept as small as possible.'

[3] §3 Bundesbank Law, July 1957; accounts of the Bundesbank's successful manipulation of the EMS can be found in David Marsh, *The Bundesbank – The Bank that Rules Europe*, London 1993, 231ff, and Ellen Kennedy, *The Bundesbank Germany's Central Bank in the International Monetary System*, London 1991, 71ff

[4] Otmar Issing, formerly chief economist and now a member of the Directorate at the Bundesbank, drew attention to these problems in his

towards EMU was strengthened by scepticism about the timing of the project and the associated ability of participants to achieve sufficient economic convergence to avoid a worsening of regional disparities and an increased need for compensatory fiscal transfers; GEMU had provided proof in miniature of such dangers.[5]

Thus, while Tietmeyer, the current President of the Bundesbank and CDU-colleague of Helmut Kohl, has expressed rhetorical support for the principle of EMU, as an institution its support has been lukewarm at best and in many respects hostile. Dyson's and Featherstone's account of the manipulation of the Bundesbank by Kohl and Genscher stresses the spirit of resistance within the Bank and the 'superb tactical skills in at once ceding a "gatekeeper" role to the Bundesbank and binding them into the web of responsibility for EMU'.[6] What remains to be seen is whether Kohl's triumph will be a real or a pyrrhic victory. What is already clear, in the view of this chapter, is that the economic and social cost of the struggle for and against EMU has been prodigious, as I seek to show below. However, while the argument will stress the culpability of the Bundesbank in incurring some of this cost, overall blame can only lie with the tangled nexus of conflicting interests, perceptions and operational imperatives which has been the framework for the Bank's actions and reactions.

EMU is being implemented in a very distinct politico-economic context and in response to a number of critical developments. In terms of economic history it is being advanced at a time when world capitalism is manifesting a number of severe structural weaknesses, particularly within the core nations of the OECD:

1) Declining rates of GDP growth; Average annual real GDP growth 1970–80 was 3.6 per cent within the OECD and 3.0 per cent within the EU; this fell to 3.03 per cent and 2.4 per cent respectively from 1981–1990 and between 1991 and 1996 has averaged 2.01 per cent and 1.53 per cent respectively.[7]

---

doctoral thesis, *Monetäre Probleme der Konjunkturpolitik*, Berlin, 1964, p.145; c.f. also Wilhelm Nölling, *Monetary Policy in Europe after Maastricht*, London 1993, 167ff

[5] See in particular the Bundesbank's warnings in its Statement of September 1990, reprinted in: *Monatsberichte*, October 1990, p.41 (section IV)

[6] Dyson and Featherstone, 'EMU and Economic Governance', op.cit. p.354

[7] Figures from: OECD *Economic Outlook* (various)

2) Stagnating or declining investment ratios; in 1970 the average proportion of GDP reinvested per annum was 24.6 per cent for 22 OECD countries (excluding the US and the UK: 25.3 per cent); by 1996 the average for the same countries had fallen to 19.4 per cent (19.7 per cent without US and UK). Declining investment is one of the strongest indicators of stagnating growth trends in the years to come.

3) Unemployment in the OECD has risen from around 7 million in 1972 to over 35 million in 1998; according to the ILO worldwide unemployment stands at around 400 million;

4) Trade and payments disparities between surplus and deficit countries increased markedly in the 1970s and 1980s (see Table 7.1 below);

5) There has been an acknowledged decoupling of global financial markets from global trade in goods and services;[8]

6) Increasing levels of corporate concentration have seen global oligopolies wielding ever greater political leverage in relation even to large and wealthy nation states, raising serious questions about the efficacy of national economic policy-making;[9]

7) The above were made significantly worse by the debt crisis of the developing world, generated largely by high levels of real interest rates in the early 1980s.[10]

In sum, these and other features represent a crisis of accumulation in which growth is both insufficient to encourage corporations to invest reserves in additional capacity and to maintain anything approaching full employment. The crisis of growth illustrates the banal but mathematically demonstrable truth that an advanced economic culture will find it more and more difficult to generate increments of 2½ per cent or more real growth per annum, where 2½ per cent is the minimum necessary merely to maintain levels of employment in modern, mature economies.[11] This is a truth rarely addressed by economists. The crisis

---

[8] See: Elmar Altvater, 'A Contest without Victors: Political Action in the Age of the Geo-Economy', *Journal of Area Studies*, No.7/ 1995, pp.57–67; Susan Strange, *Casino Capitalism*, Oxford 1986; see also Chapter 6 above.

[9] A valuable debate on the extent of trans-national corporations can be found in *New Political Economy*, Vol.3/2 (July 1998), 279ff

[10] See Chapter 6 above.

[11] For example, real economic growth in the boom years of 1951 to 1955 involved average annual real increments of 22.4 billion DM or 9.4% p.a.; the five years between 1994 and 1998 produced annual real

of accumulation corresponds to a crisis of social organisation, of politics in the broadest sense. The failure of Keynesianism (exogenous shocks and demographic disparities notwithstanding) was a function not of its theoretical inferiority to neo-liberalism or of its practical inferiority to the 'market', but rather of the declining growth trends.

The ideological context of EMU is that of a new orthodoxy deriving from the ostensible failure of Keynesianism and the collapse of some of its key global regulatory institutions: fixed exchange rates and exchange controls. The new orthodoxy is essentially neo-liberal, with significant, pragmatic national variations. Neo-liberalism favours open, deregulated markets for all factors of production, including money-capital, and therefore has a strong preference for flexible exchange rates. The die was cast by the OECD states between 1971 and 1973: 'The industrialised countries abandoned the principle of fixed exchange rates. Instead of getting the seriously sickly currency system back on the road and salvaging it, they blew it sky high to the applause of veritable hoards of liberal journalists and neo-liberal professors. The *Zeitgeist* decreed: markets are just more clever than policemen'.[12] As the previous two chapters have hopefully illustrated, the cleverness of markets was anything but apparent in the years following the abandonment of Bretton Woods. Eichengreen *et al* talk quite justifiably of 'exchange market mayhem'.[13]

The preference for flexible exchange rates (for floating) was and is not unconnected with the fact that the new liberality of currency markets increased the political and operational profile of central banks, most notably that of dominant autonomous banks like the Bundesbank and the Federal Reserve Board. Indeed the virulence of global market fluctuations made that profile even greater. Although the German Basic Law confers control over exchange rates to the Federal Government, the floating of the DM effectively handed over control of daily exchange-rate determination to the Bundesbank.[14] While – in the context

---

increments of 63 billion DM, but with growth rates averaging only 1.78 per cent.
[12] Thus Wilhelm Hankel, 'Zur Krise verführt. Ein Plädoyer für ein neues monetäres Völkerrecht', *Die Zeit*, 1 October 1998, p.44
[13] Barry Eichengreen, Andrew K. Rose and Charles Wyplosz, 'Exchange market mayhem: the antecedents and aftermath of speculative attacks', in: *Economic Policy* 1995, No. 21, pp.251–312
[14] Dietrich Dickertmann, 'Die Autonomie der Bundesbank', op.cit. 32ff

of oil crisis and stagflation in the 1970s – the Bundesbank thrived, as master of the new monetarism and beneficiary of healthy trade flows, other central banks were less successful. They were forced into a more defensive response to currency, trade and payments instability. Following the EC's 'Snake' (1972 et seq.), the 1979 EMS was designed as an attempt to neutralise ER volatility and, by implication, the one-sided politico-economic advantages enjoyed by Germany, i.e. to neutralize the currency leadership of the DM and replace it with a currency basket, the ECU as the 'pivot of the EMS'.[15] The 'intense suspicion' and initial opposition of the Bundesbank to Schmidt's and Giscard d'Estaing's scheme is well known[16], of which more later. It is sufficient here to note that the ideological hegemony of neo-liberalism and monetarism remained firmly entrenched, but was now flanked by a related but essentially subordinate ideology of central bankism.[17]

Both neo-liberalism and central bankism prioritise price stability as an economic policy goal. They share the common prejudices about the determination of prices, notably that they are closely linked to increases in the money stock. Accordingly, price increases are driven domestically by excessive wages and by fiscal deficits (crowding-out) and externally by key raw materials price rises, notably for energy. Both ideologies are remarkably silent about the effect of monopolisation and cartelisation in the industrial world on inflation, indeed on the inflationary potential of high interest rates on prices in the context of monopolism. Neo-liberalism thus has a distinct class bias in theory and in practice. The historically unprecedented redistribution of wealth and income in the 1980s[18] bear witness to this. Within this framework of a bias

---

[15] Thus David Marsh, *The Bundesbank*, op.cit. p.233

[16] See Marsh, *The Bundesbank*, p. 233; Ellen Kennedy, *The Bundesbank*, op.cit. p.80

[17] See Edward Luttwak, 'Central Bankism', in: Gowan & Anderson (eds), *The Question of Europe*, London (Verso) 1997, pp.220–33

[18] Between 1980 and 1988, the gross unadjusted profits ratio rose in all EU countries, by 6.9 percentage points in Belgium, 1.1 in Denmark and Italy, 5.0 in Germany, 4.7 in Spain and France, 5.2 in Ireland, 4.3 in Luxemburg, 6.7 in Holland, 4.3 in Portugal, 5.8 in the UK, matching corresponding falls in the gross wages ratio; c.f. Eurostat National Accounts, Luxemburg 1991. With the liberalisation of taxation, the net redistribution effects are even more marked; c.f. Dieter Eißel, 'Reichtum unter der Steuerschraube?', in E-U Huster, *Reichtum*, Frankfurt 1997

towards capital, the sanctification of price stability (or rather, low inflation) favours finance capital and rentier income.[19] Again the historically
unprecedented returns on bonds in the early 1980s and then on currency, share and derivative trading compared to returns on real goods
and services are ample proof of this dismal fact. The silence of neo-
liberals and monetarists over such contradictions has been deafening.
While the Bundesbank has continued to lecture state authorities and
workers about the inflationary potential of immoderate behaviour, it
delivered a remarkably glib judgement on the 'limited' effect of derivative markets on monetary affairs in its 1994 November report.[20]

The rhetoric of prudence thus conceals a considerable degree of intellectual dishonesty. It continues to be respected, despite the rising cost
of low real investment, bankruptcies and high unemployment a) because the accumulation crisis still only affects a minority of the developed world and b) because increasing sections of the population are
locked into the rentier system[21], dazzled by the short-term glories of
shareholder value and blind to the fundamental flaws of the system of
accumulation. Neo-liberalism and central bankism thus still enjoy a
perverse degree of legitimacy.

The immediate historical context of EMU is the extraordinary development of German unification and post-communism in central and
eastern Europe. While the idea of monetary union was mooted as early
as 1962 and was resurrected in the Werner Report of 1970 and the
Delors Report of 1988, there is little argument about the view that EMU
was accelerated by the shock of German unification and the perceived
danger of a restored German domination of central Europe. EU thinking was reinforced by fears of a European innovation-deficit in relation
to Japan and the US but it was decisively galvanized by the fear of a
new German hegemon, shifting the focus of its trade and investment to
rich new eastern pastures and diluting its commitment to multi-lateral
politics. EMU was thus 'Germany's price for unification'.[22]

---

[19]   Alan Milward, 'The Social Bases of Monetary Union', in: Gowan &
Anderson (eds), *The Question of Europe*, op.cit. 157f; Luttwak, 'Central Bankism', op.cit. p.225 etc.

[20] Deutsche Bundesbank, *Monatsberichte*, November 1994, p.54

[21]   Alan Milward, 'The Social Bases ...', op.cit. p.157

[22]   David Marsh, *The Bundesbank*, op.cit. 235f; Milward asserts that
'the single currency is the price that Germany must pay to France for
reunification', 'The Social Bases' op.cit. p.156

As such it must be seen as an extraordinary gesture by Kohl in extraordinary circumstances, akin to Odysseus binding himself to the mast: abandoning the DM, the symbol of enormous national pride for much travelled Germans in the context of an historical culture rather thin on such symbols; ceding sovereignty to a Union with a modest but not outstanding track record in economic policy, and disempowering the institution which Germans seemingly trust the most, the Bundesbank. Put another way, without German unification, without the political imperative of avoiding a new German Question, the economic imperative of currency union with all its deflationary sacrifices would have probably waited for better times. In view of the economic aftermath of German currency union in 1990, neo-liberals might have argued that it would be more prudent to wait anyway until the economic and fiscal ripples of the '*Aufschwung-Ost*' had subsided, before embarking on the mammoth task of EMU.

Finally, the institutional context of EMU needs to be sketched. Within the family of European central banks, the Bundesbank has quite clearly been the dominant force. It was dominant a) in ideological terms, being the strongest proponent of a pure monetarism based on money-supply targetting, b) in bureaucratic terms, with its 17 000 staff dwarfing counterparts in France (9 000) or Britain (4 500) (not to mention its towering superiority over Federal ministries with their average of 2 000 civil servants each) and c) in operational terms, being – in 1990 – the only major European central bank with a high degree of autonomy. It enjoyed above all the extraordinary policy advantage of presiding over a national economy of great relative strength: high skill, high productivity, high investment, universal banks, trade and payments surpluses and large currency reserves.

The result of this institutional dominance of the Bundesbank was an asymmetry of economic and specifically monetary relations which the Bundesbank was able – with little difficulty – to turn to its and Germany's short-term advantage in the 70s and 80s. 'For the Bundesbank, symmetry spelled inflation. ... The Bank was able to force asymmetry – and the stable money policies favoured by the Germans – on other members of the ERM despite the expressed objectives of the European Monetary System'.[23] World capital market volatilities – like those generated by Reagonomics and the funding of US budget and balance of payments deficits – could be fended off by the Bundesbank with greater ease and at a lower macro-economic cost than its European counterparts. That is, central bank discount rates needed to rise less dramati-

---

[23] Thus Ellen Kennedy, *The Bundesbank*, op.cit. p.86

cally in Germany than in other countries because of disparities in current account balances. This asymmetry was of crucial significance for the management of the EMS, a system designed to neutralise speculation and subordinate the Bundesbank to a collective regime, but which became a paradise for speculators[24] and (until 1992) a vehicle for maintaining Bundesbank dominance of European monetary policy.

Table 7.1   The Asymmetry of International Interest Rates: Current Account Balances and Central Bank Discount Rates in Selected Countries 1970–1990

Category	US	J	G	F	It	UK	P	Sp
Current Account Balance as % of GDP 1970	0.2	1.0	0.6	0.1	1.2	1.3	1.9	0.2
Discount Rates Dec 70 %	5½	6	6	7	5½	7	3½	6½
Current Account Balance as % of GDP 1982	−0.4	0.6	0.8	−2.2	−1.8	1.7	−11.8	−2.5
Discount Rates Dec 82 %	9	5½	5	9½	18	12[a]	19	8
Current Account Balance as % of GDP 1990	−1.6	1.5	3.3	−0.8	−1.6	−3.5	−0.3	−3.7
Discount Rates Dec 1990 %	7	6	6	9¼	12½	13 7/8	14½	8

[a] Publication of Minimum Lending Rate suspended by Bank of England in August 1981; figure in column relates to MLR of March to August 1981

Source: OECD Economic Observer (various), Bundesbank Monthly Report (various)

---

[24] See Caporale, G.M, Hassapis, C. and Pitis, N., 'Excess Returns in the EMS: Do 'weak' currencies still exist after the widening of the fluctuation bands?', in: *Weltwirtschaftliches Archiv*, 1995 (131), Nr. 2, pp.326–338; the authors note the easing of high interest rate differentials after the introduction of wide margins (p.337).

Ellen Kennedy pointedly (if misleadingly) describes the EMS as 'Germany's Bretton Woods'.[25] Karl-Otto Pöhl, the former president of the Bundesbank, confirms this perception of German dominance of the system by asserting that 'the Bundesbank turned the original concept [for the EMS} on its head by making the strongest currency the yardstick for the system'.[26]

The historical context of EMU is thus highly complex, redolent with contradictions, conflicting national and institutional perspectives. Its geopolitical thrust is counter-hegemonic, but at the same time it represents, in its current shape, a hegemonic project of an ideological kind: neo-liberal and anti-interventionist in nature, which seeks to adapt to rather than counteract the effects of globalisation.

THE STRUGGLE FOR AND AGAINST EMU IN GERMANY

The Bundesbank is generally perceived as the loser in the creation of EMU.[27] Apart from losing its legal raison d'être – its exclusive responsibility for 'safeguarding the currency' (Article 3 BBLaw) – the psychological cost of losing a cherished and respected role of supreme policy maker will weigh heavily. Public opinion polls regularly place the Bundesbank high up on the list of trusted institutions; furthermore 73 per cent of respondents to an Emnid-survey in Germany agreed that the Euro would be less stable than the Deutschmark.[28] These concerns explain in part the hostility of the Bank to EMU as such, but it is a hostility which the rules of diplomacy have generally repressed or filtered strongly in the public pronouncements of the Bank and its key representatives. There has nevertheless been an unmistakable conflict between Bank and Federal Government: 'The 'sacrificing' of the Bundesbank on the 'altars' of German *and* European unification forms the

---

[25] Ibid. p.84

[26] In a speech delivered in Frankfurt, reprinted in: Deutsche Bundesbank, *Auszüge aus Presseartikeln*, 28 August 1991, p.9

[27] Thus, for example, David Marsh, *The Bundesbank*, op.cit. p.235

[28] Dieter Balkhausen (*Gutes Geld und schlechte Politik*, Munich 1992, p.87) cites a survey by the Mannheim Institute for Praxis-Orientated Social Research which places the Bundesbank (2.1) and the Federal Constitutional Court (2.2) far ahead of the federal assembly (0.9) and government (0.6) in the public's estimation; the Emnid survey was cited by *Der Spiegel*, 2/1998

foundation for that field of conflict between Bundesbank and Federal Government, which has since then marked/influenced the struggle for the Euro, and namely because this conflict has been conducted in a 'concealed' manner.'[29] The Bundesbank's preferences were certainly made perfectly clear in its 1988 annual report which saw no need for EMU, advocating the maintenance of a successful EMS which would be perfectly adequate to allow 'the internal market to function smoothly'.[30]

Helmut Kohl's monopoly of foreign policy, his government's formal constitutional control of exchange rates and actual control of EMS-realignments gave him an inbuilt advantage in the tussle, however. Like Adenauer and Schmidt before him, the anchoring of Germany within a still suspicious continent of smaller nations via multi-lateral accords has had to take precedence over the preferences of individual sectional interests, even if they share a common ideology. Shrewd tactical manoeuvring on Kohl's part locked Bundesbank representatives into the framing process for both the Delors Report and the Maastricht Treaty, notwithstanding the Bank's deep suspicions of the shape and timing of the programme.

Nevertheless, the policy clout and institutional standing of the Bundesbank at home and abroad reduced the manoeuvrability of the Kohl administration and contributed to a 'memorable piece of German political theatre' (Marsh)[31], conveniently arranged (according to Schulmeister)[32] in five compelling 'acts', beginning with the Single Market Act of 1986 and ending with the austerity programmes of EMU-hopefuls in 1997. The Bundesbank was boxed into an uncomfortable and unexpected corner by clever manoeuvring on the part of Chancellor Kohl and Foreign Minister Genscher, who were ostensibly far stronger advocates of EMU, but both the process of EMU-qualification and the struggle between the Bundesbank and the Federal Government have inflicted untold damage on both the German and other European economies. The obsession with inflation, central bankism, the roll-back

---

[29] Thus Stephan Schulmeister, 'EURO-Projekt – Selbsterhaltungsdrang der Bundesbank und das Finale Deutschland gegen Italien', *WSI-Mitteilungen*, 5/1997, p.299

[30] Bundesbank representative, quoted in: Heisenberg, *The Mark of the Bundesbank*, op.cit. p.105

[31] Marsh, *The Bundesbank*m op.cit. p.241

[32] Schulmeister 'EURO-Projekt', op.cit., pp.299–304; Schulmeister thoughtfully provides a number of different denouements for the drama.

of the state and the efficacy of markets, mixed with the Bank's mis-guided politics of resistance, produced a cocktail of factors responsible for the 'catastrophe of Maastricht', as one Keynesian critic of the process has dubbed it.[33]

The Bundesbank did its best to parry the tactical footwork of Kohl, Genscher, Mitterrand and the Commission, firstly by defining the very strict conditions for EMU membership, which were outlined in the recommendations of the Committee for the Study of European Monetary Union and formed the basis of the 1988 Delors Report. Helmut Schlesinger, Vice-President of the Bundesbank at the time and later President, who approved the Delors Report, is reported to have been confident that 'the wording of the criteria was stiff enough to save the DM by frightening politicians away'[34]. This is good Macchiavellian stuff, as Marsh has suggested:[35]

'The Bundesbank's chosen method was to give ostensible backing to the aim of European monetary union, but to seek to obstruct it by posing conditions which would simply not be acceptable to the other countries'.

John Major, in his recent autobiography, notes that, while Kohl played the driving role in promoting EMU, he was 'not comfortable with economic detail' and, when it came to specifics, acted 'as authentic voice of the Bundesbank'.[36] This suggests, at the very least, an ambivalence in the thrust of official German policy.

The fact that the Maastricht Treaty was actually signed on 17 December 1991, was thus a surprise for the Bank and put them on the back foot. The Bank's Central Council (CBC) demonstratively raised both Lombard and Discount rates by ½ per cent each three days later. However, after December 1991, with the exception of Wilhelm Nölling (the president of the Hamburg Land Central Bank), CBC members did not proceed to a frontal public assault on EMU but rather persisted with their mildly obstructive tactics, drawing consistent attention to a number of issues:

1) the rigidity of the political timetable;

2) the related folly of proceeding with EMU while the fiscal consequences of German unification were still causing problems;

---

[33] Wilhelm Hankel, 'Zur Krise verführt', op.cit. p.44

[34] Cited by Alan Milward, 'The Social Bases of Monetary Union', op.cit. p.155

[35] Marsh, *The Bundesbank*, op.cit. p.245

[36] John Major, *The Autobiography*, London 1999, p.315 and p.325

3) the danger of conceding too much flexibility to allow Mediterranean states to join in the first wave, and

4) the culpable absence of plans for a political union, which would be better placed to achieve long-term harmonisation of fiscal policy, i.e. long-term budgetary discipline.[37]

These criticisms have been fully documented by Marsh, Dyson and Featherstone, Nölling, Heisenberg and others [38]. They are intellectually quite persuasive, and not just to neo-liberal audiences and the German general public. They do, however, pander to a kind of DM-nationalism which both the Far Right and the SPD have sought to exploit electorally.[39] But they are best assessed in the context of a full appreciation of neo-liberal preferences and alongside the one-sided fulminations of Tietmeyer and his colleagues against the social state, trade unions and profligate state authorities. These ideological preferences remain central to the new orthodoxy of central bankism, whether it is expressed by a dominant Bundesbank or a new supra-national European Central Bank.

I wish to focus more closely on the conduct of monetary policy by the Bundesbank in the period 1989 to 1993, i.e. from the first inklings of German unification through to the collapse of the EMS and its macro-economic effects. It is my contention that the Bundesbank pursued a deliberately tough monetary line with at least the indirect intention of subverting the EMU project. It has been a campaign of some subtlety which admits different interpretations. Nevertheless, the most convincing of these interpretations remains that of Stephan Schulmeister that Bundesbank behaviour was driven in large measure by a strong 'self-preservation instinct'[40].

---

[37] A fuller critical commentary of the Maastricht programme was published by the Bundesbank in its monthly report of February 1992, pp.45–54; this includes a specific statement by the Central Bank Council. See also Dyson and Featherstone ['EMU and Economic Governance', op.cit. 342f] for an exposition of the Bundesbank's preference for political union as a precondition for monetary union.

[38]   Marsh, *The Bundesbank*, op.cit. 248ff; Dyson and Featherstone 'EMU and Economic Governance', op.cit. 333f; Nölling, *Monetary Policy in Europe after Maastricht*, op.cit. 44ff

[39]   See J.Leaman, 'Central Banking and the Crisis of Social Democracy', *German Politics* 1995 4/3,   41f; also Schulmeister, 'EURO-Projekt', op.cit. p.305

[40] Schulmeister, 'EURO-Projekt', op.cit.

The period 1989–93, which coincides with the framing of the EMU project, was characterised namely by a period of unprecedented deflationary pressure on the part of the Bundesbank, amounting to overkill. The dosage and timing of the squeeze were disproportionate and dysfunctional. If one compares the four serious deflationary squeezes in Germany's post-war history (1969–71, 1972–75, 1979–83 and 89–95), it is plain that they become progressively longer and more severe (see Table 7.2).

Table 7.2   Restrictive Monetary Phases in the FRG, 1969–95

Deflationary Period	1 Discount Rate Annual Average (%)	2 Inflation Rate maximum (year on year in %)	3 Inflation Rate (RPI) Annual Average (%)	4 Ratio of 1 to 3
1969–1971:30 Months	5.85	5.2	3.5	1.69
1972–1975:31 Months	5.0	7.0	6.3	0.79
1979–1983:44 Months	6.85	6.3	4.76	1.43
1989–1995:71 Months	6.34	4.5	2.6	2.43

Source: Deutsche Bundesbank, *Monthly Reports* (various); own calculations

It is also obvious that the most recent squeeze has been considerably longer but less appropriate in terms of inflation targetting than the other three. If one takes a pattern of interest rate levels where a squeeze in Germany is defined as a period where the discount rate was 4.5 per cent or higher, the 1989–95 squeeze was 71 months long (72–75: 31 months; 79–83: 44 months). The discount rate reached a record 8.75 per cent in July 1992, accompanied by a record 9.75 per cent Lombard rate, with an average discount rate level of 6.34 per cent for the whole period. However, the cost of living index never exceeded 4.2 per cent in West Germany and averaged only 2.6 per cent for the period. The exceptional price adjustments in East Germany, pre-programmed by the removal of subsidies on rents, fuel and basic foodstuffs and by the introduction of VAT were rapidly overcome after 1993,[41] there were

---

[41] 'With the development of prices in east Germany we are dealing with processes of adaptation which are determined by unification and are thus unavoidable and which have to be accepted by monetary policy',

further increases in indirect taxation (on mineral oil products, for example) which affected price levels, but which were designed to offset
the fiscal costs of unification and, by removing liquidity, were if anything disinflationary in their medium-term effects. Table 7.3 demonstrates that key economic indicators for the German economy were con-
firming a marked downturn during 1992: investments in new machinery, industrial order books, manufacturing production and employment
were all in real decline.[42] The decline continued throughout 1993. The
figures in both Table 7.3 and Table 7.4 also indicate that price trends
were very favourable. A marginal increase of 0.4 per cent in import
prices in 1991 was followed by two consecutive years of import price
falls (1992: –3.3 per cent; 1993: –2.0 per cent). This was reflected in
factory gate prices (Table 7.4), while the cost of living index for east
Germany indicated marked improvements when the effects of removing
energy and rent subsidies are stripped out.[43]

Thus, in terms of any notional anti-inflation dosage of interest rates,
the scale of the long 1989–95 squeeze was quite inappropriate.[44] The
real central bank interest rate averaged 3.74 per cent compared to 2.09
per cent in the second oil crisis/ Reaganomics disaster, –1.3 per cent in
the first oil crisis and 2.35 per cent in the boom of 1969–71. Calculated
in terms of a simple ratio of Discount Rate to Inflation Rate (arguably a
clearer reflection of 'dosage'), the contrast is even more stark with a
ratio of 2.43 exceeding anything that had gone before (see right-hand
column in Table 7.2 above). The severity of deflation was unsurprisingly matched by the severity of the 1993 recession in west Germany
which saw a record one-year fall of 2.3 per cent in real GDP.

---

thus Deutsches Institut für Wirtschaftsforschung, 'Verfehlte Geldpolitik', *Wochenbericht,* 30 July 1992, p.386

[42] The Bundesbank's monthly statistics confirm that the downturn in
production and orders began in April 1992 and accelerated through the
last three quarters of the year.

[43] The Bundesbank in its Annual Report for 1991 (p.25) had already
acknowledged that price developments in the East do not involve 'inflationary processes, but rather adjustments of price relations to actual
conditions of scarcity and thus to the conditions of a market economy'.

[44] C.f. also Schulmeister, 'EURO-Projekt', op.cit.302ff; Eric Owen-
Smith, 'Incentives for Growth and Development' in: Stephen Frowen
and Jens Hölscher (eds), *The German Currency Union of 1990,* London
1997, 132ff

Table 7.3:   Selected Indicators for the unified German Economy, 1991–93 (Figures in per cent)

Indicator	1991	1992	1993
Gross Investments	6.5	1.1	6.9
of which: Machinery	9.1	–3.9	–15.0
Industrial Orders	+0.5	–3.5	–7.6
Gross Income of Industrial Firms	–1.1	–1.8	–2.3
Manufacturing Production	2.9	–1.9	–7.3
Unemployment	–10.3	+7.0	+25.6
Bankruptcies		+23	+38.8
Index of Import Prices	+0.4	–3.3	–2.0

Source: Deutsche Bundesbank, *Geschäftsberichte, Monatsberichte*, various

Table 7.4   Factory Gate and Consumer Price Trends in Germany, 1990–95 (Figures in per cent)

Year	Factory Gate Prices			Cost of Living Index			
	FRG	West	East	FRG	West	East	East*
1990		1.7			2.7		
1991		2.5	1.6		3.6	21.3	8.7
1992	1.4	1.4	2.3	5.1	4.0	11.2	4.4
1993	0.2	±0.0	1.9	4.5	3.6	8.8	4.0
1994	0.6	0.6	1.2	2.7	2.7	3.4	2.6
1995	1.8	1.7	1.4	1.8	1.7	2.1	n.a.
* without rent or energy							

Source: Deutsche Bundesbank, *Monatsberichte*, various

The severity of the squeeze is thus inexplicable in terms of inflation management, but also in the Bundesbank's own terms of money-supply targetting. M3 growth overshot the Bank's target corridor consistently in 1992, 1993 and early 1994.[45] However, while it raised short-term

---

[45] For a critical account of the Bundesbank's record of money supply targetting, see Peter Bofinger 'The German Currency Union of 1990 –

rates in 1992, it lowered both Discount and Lombard rates throughout 1993 and in advance of the 1994 Federal elections in small but frequent steps to 4.5 per cent by May 1994. According to the Bank's own operational principles – which involve an 11-quarter timelag between money stock increases and inflationary outcomes – this was clearly contradictory. In political terms, it nevertheless allowed Tietmeyer's party comrade, Kohl, to be re-elected on the back of a brief post-recession recovery. The long-term damage to the economy had already been done, however. Keynesian economists in Germany argued persuasively that the Bundesbank had become a 'slave to its own concept of the money supply' and that the unique situation of unification demanded above all a relaxation of money stock indicators and the provision of generous credit conditions for enterprises in the East, where external sources of credit – and not just the domestic stock of savings – should be exploited to the full.[46]

A number of economists argue convincingly that Bundesbank policy was never orientated towards the purist yardstick of money supply but towards external indicators like the exchange rate.[47] However, even using this criterion the difference between the 1979–83 squeeze and the post-unification squeeze is inexplicable. The earlier period was affected by massive increases in energy import costs, by temporary balance of payments deficits and by currency depreciation against the Dollar. In contrast, while there were also brief balance of payments problems in the 1989–95 period, import costs – notably raw material costs – fell (see Table 7.3) and the DM appreciated against both the Dollar (+31 per cent) and against a basket of 18 OECD currencies (+16 per cent).

The only convincing explanations for the exceptional behaviour of the Bank include firstly the desire to reassert its operational autonomy after the imposition by the Federal Government of a currency conversion rate of 1:1 in Germany's Currency Union of July 1990 (a decision of pure political expediency).[48] Secondly, and more plausibly, they

---

A Critical Assessment: The Impact on German Monetary Policy', in Frowen and Hölscher, op.cit. 211ff

[46] DIW, 'Verfehlte Geldpolitik', op.cit. pp.388–9

[47] C.f. Hansjörg Herr, *Geld, Währungswettbewerb und Währungssystem*, Frankfurt 1992, p.334; Bofinger, 'The German Currency Union', op.cit. p.218 suggests that the Bank has shifted to a more pragmatic inflation-targetting and away from a dogmatic adherence to M3 targetting.

[48] Thus Bofinger, ibid.

would seem to have included the desire to see the EMU project fail via the failure of its main vehicle of monetary convergence, the EMS. Lothar Müller, the President of the Bavarian LCB, supposedly urged an immediate increase in the Discount Rate after the December 1991 agreement with the words 'especially now, we must show we are serious'[49]. The quotation can clearly be interpreted in a variety of ways, and the evidence of sabotage remains anecdotal. However, it cannot be a coincidence that three days after the signing of the Maastricht treaty both Germany's main central bank rates were raised, were further raised in 1992 and maintained at levels higher than in previous, more serious inflationary periods until the EMS effectively collapsed.[50]

THE ROLLING CRISIS OF THE EUROPEAN MONETARY SYSTEM

After five years of relative exchange rate stability (1987–92), the US and several European economies were already in recession and the German economy – despite the post-unification boom in the West – had been showing signs of weakness since the end of 1991; the Dollar exchange rate against the mark fell markedly in early 1992. In this context, it was generally expected that the Bundesbank would ease the pressure on both European economies and on the currency bands of the EMS with a drop in its main rates. Instead, in July 1992, it raised the Discount Rate and the Lombard Rate to record levels. Speculation against the Pound, the Lira and the Franc increased and were arguably made worse by the significantly minor lowering of rates in September 1992 (½ per cent and ¼ per cent respectively) after a devaluation of the Lira within the EMS. When Helmut Schlesinger (who had in the meantime become President of the Bundesbank) suggested to journalists that 'one or two other currencies might come under pressure', mayhem broke out, forcing both the Lira and the Pound out of the EMS. The following summer, in 1993, when German discount rates were still twice as high as in the US, there was renewed speculative pressure on most other European currencies, notably the Irish Punt – which the Bundesbank was unwilling to protect, despite the favourable state of Ireland's external balances – and the French Franc, which the Bundesbank was prepared to support, but only to a limited extent. Nevertheless, the August adjustment of the currency bands from ± 2.5 per cent to

---

[49] Quoted in Marsh, *The Bundesbank*, op.cit. p.248
[50] Schulmeister, 'EURO-Projekt', op.cit. p.299

± 15 per cent signified the effective end of the EMS. Ironically it also ended much of the currency speculation which had been guaranteed high returns by the commitments of member states to support narrow ceilings and floors with reciprocal purchases of weaker participating currencies.

It is instructive to compare the Bundesbank's accounts of the EMS crises of 1992 and 1993 with those of other commentators and other national perspectives. The Bundesbank's view is dominated by perceptions of its obligations and its lack of manoeuvrability within the system. In October 1992 it ascribed the pressure on EMS currencies to perceptions on the part of 'foreign exchange markets ... of the unresolved economic divergences between the various EC-member states'.[51] These differences are underscored and closely defined again in August 1993 as divergent inflation rates, balance of payments levels, public debt and business cycles.[52] The specific triggers are seen as the Danish and French referendums on EMU, along with interest rate reductions in the US.[53] The Bundesbank only mentions its own Central Bank rates in terms of the specific inflationary dangers of German public debt and 'the strong explosion (sic) of wage costs'.[54] The determinants are, according to the Bundesbank view, exogenous: the contradictions of the EMS as a system of political regulation, the profligacy of states and the immoderation of trade union wage demands. The 'markets', on the other hand, are judged as reliable interpreters of economic fundamentals, whose 'disappointments' must be sympathised with and whose 'trust' must be regained.[55] The polarity of externalities and market logic, of political and market regulation, informs both the request to the Federal Government by the Bundesbank to seek a realignment of the EMS parities in 1992[56] and its approval of the widening of EMS mar-

---

[51] Bundesbank, *Monthly Report*, October 1992, p.15

[52] Bundesbank, *Monthly Report*, August 1993, 19f

[53] Bundesbank, *Monatsbericht*, October 1992, p.24

[54] Bundesbank, *Monatsbericht*, August 1993, p.21

[55] Bundesbank, *Monatsbericht*, August 1993, p.20 and p.25; Elmar Altvater, Susan Strange and others would argue that the decoupling of global financial markets from traditional trading markets makes the former just as exogenous as states and organised labour, if not more; Elmar Altvater, 'A Contest without Victors', op.cit; Susan Strange, *Casino Capitalism*, op.cit.

[56] Bundesbank, *Monatsbericht*, October 1992, p.15

gins in August 1993.[57] At the same time the Bank underlines the cost
of ostensibly flawed political regulation in terms of its 'massive' intramarginal interventions to support threatened currencies; these amounted
to some 92 billion DM from the end of August to the end of September
1992 and to 60 billion DM in July 1993.[58] The Bank's long-standing
preference for flexible exchange rates is reflected in its judgement on
the widening of EMS margins on 2 August 1993: 'The Bundesbank has
regained room for manoeuvre in monetary policy through the recent
decisions on currency policy'.[59] The 30 per cent fluctuation band indeed represented the effective return to floating exchange rates.[60]

While the Bundesbank's view of the EMS undoubtedly contains
convincing strands of argument,[61] it remains conveniently selective and
thus syllogistic. A French perspective demonstrates another kind of
selectivity which ascribes considerable blame to the Bundesbank.
Aeschimann and Riché concede that overheating had obliged the Bundesbank to raise its short-term rates from 1989, but see in the extension
of the squeeze a deliberate act of damaging deflation, reflecting the
particularly hardline attitude of Pöhl's successor, Helmut Schlesinger –
'an obsessive exponent of the struggle against inflation' who was
'never concerned about the consequences of this obsession'.[62] With
France fully committed to its 'franc fort' policy and a parity of 3.35 to
the Mark, the ratchetting up by the Bundesbank of both Discount and
Lombard rates at Schlesinger's first CBC meeting on 15 August 1991
by 1 per cent and ¼ per cent respectively created havoc in the French
economy and among its policy makers:

'Admittedly, Schlesinger was doing nothing new: German interest
rates have been rising for three years. But the situation is very different.
Up until then, the countries of Europe enjoyed solid growth and did not
suffer excessively from this hardening of monetary policy. This time,
the German cold shower hits them just as their economies – far from

---

[57] Bundesbank, *Monatsbericht*, August 1993, p.25
[58] Bundesbank, *Monatsbericht*, 10/92, p.16 and 8/93, p.25
[59] Bundesbank, *Monatsbericht*, 8/92, p.26
[60] The only exception was the bilateral commitment between the Netherlands and Germany to maintain narrow bands of fluctuation.
[61] In this context see: David Cobham, 'German Currency Union and
the Crises in the European Monetary System', in: Frowen and Hölscher
(eds), op.cit. 36ff
[62] Éric Aeschimann and Pascal Riché, *La guerre des sept ans. Histoire
secrète du franc fort 1989–1996*, Paris 1996, p.100

warming up – are beginning to slow down. Schlesinger is perfectly aware of this, but this isn't his business. On this day, Germany chooses to get its neighbours to help pay for unification. ..... The trap shuts on the French Franc.'[63]

Aeschimann and Riché document in detail the background to the bland Franco-German communiqués of 22 September 1992, 21 December 1992 and 22 July 1993, in which the appropriateness of the 3.35 parity to economic fundamentals is ritually confirmed. In doing so, they reveal not only the structural and personal subordination of French officials to their German counterparts, but also the tactical manipulation by Schlesinger and his colleagues, deriving from their double advantage: presiding over the anchor currency of the EMS and an autonomous agency of economic policy, obliged by law to resist the pressure of any elected governments whose policies run counter to their core task of stabilising the currency. The view of the French participants in the rolling crisis of the EMS from August 1991 to August 1993 sees the EMS as essentially sound but German policy as flawed and inconsistent with the spirit of European co-operation. Edmond Alphandéry, in an interview with the radio station, *Europe 1*, on 24 June 1993 was exceptionally outspoken in declaring that 'Europe is suffering from monetary policies that are too restrictive ... The Germans must accelerate their lowering of interest rates'.[64] Alphandéry's 'gaffe' in fact generated outrage in Bonn and Frankfurt, caused the cancellation of a planned Franco-German meeting in Paris and stiffened the Bundesbank's resolve not to be hurried.[65] In the face of German resistance to such re-

---

[63] Aeschimann and Riché, *La guerre de sept ans*, op.cit., 100f; it is perhaps worth noting that this French account neglects to point out that the British economy was already in recession in 1991.

[64] Quoted in Aeschimann and Riché, *La guerre de sept ans*, op.cit., p.208

[65] Dyson and Featherstone assert that the 'lesson' from this episode 'was that neither side must ask what the other cannot domestically deliver', ['EMU and Economic Governance', op.cit. p.352]; this implies firstly that Kohl and Waigel had the same agenda as Schlesinger and Tietmeyer, although there are strong indications that the Federal Government would have preferred a loosening of monetary policy at an earlier stage; secondly, that Bundesbank policy was appropriate to German conditions, that they were 'unable' to respond to French requests because of their domestic legal obligations. A closer reading of the various discourses taking place during this period would take a less

quests, Alphandéry and Balladur seriously considered proposing that Germany should be obliged to withdraw from the EMS.[66] This is essentially the mirror image of the Bundesbank's repeated demands for realignments *within* the EMS and of its final successful bid to widen the margins of fluctuation, first floated on 22 July 1993 and then agreed at the crisis summit in Brussels on 1 August 1993.

What is clear from the EMS episode is that the Central Bank Council was quite happy to see its demise as the main vehicle for exchange rate convergence, indeed eager to accentuate the disparities between the participating countries. What is also plain is that – in the medium term – the unprecedented squeeze made it much more difficult for European economies and their state authorities to achieve the convergence criteria set by the Bundesbank for EMU even within the more generous of the two timetables (1999 as opposed to 1997). The competitive monetary deflation of 1989–1993 reduced growth, investment and employment and increased both the overall debt burden of states and the ratio of debt servicing to GDP[67]. It represented, at the European level, a chronic misallocation of resources. Stages Two and Three of the Maastricht Programme have meant, however, that the deflationary baton has been passed on from central banks to the fiscal authorities of the member states, as they seek to reduce both their annual borrowing requirements and their overall debt ratios. Interest rates in Germany have fallen to historic lows, as fiscal consolidation by the Kohl administration ensures that state investment, domestic demand, wage settlements place no pressure on prices. Monetary deflation, followed by fiscal deflation dictated by the monetarist imperatives of Maastricht, produced a deflationary continuum from 1989 throught to 1998, which can be observed in Table 7.5.

---

benign view of Bundesbank behaviour and would point to both its track record of scepticism/resistance to EMU and also to its habit of rejecting public appeals for policy changes as a symbolic confirmation of its independence.

[66] Aeschimann and Riché, *La guerre de sept ans*, op.cit., 222ff

[67] Between 1989 and 1995 net debt interest payments by EU governments rose from 3.5 per cent to 5 per cent of GDP, from 2.2 per cent to 3.2 per cent in Germany and 2.2 per cent to 3.5 per cent in France; see OECD *Economic Observer*, December 1997

Table 7.5   Deflationary Continuum: Macro-Economic Policy
                   Effects on East German Economy, 1989–98
                   (Contractive effects in bold)

19..	89	90	91	92	93	94	95	96	97	98*
FDE**		26.6	72.1	30.2	6.1	**-54.9**	**-5.2**	**-12.2**	**-7.5**	**-28.2**
MSE***	2.1	3.3	2.7	**2.85**	**3.4**	**3.1**	1.95	1.2	0.7	1.3
GDP+	100	78	56	62	66	71	74	76	77	79

* Estimate; ** Fiscal Demand effects in DM Bill. without interest payments; *** Monetary Supply effects. Real Interest Rate (average annual
discount rate minus annual rate of consumer price inflation) in per cent;
+ East German GDP (1989 = 100)

Sources: Deutsches Institut für Wirtschaftsforschung, Bundesbank
Monthly Reports (various)

The long-term damage that has been inflicted on Germany, in particular
east Germany, and the societies of other EU-member states can only be
guessed at. The struggle by the Bundesbank against EMU can be convincingly defended intellectually, for the reasons outlined above. However, the deployment of monetary deflation during the crucial transition
period 1990–93 and the continuing dominance of the monetarist imperative have arguably extended the period necessary for the alignment
of the eastern Länder to western levels of productivity and employment
by many years. The *speed* of alignment was always going to be a crucial factor in determining the extent of economic dependence of the
new Länder on the old. With that it would decisively influence both the
extent of the political and social psychological subordination of the
people of the East to the supporting population of the West and the degree of political resentment felt by the West towards the East. The initial calculations of even optimistic observers of German unification
involved at least ten years of fiscal dependence, as the East's regional
GDP grew at 9–10 per cent per annum to catch up the West within an
economically and politically sustainable period. The real GDP performance of the East is instructive: After the catastrophic years of
1990–91, the new Länder have only approached the target of 10 per
cent per annum in two of the 8 years (in 1992 and 1994; see Table 7.6).
Since then east German growth has declined to a level in 1997 which,
at 1.6 per cent, was even below the modest 2.2 per cent achieved in the
West. The crucial catching-up process of 1992–96 has stopped, long

before even the post-unification slump has been made good; far from decreasing, the dis-parities in GDP levels and other macro-economic variables remain stubbornly wide (see Table 7.6), unemployment in the East (at 21.1 per cent in January 1998) is double the level in the West (10.5 per cent). With the Federal Republic's constitutional obligation to ensure 'uniformity of living standards' throughout its territory, the level of social insurance and other social benefits in the West must also apply in the East; consumer demand in the East, while not as high as in the richer West, is nevertheless far higher than the economic product generated by the population in the East. The resulting demand-output gap has had to be plugged by large-scale fiscal transfers from the West equivalent to 4–5 per cent of GDP per annum. Because of the double burden of monetary and fiscal deflation, the East will continue to need such transfers for far longer than might have been necessary, had Germany's federal authorities adopted a more coherent set of macro-economic policies to address the extraordinary circumstances of unification. There are a variety of estimates concerning the date at which the East will have finally converged with the old FRG. The early Goldmann-Sachs timescale of ten years has already been proven ridiculously optimistic. The most optimistic forecast, by Lange and Pugh[68], sees convergence taking some 25–30 years; Dornbusch and Wolf reckon on 50 years, Barro and Sala-i-Martin 84 years.[69] Assuming an average growth rate for the West of 2½ per cent (the level which currently ensures no further increases in unemployment), and of 3½ per cent in the East, it would take roughly 78 years for complete convergence to be complete.[70] The lack of structural planning, be it of an industrial or regional nature, was bad enough but to add monetary and fiscal deflation to the neo-liberal anti-interventionist recipe will be judged severely by future generations of economic historians.

---

[68] Thomas Lange and Geoffrey Pugh, *The Economics of German Unification*, Cheltenham 1998, 150f
[69] The data from Dornbusch and Wolf, and Barro and Sala-I-Martin is cited by Michael Burda and Michael Funke, 'Eastern Germany: Can't we be more optimistic', *Centre for Economic Policy Research Discussion Paper*, No 863, December 1993
[70] The convergence problem is dealt with in greater detail in a conference paper I presented in April 1998, 'Bad Policies, Bad Timing: The Failure of Germany's Neo-Liberal Transformation Strategy', Southampton Conference: Dis-Unification. Competing Constructions of Contemporary Germany, April 16–17 1998

The analogy with Brüning is arguably unfair on Brüning. While the collapse of the east German economy in 1990 and 1991 was similar to the German recession of 1930–32, Germany's authorities are today operating in a strong and supportive multi-lateral environment; unification has manifested enormous potential for national solidarity and international co-operation, while the Versailles Treaty and international protectionism in the early 1930s continued both to polarise national opinion and divide Germany from its neighbours. Above all, Brüning did not have the advantage of hindsight, which would have allowed him to see that the continuing primacy of inflation-control – be it under a dominant Bundesbank within the EMS or under the restrictive conditions of Maastricht monetarism – defies the reality of a) a global environment in which inflation has ceased to be an immediate problem[71], b) global structural unemployment which increases with every cycle and c) a national German transformation crisis which from the start cried out for a coordinated and refined economic policy.

Table 7.6   Annual Real GDP Growth in Old and New Länder, 1990-97 in per cent

	1990	1991	1992	1993	1994	1995	1996	1997
GDP growth in Five New Länder	-22.0	-28.4	9.7	6.3	9.2	5.3	1.9	1.6
GDP in FNL (1989=100)	78	56	61	65	71	75	76	77
GDP growth in Old Länder	4.9	4.9	1.2	-2.3	2.3	1.8	1.3	2.2
GDP in OL (1989=100)	105	110	111	109	111	113	115	117

Source: Deutsches Institut für Wirtschaftsforschung, *Wochenberichte*, various; own calculations.

---

[71] C.f. Roger Bootle, *The Death of Inflation. Surviving and Thriving in the Zero Era*, London 1996

As such, the struggle for and against EMU in Germany has been an irrelevant discourse between camps committed to neo-liberal principles but at odds over the modalities for implementing those principles. Accordingly, the outcome to that discourse – be it EMU or non-EMU – will not alter the dominance of its orthodoxy at this point in time: economic policy under EMU or non-EMU will be dominated directly or indirectly by an independent central bank (ECB or the Bundesbank) statutorily obliged to pursue one primary macro-economic goal before all others. This means the structural subordination of fiscal policy to the fiscal targets dictated by monetary authorities, a continued weakening of policy coordination and, not least, the continued marginalisation of democratic institutions in the shaping of economic policy. The theoretical and practical shambles of neo-liberalism should rather alert us to the dangers of either variant (EMU or non-EMU) and the irrelevance of current orthodoxy to the problems of the 21st century.

8 Concluding Remarks: Breaking the Myth

We live increasingly interdependent lives, not just in the advanced capitalist societies of Europe and the rest of the OECD but in the emerging and developing countries of the – no longer separate – 'Third World'. The global trans-national corporations, operating on the basis of just-in-time management techniques, the optimal use of geographically disparate locations and the relative cheapness of transport, have established a highly complex mesh of production, distribution, consumption and servicing networks, linking all continents. As a result of global deregulation of financial markets and new communications technologies, capital no longer has strong territorial roots, but operates in large measure as an interlinked whole; indeed the drive to shed territorial restrictions has gone beyond even the lure of offshore locations for 'portfolio management' to generate the utterly bizarre (but apparently serious) notion of 'off-planet banking'.[1]

We depend on the labour and cooperative behaviour of other people to a greater degree than at any time in human history; the lifestyles in highly modern societies like those of Germany and Britain manifest all the elements of this dependence, be it in what we consume, how we work, how we inform ourselves, how we make decisions about our future. Interdependence is ineluctable. And yet the dominant ideology that has accompanied us into the twenty-first century is of autonomous self-determination, the efficacy of self-reliance, self-help, individual welfare provision, individual rational choice. We are encouraged to act in terms of an atomised self-interest when the reality of global economics and global culture is of dependence and external determination. The rhetoric of capitalism, of the self-adequate entrepreneur, thus collides head-on with the reality of integrated global capitalism. Perversely, the new insecurities of employment are translated ideologically into the need for self-promotion and self-stylisation, assisted by armies of (organised and corporate) style

---

[1] See Dan Atkinson, 'The pie in the sky nightmare', *The Guardian*, 4 February 1999, p.17

engineers in the mass media. The organised capitalism of the 21st century legitimates itself by reference to a (largely mythical) frontier existence of white American settlers; mythical, because even frontier existence depended on refined networks of support.

Within the popular new rhetoric of human existence, there has emerged the preference in politics for single agencies to be responsible for supposedly separable areas of policy formulation and/or policy implementation. A dominant place among these preferences is accorded to the independent central bank and the conduct of anti-inflationary monetary policy. In this book I have attempted to expose a series of syllogisms which have contributed to the popularisation of independent central banks. I have examined the complex and changing role of money in human society and the specific historical, ideological, economic, political and social contexts within which the particular German preference for an autonomous central bank evolved. What is revealed by the, often very brief, sketches of central bank history in Germany is not a picture of overwhelming evidence in favour of the institution with which so many nations have chosen to enter the new century. Rather, the evidence points strongly towards the collective self-delusion of both political and academic elites within capitalist countries, where they identify the independent Bundesbank (and Bank deutscher Länder before it) as the key to German politico-economic success. It should have been clear to all intelligent observers of modern economic history that the strengths of Germany's political economy are rooted above all in its culture of long-termism, investment in human capital, research, machinery and (export-) marketing, in the quality of traded goods, in supportive financial and political institutions and the political leverage associated with the success of the secular economy. Yes, of course, monetary policy contributed to the success of the secular economy, particularly in the early years of the federal republic, but in quite different contexts an independent German central bank has been decidedly unhelpful: in the struggle against hyper-inflation between May 1922 and November 1923, in the struggle against recession and politico-economic meltdown in the Great Depression (in both cases the Reichsbank made things deliberately worse); in the timing of policy, when all too often (1966, 1974–75, 1979–82) monetary deflation coincided with cyclical downturns, and most culpably in the politico-economic mess of German unification, where a seemingly blind and dogmatic Bundesbank put paid to the dim hopes of a rapid convergence of the east German economy with the economy of the old Federal Republic. The German economy has remained relatively robust since 1990 not because of resolute and prudent Bundesbank policy but because of the resilience of its other agencies and despite a wrong-headed approach to monetary and fiscal policy, driven by the Bundesbank and its neo-liberal allies. The price of the non-convergence of the east German economy, severely compounded by the Bundesbank, will be heavy in the years to come and will be measured not just in terms of the continuing misallocation of national resources to plug the demand-output gap in the East. It will be measured in the social and political tensions which result from the long-term dependence of one region on another. The example of the Italian mezzogiorno is not over-dramatic. More worrying is the decision by individual countries and by the EU collectively to adopt the institutional structures and operational procedures of Germany's Bundesbank as their model. As the above chapters have sought to demonstrate, public concern about the popularisation of autonomous central banking can be targetted at either the technical appropriateness or at the political appropriateness of the institution. The conclusion by a number of academic observers that autonomous central banks deliver not just optimal results in respect of price developments but also solid outcomes for all macro-economic indicators (including growth and employment),[2] is based on a rather narrow sample of one, namely the Bundesbank, as Gerald Holtham has rightly pointed out.[3] Notwithstanding the absurdity of any mono-causal explanations for macro-economic phenomena, it would be no less syllogistic to assert that dependent central banks have had a better record of consumer price inflation since 1980, using the single example of the Bank of Japan which, up until 1999, was heavily integrated into state/government coordinated economic policy-making, and seemingly out-performed all other countries in the IMF's table of compared inflation rates.[4] It would be more honest to assert, firstly,

---

[2] Cukierman, Alex, Steven B. Webb and Bilin Neyapti, 'Measuring the Independence of Central Banks and Its Effect on Policy Outcomes" in: *World Bank Economic Review*, Vol.6, no.3; Alesina, Alberto and Summers, Lawrence, 'Central Bank Independence and Macroeconomic Performance: Some Comparative Evidence, in: *Journal of Money, Credit and Banking*, 25 (1993), pp.151–162

[3] Holtham, Gerald, Economic *Integration after Maastricht*, IPPR Occasional Paper, London 1993

[4] See: IMF, *International Financial Statistics* (CD-Rom), September 1996; Japanese consumer price inflation between 1980 and 1989 averaged 2.53 per cent, compared to Germany's 2.9 per cent and the

that economics is an approximative 'science' which should avoid the application of syllogisms – which exclude historical, contextual and countless other cultural co-determinants – to the design of national or supranational institutional architecture. Secondly, it would more appropriate to point out that economists are entirely divided about the nature and causes of inflation. In an extensive survey of almost 1000 economists in 1990, Martin Ricketts and Edward Shoesmith found an equal number of academics who were prepared to reject the thesis that 'inflation is primarily a monetary phenomenon' as were prepared to support it.[5] A later survey of British and German social-democratic politicians produced similar collisions of opinion.[6] The important lesson from any study of this kind is of extreme uncertainty, taking the view of 'economic science' as a whole. It is simply not justifiable to separate out one factor (CB autonomy) from the broad set of determinants to assert its primacy/efficacy in producing the outcome of one variable, be it inflation, growth, unemployment or investments. Entirely contradictory views may be asserted with conviction and authoritative certainty, but with the dubious comfort of knowing that there are no tests to establish the absolute correctness or absolute incorrectness of any hypothesis in the 'dismal' science.

The institutional and operational principles of the independent central bank rest on a chain of logic, developed essentially by monetarists, which breaks down in any honest empirical test (see above p.7f). Purely at the conceptual level, the Bundesbank has conceded that

---

USA's 5.5 per cent; between 1990 and 1995 it was a mere 1.66 per cent, compared to Germany's 3.17 per cent and the USA's 3.5 per cent.

[5] Ricketts, M. and Shoesmith, E., *British Economic Opinion*, London 1990; 41.1 per cent rejected the hypothesis, 41.9 per cent accepted it

[6] See J. Leaman, 'Central Banking and the Crisis of Social Democracy', *German Politics*, December 1995, pp.22–48; 39.2 per cent of all respondents (Labour Party and SPD MPs and MEPS) rejected the thesis that inflation was primarily a monetary phenomenon, with only 29.1 per cent supporting it; 92.4 per cent agreed with the hypothesis that 'inflation was caused by a variety of factors'; 65.2 per cent rejected the view that 'the control of inflation should be the responsibility of a single, independent monetary agency', although the German sample produced only 43.0 per cent rejecting this view and 34.7 per cent accepting it. On the other hand, over 80 per cent of all respondents in each group supported the view that the control of inflation should be the responsibility of all agencies of the state.

key variables of the monetarist hypothesis MV = PT have shaky foundations: firstly, by adopting a wide variety of definitions of money stock (M) – M1, CBMS, M3, M3 extended – the solidity of the concept of quantity in Quantity Theory looks dubious by implication; secondly, the Bundesbank's own Hoffmann Report (1998) concluded that standard calculations of price changes consistently overestimate inflation, or distort the relationship between price (P) and commodity value (see above p.12). If at least two elements either side of the MV=PT equation are wrong and the other two (V and T) are also cast into doubt by the increased size of the black economy,[7] the value of the equation is at best only approximative and certainly not appropriate for formulating precise quantitative or temporal adjustments to the cost of refinanced credit. The failure by the Bundesbank to hit annual money stock targets more often than it missed them is indicative of this problem, as was the persistent inability to avoid stability crises by timing the end of credit squeezes appropriately.

Another problem attaching to the Bank's view of the dynamics of inflation is its selective view of the major causal factors. Quantity theory essentially predefines a narrow focus on the demand for and the supply of money. The 'culprits' in driving inflation are persistently seen on the demand side and no less persistently are narrowed down to trade unions in the annual round of wage negotiations and state authorities in the development of their expenditure and borrowing plans. Decisions to raise short-term interests have been frequently justified by reference to one or both of these culprits. Neither, however, is directly involved in the setting of prices, if one disregards local authority service fees and the price effects of indirect taxation; the latter has, in any case, a potentially deflationary effect by removing liquidity from circulation. The actual price-setters, private companies and the self-employed, are regarded as less culpable agents in the transmission of demand by workers/households and the state. They merely respond to market conditions or rather – and this is the dominant neo-liberal sub-text of Bundesbank policy – to the externalities, represented by the collective, non-market institutions of trade unions and the state.

---

[7] The size of the black economy is estimated to be at least 10 per cent of German GDP; during the period of preparation for EMU qualification, there were suggestions from various quarters in various countries to include a notional additional figure for the black economy in calculations of real GDP, so that PSBR and overall debt ratios would slip down below the permitted threshholds!!

Consistently excluded from the critical gaze of the Bundesbank and its allies is any notion that companies, as price-setters, abuse market power either during cyclical peaks when strong demand partly suspends price competition or at any time during the cycle if they possess strategic power positions within the market – be it as monopolies/ oligopolies, as monopsonies or as members of legal or illegal cartels. The neglect of the effects of economic concentration on price-setting – not just by the Bundesbank but by neo-liberal thinking in general – is simply staggering. One seeks in vain in the copious press statements, monthly reports, annual reports and special publications of the Bundesbank for any comment on the price effects of the most dramatic period of national and trans-national mergers the world has ever known. There is no suggestion that corporate planners are ever motivated by the desire to increase market power over either customers or over suppliers, no hint that mergers frequently involve the 'downsizing' of the workforce with resultant (and intended) boosts to share-values and therefore the wealth of directors and shareholders. The selective blaming of non-market actors and the implicit exculpation of the dominant actors on national and global markets reflects not the neutrality of the autonomous institution but an extreme partisanship for an extreme economic orthodoxy and its main class beneficiaries.

While the Bundesbank persisted officially with quantitative targetting, its top personnel has more frequently stressed that monetary policy is more of an 'art form' than a science.[8] Apart from sounding suspiciously disingenuous, this view does draw the observer's eye to the increasingly obvious fact that a significant element of monetary affairs is driven not by well calibrated transmission mechanisms but above all by perceptions of behaviour on the part of both market agents and political authorities. The market agents include both domestic financial institutions and, more notably in the era of flexible exchange rates, international deals on currency, bond and derivatives markets. The political agents include both the Bundesbank as domestic monetary authority and other major central banks like the Federal Reserve Board and the Bank of Japan.

---

[8] David Marsh quotes Helmut Hesse, head of the Land Central Bank in Lower Saxony who stated that '(a) lot of the decisions were not scientifically founded, but depended on politics. I learned in my second year that monetary policy is also high politics'. In: Marsh, *The Bundesbank*, op.cit. p.76

The core problem in the relationship between market agents and monetary authorities is that while the latter are politically committed to the long-term stability of economic fundamentals like domestic price levels and exchange rates, the former operate in the very short term, such that 'economic fundamentals do not enter into most traders' behavior'.[9] Market perceptions and political perceptions of economic developments are critically different. As the exchange rate crises of the 1980s and the 1990s demonstrated, the decision to buy and sell a given currency bore little relation to the solidity or frailty of that currency's national economy and was rather driven by the expectation that, as a result of the collective decisions of the bulk of currency dealers, a currency would fluctuate by amounts sufficient enough to make short-term profits. The key to the speculator's success, as Keynes correctly pointed out, is not to understand the intricacies of macro-economics but to be ahead of the game, to anticipate market behaviour or, as in the case of George Soros, to command a sufficient critical mass of liquid capital to be able to nudge exchange rates (or other security values) in the direction one wishes. In the absence of an effective regulatory framework for capital markets, the behaviour of monetary authorities, even the key institutions like the Bundesbank, the Federal Reserve and now the European Central Bank, becomes secondary: disempowered from exercising 'rational' control over monetary affairs by the dominant behaviour of actors who are driven by another kind of rationality, that of short-term profit-seeking. The 'absolute contradiction' between unregulated capital transactions and national policy-making[10] is resolved by the subjugation of national monetary authorities to the will of financial markets. It is not simply that the stabilising effect of speculation, postulated by Milton Friedman, H.G. Johnson, the Bundesbank and others, does not take place. Rather, speculation generates economic instability and insecurity and neutralises political action. The conclusion of Herr and Voy is that flexible exchange rates have a negative effect on economic development.[11]

Within the general framework of increased disequilibrium, however, some central banks – like the Bundesbank and the Fed – were able to exploit their autonomous power to extract some institutional and

[9] Dornbusch, R. and Frankel, J. 'The Flexible Exchange Rate System', paper quoted by Herr and Voy, *Währungskonkurrenz*, op.cit. p.76.
[10] Herr and Voy, *Währungskonkurrenz*, op.cit. p.78
[11] Ibid.

national economic advantage compared to other countries, as discussed in Chapters Six and Seven. This, again, cannot be taken to constitute a valid demonstration of the technical superiority of the autonomous central bank. It simply demonstrates the disparity of leverage within a distinct hierarchy of national monetary institutions worldwide. More important in the context of this conclusion is to recognize the fraudulence of the claim by the Bundesbank to have either quantitative or qualitative (intuitive, artistic) control of monetary behaviour, in a way which makes the translation of its institutional and operational structures onto other central banks feasible, be they at supra-national or national level, as long as capital can be shifted at high speed and at no transactional cost (qua Tobin Tax) from one economic space to another.

This brings us to a consideration of the political case for central bank independence. The core argument revolves around the potential abuse of monetary policy by democratically elected governments to secure economic advantage, legitimacy or re-election; the main evidence is derived from Germany's two hyper-inflations and from studies of so-called political cycles. While there is some evidence to suggest that dependent central banks – in Britain and France, for example – have been used to stimulate economic activity in advance of elections, there is also evidence to suggest that the behaviour of the Bundesbank was influenced by the political composition of the Central Bank Council:

'The members of the Bundesbank council, like most ordinary citizens, seem to derive utility from the election of their preferred party. If they are independent and if they are not rewarded for stable monetary growth nor punished for monetary policy cycles, they use their power to improve the electoral chances of their preferred party. .... The central bank and the political parties preferred by it have an interest in maintaining the appearance of central bank neutrality because a central bank that is believed to be neutral needs a smaller increase in monetary expansion and inflation to generate the intended pre-election boom and because it is a better "scapegoat" for the stabilization recession thereafter.'[12]

Vaubel's conclusion runs counter to the mythology of neutrality which is so assiduously cultivated by the Bank and its supporters and underscores the view expressed above of ideological partisanship; from

---

[12] Roland Vaubel, 'The bureaucratic and partisan behaviour of independent central banks: German and international evidence', author's manuscript, December 1995, p.14.

1958 to 1991 the central bank council enjoyed a CDU majority in 25 out of 35 years.[13]

The mythology, however, remains potent. The repeated contrast of 'good money' and 'bad politics',[14] the repeated incantation of the value of the Bundesbank as a counter-weight or 'countervailing-power' ('Gegenmacht'), as 'protection of the Federal Republic from itself' (sic),[15] found strong resonance in Germany and beyond, particularly in the last quarter of the 20th century when economics suddenly took against fiscalism, and when corruptibility and sleaze in party politics seemed regularly to hit the headlines. The analysis was strongly reminiscent of discourse in the Weimar Republic, where the dissonance and clientelism of democratic party politics was contrasted with a state form that would put nation and the common weal above sectional interest, strong leadership, 'folk community' etc. One author sees the Bundesbank as a core institution of a 'contemporary concept of democracy':

'In the light of a realistic theory of democracy and more recent approaches to the common good, to the separation of powers and the organisational guarantee of basic rights, the independence of the German Bundesbank is not a foreign body in the constitutional order of the Basic Law, but an indispensable counterweight to the threat of abortive developments'.[16]

The article from which this passage is taken is based on the double assumption that the single agency approach is appropriate to the purpose and that the 'common good' (qua national interest) argument is demonstrated. Both assumptions are at least in part contestable, as this book has attempted to demonstrate. More problematic still is the generalisation of this assumption to cover other institutions of social organisation. Bryan Hopkin and Douglas Wass underscored the danger of generalising the efficacy of autonomy in a brief but utterly

---

[13] Vaubel, ibid. p. 10a; the notion of political partisanship towards conservative-liberal politics is, in any case, strengthened by the operational principles of the Bank which were designed to curtail the inclinations of deficit-spending fiscal authorities, i.e. to counteract Keynesian tendencies.

[14] Balkhausen, *Gutes Geld und schlechte Politik*, op.cit.

[15] Arnim, Hans Herbert von, 'Die Deutsche Bundesbank – Pfeiler der Demokratie', in: *Zeitschrift für Wirtschaftspolitik*, Vol.1 (1988), p.61, p.62

[16] Arnim, 'Die deutsche Bundesbank', op. cit., p.61

convincing article in the Financial Times: 'If beating inflation is so important and the politicians cannot be trusted to give it the priority it deserves, logically we should take out of their hands not only monetary policy but a range of other policies as well.'[17] The danger of this logic is reflected in the new 'realistic theory of democracy' expounded by von Arnim and others: 'The solution can therefore not consist of removing or weakening counterweights like the independent Bundesbank. Rather, consideration must be given to the creation of further counterweights. This seems to be particularly urgent in relation to state indebtedness.' An independent agency or constitutional rule, enforcable by the Constitutional Court therefore, would further prevent the abuse of debt by elected governments: 'Politics would thereby, to a certain extent, protect itself from itself, like Odysseus who once bound himself to the mast of his ship, so that he did not succumb to the singing of the Sirens'.[18]

The list of state functions which would be more appropriately run by agencies which were free from the instructions of an elected government could be extended at will. The popularisation of the 'quango' – the quasi autonomous non-governmental organisation – in many advanced industrial societies is a monument to this logic: single autonomous agencies are supposedly more efficient at allocating state resources and managing specific areas of social and economic concern and they are not subject to the abuse of politicians who might be tempted to buy electoral success with fiscal gifts or promises of fiscal gifts. 'Leave it to the experts' is a plausible clarion call, appealing to the good sense of the well-informed citizens of societies based on the highly specialised technical knowledge; it would be absurd to put gardeners in charge of a nuclear power station or children in charge of jumbo jet. It does not and cannot follow, however, that macro-political decision-making in a democratic society should be placed in the hands of independent and largely unaccountable agencies. What, one must ask, is the purpose of democratic structures if not to influence the decision-making of state bodies and to hold those bodies to account at regular intervals? What is the purpose of the democratic state other than to reflect the preferences of the majority of its citizens and to ensure that those citizens are well informed, able to form reasoned judgements and motivated to participate in democratic politics. The

---

[17] Bryan Hopkin and Douglas Wass, 'The flaws of central bank freedom', *Financial Times*, 22 January 1993

[18] von Arnim, 'Die deutsche Bundesbank', op.cit. p.62

removal of key institutions of the state from democratic influence represents a dangerous precedent for the future of human society:

firstly, and obviously, it creates the potential for bad principles, partisan policies and self-serving bureaucracies to be set in stone;

secondly, it denies the key virtue of democratic culture, namely to identify and rectify mistakes, as perceived by the majority of a given electorate;

thirdly, it generates a political culture in which the focus of democratic attention can only be partial – the unaccountable institution is seen as being unalterable, like the monsoon, criticism of that institution becomes pointless and it is either tabuised as a subject of political discourse or sanctified as a repository of virtue, incorruptibility and infallibility; the only reasonable candidates for criticism are those institutions which can be influenced by lobbying or electoral preferences, such that blame for problems in part determined by the autonomous agency is loaded (unfairly) onto elected bodies, i.e. those that are accessible to blame;

fourthly, the sanctification of institutions like the Bundesbank ('not all Germans believe in God but all Germans believe in the Bundesbank')[19] in turn creates a mythology of power and effectiveness which is internalised by its exponents.

The rhetoric of this mythology is a potent one. In his hagiography of the Bundesbank, Balkhausen quotes a long passage from Wilhelm Röpke, one of the early leading figures in German ordo-liberalism, which had in turn been used by Hans Tietmeyer in a speech in 1990 in celebration of Kurt Biedenkopf. The passage is redolent of the fundamentally elitist view of leading servants of the state and is worth revisiting:

'It is of decisive importance – and this is increasingly a generally held conviction – that there is in society a group of leaders, however small, that sets the tone and feels a responsibility in the name of the whole of society for the inviolable norms and values of society and which lives up to this responsibility in the strictest fashion. What we need at any time and what we need all the more urgently today, when so much is crumbling and tottering, is a genuine nobilitas naturalis with its authority comfortingly acknowledged by the people of their own free will; an elite which derives its aristocratic title only from the most supreme achievements and from an unsurpassable moral example and

---

[19] This quotation is ascribed to Jacques Delors, erstwhile President of the EU Commission

which is cloaked in the natural dignity of such a life ... To belong to this stratum of moral notables has to become the highest and most desirable goal, against which all life's other triumphs pale into insignificance'.[20]

Balkhausen and, by implication Tietmeyer himself, urge citizens to accept the unanswerable authority of the Bundesbank on the grounds of the natural nobility and highest morality of its directors, as an act of faith. That faith is indeed confirmed in a number of surveys of public opinion, where elected authorities are accorded far less public confidence than autonomous agencies like the Bundesbank or the Federal Constitutional Court. The mythology is occasionally ironised in terms of religious systems. The Central Bank Committee is likened to Olympus, 'the throne of the Gods', its members appear to have 'all the moral certitude of Aztec priests' in the service of the religion of central bankism.[21] The commonly used term 'Währungshüter' (guardians of the currency) is reminiscent of the notion of the 'guardians of the Holy Grail' ('Gralshüter'). The aristocratic metaphor is frequently used to describe the presidents of the Land Central Banks ('angry' or 'rebellious princes' etc.).[22]

The most subversive feature of the mythology and rhetoric of Bundesbank effectiveness and 'success' remains the temptation both to copy the institution's structures and procedures for other systems of central banking in differing and possibly inappropriate contexts, and to generalise the notion of the efficiency of autonomous, technocratic agencies which perform state functions without being subject to democratic checks and balances. The new century arguably needs both refined processes of policy co-ordination in economic and social policy and the broadest degree of democratic participation that can be realistically achieved. Autonomous central banks and other quangos are driving us in the opposite direction, towards a new particularism which neutralises democratic influence. While it would be rash to suggest that 'inflation is dead' – given the price-fixing potential of mega-corporations – but the key problems facing humanity in the

---

[20] Wilhelm Röpke, Jenseits von Angebot und Nachfrage, Erlenbach-Zürich/ Stuttgart, 1966, p. 192; also quoted in Balkhausen, Gutes Geld und schlechte Politik, op.cit. p.187.

[21] See *Der Spiegel*, no.35, 1980, p.32, 'Thron der Götter'; Edward Luttwak, 'Central Bankism', op.cit. 220ff; the *Financial Times*, 1 October 1993 dubs Tietmeyer the 'high priest of hard money doctrine'.

[22] 'Zornige Fürsten', *Die Zeit* 1 February 1991; 'Elf aufsässige Prinzen im Reich der D-Mark', *Frankfurter Rundschau*, 24 October 1992

immediate future will, in the view of this author, be distributional and environmental. The last quarter of the twentieth century witnessed a significant regression in the development of income and wealth distribution both within most countries and between those countries. The share of the poorest sections of society has dropped to the advantage of more affluent sections; the ratio of the income of the top twenty per cent of the world's population to that of the bottom twenty per cent rose from 32:1 to 61.1 between 1970 and 1991.[23] With the exception of South and East Asia, distribution ratios within the developing world have deteriorated further. As was noted above, the share of developing countries in global wealth has suffered markedly by the deterioration of terms of trade and the net transfer of capital back to the rich countries of the North. It is no coincidence that this dramatic process of redistribution was accompanied by a shift in global economic orthodoxies away from Keynesian demand management and welfarism towards neo-liberal supply-sidism and monetarism. Neo-liberalism is built on the assumption that the wealth-creators (qua enterprises/employers) should be rewarded better for their contribution to economy and society and that the costs of taxation (state ratio) and of labour (wages ratio) should be reduced, as a pre-condition for reversing the negative trends of growth and employment. The problem with neo-liberal prescriptions is, as was observed above, that the virtuous chain (cost relief > higher profits > higher investment > higher growth > higher employment) has repeatedly broken down after the second link. Investment ratios within the OECD have declined, growth rates have continued to stagnate, unemployment has continued to rise. More perniciously, the capital surpluses generated by cost relief and higher profits have been re-channeled into the mysterious waters of financial services, generating a de-coupled sphere of monetary accumulation which is based predominantly on speculation and fictitious values rather than on the production/provision of goods and services. Monetary accumulation and its client class of rentiers are serviced in part by (independent) central banks. The potential for economic and social catastrophe is made far greater by the perpetuation of the system of monetary accumulation and of the particularist institutions which encourage it. It diverts resources away from socially necessary investment, undermines employment – through the one-sided emphasis on 'shareholder value' – and creates a perverse framework of expectations, in which meaningful and productive work in society is

---

[23] Figures from: *Globale Trends*, Frankfurt am Main 1995, 40ff

accorded a lower value than gambling with financial assets. Above all, the new monetary accumulation – as an extraordinary attempt to breathe life into an otherwise crisis-ridden process of accumulation – diverts the attention of economic and political elites in the developed world from the critical challenge of the limits of growth. The limits of human consumption, together with simple mathematics make the assumption of incremental real growth of 2–3 percent per annum an absurdity, and yet it is an absurdity to which the political and economic establishment clings. 3 per cent of 97.8 billion DM (the gross national product of the Federal Republic in 1950) is considerably less in absolute terms (2.93 billion DM) than 3 per cent of 3833 billion DM (Germany's GNP in 1999), even accounting for price inflation. In fact, at 114 billion DM (3 percent of 1999 GNP), it exceeds even total GNP from 50 years earlier (albeit in nominal terms). Given the increasing saturation of markets, expressed in the declining trend in growth rates in any case, the growth trajectory assumed by both orthodox economists and politicians is simply unsustainable. If one adds the material/environmental dimension to the equation, the absurdity of growth ad infinitum becomes even more apparent: 'If all countries were to follow the example of the industrialised states, five or six planets would be required as sources for the inputs and as dumps for the waste of economic progress. A situation has evolved therefore, in which that certainty which sustained economic growth for two hundred years, is exposed as an existential lie: that growth involves an infinite and open process. For economic growth is already confronted with its bio-physical limits.'[24]
I have yet to read a plausible riposte to this seemingly uncontestable statement. In the context of a critique of autonomous central banking, it helps us focus on the serious challenges facing humanity which are arguably not served by the fashionable creed of neo-liberalism, central bankism and monetary accumulation. Coping with declining trends in the growth of domestic demand, with the virtual elimination of the pattern of economic activity typical of the last two centuries, requires national and supra-national policy co-ordination and the highest degree of democratic participation on the part of motivated, well-informed electorates. In this context of systemic upheaval, marked disparities of income, wealth, resources, access to employment, education and power,

---

[24] Thus Wolfgang Sachs, 'Globale Umweltpolitik und Entwicklungsdenken', *Blätter für deutsche und internationale Politik*, 11/1994, p.1369

will hinder the resolution of acute common problems. It is the contention of this book that the voguish architecture of autonomous central banking, modelled on the Bundesbank, is quite unsuitable to help manage that process. It is therefore a pressing priority for Europe and the international community to begin the process of intellectual and real dismantling of that architecture before economic, social and environmental disintegration gets any worse.

Bibliography

PRIMARY SOURCES

Akten der Reichskanzlei Weimarer Republik Boppard (Harald Boldt)
    Kabinett Müller
Akten der Reichskanzlei, Regierung Cuno Boppard (Harald Boldt)
Akten der Reichskanzler, Kabinett Stresemann Boppard (Harald Boldt)
Bundesarchiv (ed.), *Die Kabinettsprotokolle der Bundesregierung*,
    Vol.9, Boppard am Rhein
Deutsche Bundesbank (ed.), *Auszüge aus Presseartikeln*
Deutsche Bundesbank (ed.), *Monthly Reports (Monatsberichte)*, various
Deutsche Bundesbank (ed.), *Vierzig Jahre Deutsche Mark. Monetäre
    Statistiken 1948–1987*, Frankfurt 1988
Deutsche Reichsbank, *Verwaltungsbericht* (various)
Deutscher Reichstag, *Stenographische Berichte über die Verhandlun-
    gen des Deutschen Reichstages*
Deutsche Bundesbank (ed.), *Annual Reports (Geschäftsberichte)*,
    various
Verhandlungen des deutschen Bundestags (Stenographische Berichte)
Zentrales Staatsarchiv, Nl Havenstein

SECONDARY SOURCES

Abelshauser ,Werner, *Wirtschaftsgeschichte der Bundesrepublik
    Deutschland 1945 bis 1980*, Frankfurt am Main 1983
Aeschimann, E and Riché, P. *La Guerre de Sept Ans. Histoire Secrète
    du franc fort 1989–1996*, Paris 1996
Alesina, Alberto and Summers, Lawrence, 'Central Bank Independence
    and Macroeconomic Performance: Some Comparative Evidence, in:
    Journal of Money, Credit and Banking, 25 (1993), pp. 151–162
Altvater, Elmar, *Die Zukunft des Marktes*, Münster 1992
Altvater, Elmar, 'A Contest without Victors', *Journal of Area Studies*,
    No.7, 1995
Arblaster, A., *The Rise and Decline of Western Liberalism'*, London
    1984

Bach, G.L., *Inflation. Causes, Effects, Cures*, Englewood Cliffs 1958
Balderston, Theo, *The Origins and Course of the German Economic Crisis, November 1923 to May 1932*, Berlin 1993
Balkhausen, Dieter, *Gutes Geld und Schlechte Politik*, Düsseldorf 1992
Barry, Brian, *Democracy and Power*, Oxford 1991
Bendixen, Wilhelm *Geld und Kapital*, collected essays, Jena 1920
Bendixen, Wilhelm, 'Die Inflation als Rettungsmittel', in: *Bank-Archiv*, Vol.19 (1919/20)
Bendixen, Wilhelm, 'Die Parität und ihre Wiederherstellung', in: *Bank-Archiv*, Vol.18 (1918/19)
Bendixen, Wilhelm, *Kriegsanleihen und Finanznot. Zwei finanzpolitische Vorschläge*, Jena 1919
Bennett, Robert J. 'Trade Associations: new challenges, new logic', in: Bennett, R.J. (ed.), *Trade Associations in Britain and Germany: responding to internationalisation and the EU*, London 1997
Berlin, Jörg, (ed.) *Die Deutsche Revolution 1918/19*, Cologne 1979
Blackbourn, David and Eley, Geoff *The Peculiarities of German History*, Oxford 1984
Blanke, B., Jürgens, U. and Kastandiek, H. *Kritik der Politischen Wissenschaft*, (2 vols), Frankfurt 1975
Bofinger, Peter, 'The German Currency Union of 1990 – A Critical Assessment: The Impact on German Monetary Policy', in: Frowen and Hölscher, *The German Currency Union*, Basingstoke 1997
Böhm, Franz, *Die Ordnung der Wirtschaft als geschichtliche Aufgabe und rechtschöpferische Leistung*, Stuttgart 1937
Böhm, Franz, *Wettbewerb und Monopolkampf*, Berlin 1933
Böhret, Claus, *Aktionen gegen die 'kalte Sozialisierung' 1926–1930. Ein Beitrag zum Wirken ökonomischer Einflußverbände in der Weimarer Republik*, Berlin (Duncker and Humblot) 1966
Bonin, Konrad von, *Zentralbanken zwischen funktioneller Abhängigkeit und politischer Autonomie*, Baden-Baden 1979
Bootle, Roger, *The Death of Inflation*, London 1977
Borchardt, Knut, 'Währung und Wirtschaft', in: Deutsche Bundesbank (ed.), *Währung und Wirtschaft in Deutschland 1876–1975*, Frankfurt am Main 1976
Boskin, Michael J. and Jorgenson, Dale W., 'Implications of Overstating Inflation for Indexing Government Programs and Understanding Economic Progress', *American Economic Review 87, Papers and Proceedings*, pp. 89–93
Bower, Tom, *Blind Eye to Murder*, London 1981

Buchheim, Christoph, 'The Establishment of the Bank deutscher Länder and the West German Currency Reform', in: Deutsche Bundesbank (ed.), *Fifty Years of the Deutsche Mark*, Oxford 1998

Büscher, G., *Die Inflation und ihre Lehren*, Zürich 1926

Cassen, Bernard, 'Au nom de l'orthodoxie monétaire', *Le Monde Diplomatique*, 17 June 1992

Coricelli, Fabrizio, Cukierman, Alex and Dalmazzo, Alberto, 'Monetary Institutions, Monopolistic Competition, Unionized Labor Markets and Economic Performance', ms 27 January 2000

Cukierman, Alex, Steven B. Webb and Bilin Neyapti, 'Measuring the Independence of Central Banks and Its Effect on Policy Outcomes'' in: *World Bank Economic Review*, Vol.6, no.3

Dahrendorf, Ralf, *Die Chancen der Krise*, Stuttgart 1983

Dahrendorf, Ralf, *Gesellschaft und Demokratie in Deutschland*, Munich 1965

Dawson, W.H. *The Evolution of Modern Germany*, London/New York 1908

Desai, Meghnad, 'The scourge of monetarism: Kaldor on monetarism and on money, *Cambridge Journal of Economics* 1989, Vol. 13, pp.171–82

Deutsches Institut für Wirtschaftsforschung, 'Muß der deutsche Zins im Schlepptau Amerikas bleiben?, *Wochenbericht* 13, March 1984

Deutsches Institut für Wirtschaftsforschung, 'Geldpolitik nicht wachstumsgerecht: Hoher Realzins hemmt Investitionen', *Wochenbericht* 52, 1985

Deutsches Institut für Wirtschaftsforschung, 'Verfehlte Geldpolitik', *Wochenbericht* pp.31–32, July 1992

Dodd, Nigel, *The Sociology of Money*, New York 1994

Döhn, Lothar 'Liberalismus', in: Neumann, F. (ed.) *Handbuch politischer Theorien und Ideologien*, Opladen 1995

Duckenfield, Mark, 'Bundesbank-Government Relations in Germany in the 1990s: From GEMU to EMU', *West European Politics*, Vol.22, No.3, July 1999

Ebster-Grosz , Dagmar and Pugh, Derek, *Anglo-German Business Collaboration. Pitfalls and Potentials*, London 1996

Ehrenberg, Herbert, *Abstieg vom Währungsolymp. Zur Zukunft der Deutschen Bundesbank*, Frankfurt 1991

Ehrenberg, Herbert, 'Wie unabhängig kann die Bundesbank sein?, *Wirtschaftsdienst* 1988/III, pp.119–29

Eichengreen, B, Rose, A.K. and Wyplosz, C, *'Exchange market mayhem: the antecedents and aftermath of speculative attacks'*, in: *Economic Policy*, No 21, pp.251–312

Eichengreen, B. and Wyplosz, C., 'Stability Pact. More than a Minor Nuisance?', *Economic Policy*, April 1998

Eisermann, Gottfried, *Bedeutende Soziologen*, Stuttgart 1968

Elgie, R and Thompson, H., *The Politics of Central Banks*, London 1998

Eucken, Walter, *Grundsätze der Wirtschaftspolitik*, Tübingen 1960

Eucken, Walter, 'Staatliche Strukturwandlungen und die Krise des Kapitalismus', in: *Weltwirtschaftliches Archiv*, 36/2

Eucken, Walter, *This Unsuccessful Age (or the Pains of Economic Progress)*, London 1951

Feldman, Gerald, *The Great Disorder: Politics, Economics and Society in the German Inflation 1914–1924*, New York 1993

Ferguson, Adam, *When Money Dies: The Nightmare of the Weimar Collapse*, London 1975

Flechtheim, O. (ed.), *Dokumente zur parteipolitischen Entwicklung in Deutschland seit 1945*, Vol. III, Berlin 1963

Flink, Salomon, *The German Reichsbank and Economic Germany*, New York 1930

Frazer, Elizabeth and Lacey, Nicola,*The Politics of Community*, Toronto 1993

Freund, Michael , *Deutsche Geschichte*, Munich 1969

Friedman, Milton, 'Inflation and Unemployment', *Journal of Political Economy*, Vol.85, 1987

Friedman, Milton, 'Should there be an independent monetary authority?', in: Yeager, L.BV. (ed.), *In Search of a Monetary Constitution*, Harvard 1962

Frowen, Stephen and Hölscher, Jens (eds), *The German Currency Union of 1990. A Critical Assessment*, Basingstoke 1997

Frowen, Stephen (ed.) *Inside the Bundesbank*, London 1998

George, Susan, *A Fate Worse Than Debt*, London 1988

Gneist, R. *Der Rechtsstaat*, Berlin 1872

Godley, Wyn, 'The Hole in the Treaty', in: Gowan, Peter and Anderson, Perry (eds) *The Question of Europe*, London 1997

Gossweiler, Kurt, *Großbanken, Industriemonopole, Staat. Ökonomie und Politik des staatsmonopolistischen Kapitalismus in Deutschland 1914–1932*, Berlin (E), 1971

Gowan, Peter and Anderson, Perry (eds) *The Question of Europe*, London 1997

Graham, D., *Exchange, Prices and Production in Hyper-Inflation: Germany 1920–1923*, Princeton 1930

Gray, John, *The Moral Foundations of Market Institutions*, London 1992

Gutmann, Robert, 'Die Transformation des Geldkapitals', *Prokla*, Nr.103, Vol.26/2

Haan, Jakob de, Amtenbrink, Fabian and Eijffinger, Sylvester, *Accountability of Central Banks: Aspects and Quantification*, Tilburg 1998

Hallgarten, G. and Radkau, J., *Deutsche Industrie und Politik*, Cologne 1974

Hankel, Wilhelm, *Währungspolitik, Geldwertstabilisierung, Währungsintegration und Sparerschutz*, Stuttgart 1972

Hansmeyer, Karl-Heinrich and Caesar, Rolf, 'Kriegswirtschaft und Inflation (1936–1948)', in: Deutsche Bundesbank (ed.), *Währung und Wirtschaft in Deutschland 1876–1975*, Frankfurt am Main 1976

Hardach, Gerd, *Weltmarktorientierung und relative Stagnation: Währungspolitik in Deutschland 1924–1931*, Berlin 1976

Haselbach, Dieter, *Autoritärer Liberalismus und soziale Marktwirtschaft*, Baden-Baden 1991

Heiber, Helmut, *Die Republik von Weimar*, Munich 1977

Heine, M. and Herr, H., 'Verdrängte Risiken der Euro-Einführung', *WSI-Mitteilungen*, 8/1999

Heise, Arne, 'Geldpolitik im Disput', *Konjunkturpolitik*, Vol. 38, No.4, 1992

Heller, Hermann, 'Autoritärer Liberalismus?', in: *Die neue Rundschau*, 44/1

Hentschel, Volker, 'Die Entstehungsgeschichte des Bundesbankgesetzes 1949–1957' (Part I), *Bankhistorisches Archiv*, Vol.14 (1988)

Herr, Hansjörg and Voy, Klaus, *Währungskonkurrenz und Deregulierung der Weltwirtschaft*, Marburg 1989

Herr, Hansjörg, *Geld, Währungswettbewerb und Währungssysteme*, Frankfurt am Main 1992

Hofer, W (ed.), *Der Nationalsozialismus. Dokumente 1933–1945*, Frankfurt am Main 1957

Hölscher, Jens, *Entwicklungsmodell Westdeutschland. Aspekte der Akkumulation in der Geldwirtschaft*, Berlin 1994

Holtfrerich, Carl-Ludwig, 'Relations between Monetary Authorities and Governmental Institutions: The Case of Germany from the 19th Century to the Present', in: Toniolo, G (ed.), *Central Banks' Independence in Historical Perspective*, Berlin/ New York 1988

Holtfrerich, Carl-Ludwig, *Die deutsche Inflation 1914–1923*, Berlin 1980

Holtham, Gerald, *Economic Integration after Maastricht*, IPPR Occasional Paper, London 1993

Hopkin, Bryan and Wass, Douglas 'The flaws of central bank freedom', *Financial Times*, 22 January 1993

Hörster-Philipps, Ulrike,'Großkapital, Weimarer Republik und Faschismus', in: R.Kühnl and G. Hardach (eds), *Die Zerstörung der Weimarer Republik*, Cologne 1979

Hortleder, Gerd, *Das Gesellschaftsbild des Ingenieurs. Zum politischen Verhalten der Technischen Intelligenz in Deutschland*, Frankfurt 1970

Huffschmid, Jörg, *Die Politik des Kapitals*, Frankfurt 1972

Huster, E-U, Kraiker, G. et. al., *Determinanten der westdeutschen Restauration 1945–1949*, Frankfurt 1975

James, Harold, 'The Reichsbank 1876–1945', in: Deutsche Bundesbank (ed.), *Fifty Years of the Deutsche Mark. Central Bank and the Currency in Germany since 1948*, Oxford 1999

Kaiser, Rolf H. ,*Bundesbankautonomie, Möglichkeiten und Grenzen einer unabhängigen Politik*, Frankfurt am Main 1980

Kant, Immanuel, *Kritik der Praktischen Vernunft*, Vol. 1

Kitchen, Martin, *The Political Economy of Germany 1815–1914*, London 1978

Knauss, Robert, *Die deutsche, englische und französische Kriegsfinanzierung*, Berlin 1923

Köhler, H. *Adenauer*, Munich (Ullstein) 1994

Kohler, Reinhold, 'Die Bremspolitik der Bundesbank hat nie richtig funktioniert', *Frankfurter Rundschau*, 27 June 1979

Krieger, Leonard, *The German Idea of Freedom. History of a Political Tradition*, Chicago 1957

Krohn, Claus-Dieter, *Die große Inflation in Deutschland 1918–1923*, Cologne 1977

Krohn, Claus-Dieter, *Stabilisierung und ökonomische Interessen. Die Finanzpolitik des Deutschen Reiches 1923–1927*, Düsseldorf 1974

Kuzcynski, Jürgen, *Die Bewegung der deutschen Wirtschaft von 1800 bis 1946*, Meisenheim 1948

Langewiesche, Dieter, *Liberalismus in Deutschland*, Frankfurt am Main 1988

Laubach, Ernst, *Die Politik der Kabinette Wirth 1921/22*, Lübeck/Hamburg 1968

Laursen, K. and Pedersen, J. *The German Inflation 1918–1923*, Amsterdam 1964

Leaman, J. 'The "Gemeinden" as Agents of Fiscal and Social Policy in Twentieth Century Germany', in: Robert Lee and Eve Rosenhaft (eds), *State and Social Change in Germany*, New York/Oxford/Munich (Berg) 1990

Leaman, J. 'Central Banking and the Crisis of Social Democracy – A Comparative Analysis of British and German Views', *German Politics*, Vol.4, No.3, 1995

Leaman, J. *The Political Economy of West Germany 1945–1985*, London 1988

Lohmeier, Susanne *Federalism and Central Bank Autonomy: The Politics of German Monetary Policy 1957–1992*, Mimeograph, University of California at Los Angeles

Lukacs, Georg, *Ontologie der Arbeit*, (reprint) Darmstadt 1973

Luther, Hans, *Politiker ohne Partei*, Stuttgart 1960

Luttwak, Edward, 'Central Bankism', in: P. Gowan and P. Anderson, (eds), *The Question of Europe*, London 1997

Manfred Neumann, 'Monetary Stability: Threat and Proven Response' in: Deutsche Bundesbank (ed.) *Fifty Years of the Deutsche Mark*, Frankfurt 1999

Marsh, David, *The Bundesbank. The Bank that Rules Europe*, London 1992

Marx, Karl, *Grundrisse. Foundations of the Critique of Political Economy*, London 1973

Marx, Karl, *Capital* Vol. 1, London 1954

McGouldrick, Paul, 'Operations of the German Central Bank and the Rules of the Game 1879–1913', in: Michael Bordo and Anna Schwartz (eds), *A Retrospective on the Classical Gold Standard 1821–1931*, Chicago 1984

Mendershausen, Horst, 'Prices, Money and the Distribution of Goods in Postwar Germany', in: *The American Economic Review*, Vol.39, 1949

Milward, Alan S., 'The Social Bases of Monetary Union', in: Peter Gowan and Perry Anderson (eds), *The Question of Europe*, London 1997

Moers, Colin, *The Making of Bourgeois Europe*, London 1991

Möller, Alex, 'Die westdeutsche Währungsreform von 1948', in: Deutsche Bundesbank (ed.), *Währung und Wirtschaft in Deutschland 1876–1975*

Mommsen, W. 'Deutscher und britischer Liberalismus. Versuch einer Bilanz', in: Langewiesche (ed.) *Liberalismus im 19. Jahrhundert*

Mooers, Colin *The Making of Bourgeois Europe. Absolutism, Revolution and the Rise of Capitalism in England, France and Germany*, London 1991

Müller, Detlev K., *Sozialstruktur und Schulsystem. Aspekte zum Strukturwandel des Schulwesens im 19. Jahrhundert*, Göttingen 1977

Müller, Heinz, *Die Politik der deutschen Zentralbank*, Tübingen 1969

Müller-Armack, Alfred., *Staatsidee und Wirtschaftsordnung im neuen Reich*, Berlin 1933

Netzband, and Widmaier, *Währungs- und Finanzpolitik der Ära Luther 1923–1925*, Tübingen 1964

Nicholls, Anthony, *Freedom with Responsibility. The Social Market Economy in Germany 1918–1963*, Oxford 1994

Nölling, Wilhelm, *Goodbye to the Deutschmark*, Hamburg 1993

Nölling, Wilhelm, *Monetary Policy in Europe before and after Maastricht*, London 1993

Nölling, Wilhelm, *Unser Geld*, Berlin/ Frankfurt 1993

Nordhaus, William D., 'The Political Business Cycle', in: *Review of Economic Studies*, Vol 42

North, Douglas 'International Capital Movements in Historical Perspective', in: Raymond Mikesell (ed.), *US Private and Government Investment Abroad*, Eugene 1962

Nussbaum, Manfred, *Wirtschaft und Staat in Deutschland während der Weimarer Republik*, Vaduz 1978

Oberhauser, Alois, 'Geld- und Kreditpolitik', in: Deutsche Bundesbank (ed.), *Währung und Wirtschaft in Deutschland 1876–1975*, Frankfurt am Main 1976

OECD, *Economic Surveys* (various), Paris

Owen-Smith, Eric, 'Incentives for Growth and Development', in: Frowen and Hölscher, *The German Currency Union*, Basingstoke 1997

Petzina, Dietmar, *Deutsche Wirtschaft in der Zwischenkriegszeit*, Wiesbaden 1977

Pfleiderer, Otto, 'Das Prinzip "Mark=Mark" in der deutschen Inflation 1914 bis 1924', in: Büsch, O. and Feldman, G. (eds), *Historische Prozesse der deutschen Inflation*, Berlin 1978

Prion, Willi, *Kreditpolitik*, Berlin (Springer) 1926

Pritzkoleit, Kurt *Das kommandierte Wunder*, Vienna/Munich/Basle 1959

Reich, Robert, 'Deflation, the real enemy', *The Financial Times*, 15 January 1998

Röpke, Wilhelm *The Social Crisis of our Time*, Erlenbach-Zürich 1942

Röpke, Wilhelm, *Jenseits von Angebot und Nachfrage*, Erlenbach-Zürich/ Stuttgart 1966

Rüstow, Alexander, *Rede und Antwort*, Ludwigsburg 1963

Schacht, *End of Reparations*, Glasgow 1931

Schacht, Hjalmar, 'Selbstkontrolle', *Der deutsche Volkswirt*, Vol.2. (1927), Nr.7

Schacht, Hjalmar, *Confessions of the 'Old Wizard'*, Boston 1956

Schacht, Hjalmar, *Die Stabilisierung der Mark*, Stuttgart/Berlin/ Leipzig 1927

Schlesinger, Helmut, 'Geldpolitik in der Phase des Wiederaufbaus', in: Deutsche Bundesbank (ed.), *Währung und Wirtschaft in Deutschland 1876–1975*, Frankfurt am Main 1976

Schmidt, Helmut, 'Offener Brief an Bundesbankpräsident Hans Tietmeyer', *Die Zeit*, Nr 46, 8 November 1996

Schmidt-Klingenberg, Michael, 'Der schwere Abschied', *Der Spiegel*, 18/1998

Schuker, Stephen, 'Finance Policy in the Era of the German Inflation: British, French and German Strategies for Economic Reconstruction after the First World War', in: Büsch, O. and Feldman, G. (eds), *Historische Prozesse der deutschen Inflation 1914 bis 1924*, Berlin 1978

Schui, Herbert, 'Ökonomische Stabilisierung durch Monetarismus?, *Blätter für deutsche und internationale Politik*, 6/1975

Schulmeister, Stephan, 'EURO-Projekt – Selbsterhaltungsdrang der Bundesbank und das Finale Deutschland gegen Italien', *WSI-Mitteilungen*, 5/1997

Schumpeter, Joseph, *Theorie der wirtschaftlichen Entwicklung*, (2. Edition), Munich 1926

Schwartz, H.P. *Die Ära Adenauer. Gründerjahre der Republik 1949–1957*, Stuttgart 1981

Shapiro, J.S., *Liberalism, Its Meaning and History*, Princeton/London/New York 1958

Sheehan, James Sheehan, *German Liberalism in the Nineteenth Century*, Chicago 1978

Simmel, Georg, T*he Philosophy of Money*, London 1978

Smith, Adam, *Wealth of Nations*, Vols I and II, London 1904

Smith, David, *The Rise and Fall of Monetarism*, London 1987

Somary, Felix, *Erinnerungen aus meinem Leben*, Zürich 1959

Stern, Klaus, 'The Central Bank in the Constitutional and Financial Set-Up of the Federal Republic of Germany', in: Deutsche Bundesbank (ed.), *Fifty Years of the Deutsche Mark*

Stolper, Gustav, *Deutsche Wirtschaft seit 1870*, Tübingen 1964

Stremme, Marcel, 'The Scope for National Monetary Policy in the Face of Globalised Financial Markets', Deutsches Institut für Wirtschaftsforschung, *Economic Bulletin* 11, April 1995

Sturm, Roland, 'How Independent is the Bundesbank?', *German Politics*, Vol.4 (1995)

Tawney, R.H., *Religion and the Rise of Capitalism*

Toniolo, Gianni (ed.), *Central Banks' Independence in Historical Perspective*, Berlin/ New York 1988

Treue, Wilhelm (ed.), *Deutsche Parteiprogramme seit 1861*, Göttingen, Zürich, Frankfurt 1954

Vaubel, Roland 'The Bureaucratic and Partisan Behaviour of Independent Central Banks: German and International Evidence', ms.December 1995

Vaubel, Roland, 'Eine Public-Choice-Analyse der Deutschen Bundesbank und ihre Implikationenen für die Europäische Währungsunion', in: Duwendag, Dieter et.al. (eds), *Europa vor dem Eintritt in die Wirtschafts- und Währungsunion*, Berlin 1993

Wallerstein, Immanuel, *Historical Capitalism and Capitalist Civilization*, London 1983

Weißbecker, Manfred, *Macht und Ohnmacht der Weimarer Republik*, Freiburg/ Berlin 1990

Wolff, Robert Paul, *The Poverty of Liberalism*, Boston 1968

Zapf, Michael, 'Good news is bad news. Kapitalmärkte als paradoxe Systeme', *Kursbuch*, Nr.13

Index

Metallurgische
Forschungsgemeinschaft
(Mefo), 89
Minimum reserve ratios, 132
Mitterrand, François, 20, 214,
231
Monetarism, 2, 6, 20, 28, 143,
154, 157, 161, 165, 176–7,
179–80, 193–4, 196, 199–
203, 211, 214, 219, 225, 227,
245, 258
blindness of, 220
compounds fiscal crisis, 203
hegemony of, 219
primacy of, 161
Third World debt crisis and,
179–180
transmission   mechanisms,
164, 211, 251
monetarist doctrine, 7, 213
monetarist orthodoxy, 188,
192, 195
monetary accumulation, 16,
157, 180, 193, 196–7, 202,
204, 207–12, 214, 218, 220,
258–9
distribution ratios and, 148,
169, 206, 258
monetary policy, 1–2, 7, 12,
21, 25–6, 28, 51, 61–2, 75–6,
91, 94, 96–7, 100, 103, 106,
112, 115, 117, 119, 121, 123,
129, 131, 137, 141, 144, 146,
150, 153, 155, 156, 159, 162,
164–5, 170, 172, 180–1, 183,
185–6, 196, 209, 211, 213,
220, 228, 232, 234, 239–41,
247, 251, 253, 255
capital concentration and,
34, 39, 45, 86

corporate time horizons and,
162, 186
deflationary squeezes, 233
immunity to, 209–10
leverage problems, 120
pro-cyclical, 159
pro-cyclical effects of, 170
slow relaxation of, 171
stagflation and, 159
monetary protectionism, 115
monetary targeting
Bundesbank doubts, 165
monetary theory, 2, 123, 171
money, 1–5, 7, 8, 9–20, 26, 28,
30, 52, 54–5, 59–60, 63, 65,
67, 70, 74, 76–7, 80, 90–1,
95, 103, 113, 120–2, 125,
128, 131, 135, 137, 145, 149,
153, 155, 162, 164–6, 168,
188, 194, 196–7, 199, 204,
207, 210, 213, 225, 227, 236,
247–8, 250, 254, 257
stock, 2, 7–8, 13, 55, 63, 95,
120–2, 128, 131, 155,
164–6, 188, 213, 225, 236,
250
stock targeting, 155
valuation of, 8
monopolies, 167, 181
Müller, Lothar, 32, 85–9, 104,
237
Müller-Armack, Alfred, 44,
46–7
Mundell, Robert, 155
Mürdel, Karl, 97

National Liberalism, 41
National Liberals, 37, 39, 42–4,
50, 57
neo-liberalism, 2, 22, 24–6, 45,
157, 176, 189, 192, 194–6,